BY MICHAEL WALKER

Laurel Canyon

What You Want Is in the Limo

WHAT YOU WANT IS IN THE LIMO

WHAT YOU WANT IS IN THE

LIMO

On the Road with Led Zeppelin, Alice Cooper,
and the Who in 1973, the Year the Sixties
Died and the Modern Rock Star Was Born

MICHAEL WALKER

SPIEGEL & GRAU

Copyright © 2013 by Michael Walker

Published in the United States by Spiegel & Grau,
an imprint of The Random House Publishing Group,
a division of Random House, Inc., New York.

SPIEGEL & GRAU and Design is a registered
trademark of Random House, Inc.

Library of Congress Cataloging-in-Publication Data
Walker, Michael.
What you want is in the limo : on the road with Led Zeppelin, Alice Cooper, and the
Who in 1973, the year the sixties died and the modern rock star was born /
Michael Walker.
pages cm
Includes blbliographical references and index.
ISBN 978-0-8129-9288-5
eBook ISBN 978-0-679-64415-6
1. Concert tours. 2. Led Zeppelin (Musical group) 3. Who (Musical group) 4. Alice
Cooper (Musical group) 5. Rock music—1971–1980—History and criticism. I. Title.
ML3534.W286 2013
781.6609'047—dc23
2013009095

Printed in the United States of America on acid-free paper

www.spiegelandgrau.com

2 4 6 8 9 7 5 3 1

First Edition

Book design by Christopher M. Zucker

CONTENTS

INTRODUCTION

In 1973, three legendary bands embark upon tours of North America.

Led Zeppelin, the Who, and Alice Cooper already rule the eight-track players in high school parking lots across America. Each band's previous album sold more than one million copies in the United States; each band is still endowed with its original lineup. And although they don't know it, in 1973 each has just released a career-defining album that will turn out to be a commercial and creative watershed: Zeppelin's *Houses of the Holy,* the Who's *Quadrophenia,* and Cooper's *Billion Dollar Babies.*

What the bands also can't know is that their 1973 tours in support of these albums, which will collectively touch nearly every metropolitan area in the United States and Canada, represent the apogee for a certain type of rock stardom that has been building—indeed, that each of these bands has helped to build—which the world has not seen since and probably never will again.

Subsequent generations of rock musicians will literally kill themselves trying to emulate the example set in 1973, be it the attendance records smashed, the quantity and quality of drugs, the booze and groupies harvested, the hotel rooms and vital organs ravaged or—most elusive—the evanescent aesthetic and sexual heat generated. Why? Because, in this brief and shining moment in 1973, modern rock stardom is born.

This is not to be confused with rock and roll stardom as defined by

Elvis and Chuck Berry in the 1950s or by the Beatles in the 1960s. The rock star of 1973 is a new animal in every respect—both creator and beneficiary of a post-Beatles, pre-MTV, what-you-want-is-in-the-limo, halter-topped, lude-dropping, coke-and-glitter-flecked Midwestern-arena-backstage-blowjob shindig. The template created in 1973 will, three years later, metastasize into mega-albums by Peter Frampton and Fleetwood Mac and, in the eighties and nineties, tours upsized from civic arenas to Jumbotronned stadia and records shipped in the tens of millions—though by then the rituals, commodified by corporate patronage, will seem increasingly scripted. But while it lasts, the Spirit of '73 burns hot, blue, and righteous—the title of a ZZ Top classic released that summer—throughout rock and the culture beyond.

How did this moment, so estranged from the rock culture of the 1960s, arrive only four years after the supposed hippie pastoral of Woodstock? How did rock go from Beatles in tab-collar suits and fans throwing jelly babies to Led Zeppelin careering through the provinces by limo and private jet trailed by—good morning, little schoolgirl!—feral fourteen-year-olds with fake IDs? How do the same musicians who once espoused, or pretended to espouse, tie-dyed collectivism suddenly conjure a backstage culture more Weimar Berlin than Woodstock Nation? And what does this say about the popular culture of those times? Or the fact that forty years later it still makes us wonder?

The sixties created an outsize hunger for rock culture but lacked the infrastructure to deliver it; in 1973 supply finally catches up with demand. As the sixties bled into the seventies, the naïve counterculturalism that bound rock bands in generational solidarity to their audience began to fray. A new generation of fans too young for Woodstock inherited the tropes of the sixties minus the boring poli-sci socio-overlay. Thus do peace, love, and understanding devolve into sex, drugs, and rock and roll—the sex being younger, the drugs harder, and the rock and roll louder, longer, and infinitely more belligerent.

By 1973, largely on the strength of this new demographic, the Who, Alice Cooper, and especially Led Zeppelin are outselling the Beatles (who disbanded three years earlier) and the Rolling Stones, who toured the year before and upped the ante considerably in regard to on-the-road outrage. "The Sixties," as they are already sentimentalized, are finally over, replaced by an altogether colder and more cynical epoch: by 1973, the United States is in the grip of crippling inflation and an unrelenting energy crisis; Richard Nixon, inaugurated in January and in danger of impeachment by December, famously asserts he is "not a crook"; *Bonanza* is canceled.

In the midst of this, the money suddenly pouring into the record industry's coffers confers upon rock bands the status of young princes. In the sixties, a convincing show of empathy with the rank-and-file audience was compulsory; the newly flush rockers of the early 1970s dispense with the charade and start behaving like, well, stars. Not for them the aw-shucks of Elvis, the cheek and charm of the Beatles, however feigned; no, they are *rock stars*—a taxonomy and work in progress that manifests in limos and Learjets and contract riders specifying vintage cognacs, which in turn feed a galloping sense of entitlement that breeds contempt for anyone not in the inner sanctum.

Backstage depravity in the sixties was carried out with a modicum of discretion; now it is in the open. Groupies who once pursued a single performer and became his "road wife" now willingly trade down to group sex, fetishism, whippings, zoophilia—whatever the boys fancy. Several are immortalized in song. Connie Hamzy of Little Rock—the "sweet, sweet Connie" of Grand Funk Railroad's number one 1973 single "We're an American Band," itself a manifesto for the new party-down rock star—makes it clear that she will do pretty much anything and apparently does with everybody from Grand Funk's Mark Farner to Peter Frampton and, twenty years later, then-governor William Jefferson Clinton, whom she accuses of propositioning *her*.

Into this supercharged atmosphere Led Zeppelin, Alice Cooper, and the Who launch the most ambitious tours of their careers. It is a measure of the times that the bands emerge from these voyages utterly changed. Following its '73 tour, Led Zeppelin retreats from the road for a year and a half and—1975's semicelebrated *Physical Graffiti* notwithstanding— spends the rest of the seventies in a creative funk interspersed with personal calamities that stoke rumors that the band is cursed before its drummer, John Bonham, dies in his sleep after downing forty ounces of vodka before and during rehearsals for a comeback tour. Emotionally and creatively spent, Alice Cooper disintegrate at the peak of their success within months of playing their last gig of 1973, on New Year's Eve in Buffalo. The Who never revisit the creative muse of *Quadrophenia* on record or onstage and exit the decade after a pair of desultory albums that culminate in drummer Keith Moon's death by overdose of the drug weaning him from alcohol and the tragedy of eleven fans trampled to death in a stampede at a Who concert in Cincinnati.

Like a power chord struck on a Les Paul, the electric guitar favored by Zeppelin's Jimmy Page for its endless sustain, the impact that these three 1973 albums and tours have on rock and popular culture continues to reverberate today.

The Billion Dollar Babies tour will prove especially influential: Kiss's fire-breathing theatrics, Marilyn Manson and Slipknot's calculated horror shows, Lady Gaga's self-conscious role-play—all are deeply indebted to the example Alice Cooper set in the spring and summer of 1973. Likewise, every hair band who trashes a Days Inn or snorts PCP off a Gulfstream's tray table, every David Lee Roth who caterwauls bare-chested and every Slash who slings a Les Paul low over his hip, owes a tip of the top hat to Robert Plant and Jimmy Page's onstage duende, perfected on Led Zeppelin's '73 tour. And every time a Bono gets a stadium full of disaffected youth shouting along to parables about Martin Luther King Jr., he can thank the Who's Quadrophenia tour for demonstrating that rock can deliver a thinking man's agenda and still crank the amps to 11.

All of which makes it essential to dust off the metaphorical coke mirror, rouse the groupie passed out in the Holiday Inn of the mind, and make sense of this chaotic, hilarious, decadent, and, it must be said, unprecedented and important year in American popular culture. "So you wanna be a rock 'n' roll star?" the Byrds ask, all smugness, in prehistoric 1967. They have no idea. It isn't until '73 that bands like Led Zeppelin, the Who, and Alice Cooper supply the correct answer—"*Fuck, yeah*"—and then write the manual. Dancing days may never be here again, but it's instructive to revisit the time and place when they unquestionably are.

• • •

Welcome to 1973—the year the sixties die. *O father of the four winds fill our sails . . .* and please blast the patchouli out of the room once and for all while you're at it. And so it is done. Cleansed of the 1960s cultural jetsam, rock and pop are reborn in ravishing new duds: glam, prog, protopunk, metal, you name it—the gang is suddenly all here, at the top of their game, hurling hits like fastballs. It is an unbelievably fecund year. Albums later garlanded as classics arrive weekly: *The Dark Side of the Moon, Berlin, Innervisions, Goat's Head Soup, Brothers and Sisters, Don't Shoot Me I'm Only the Piano Player* and *Goodbye Yellow Brick Road, Greetings from Asbury Park N.J.* and *The Wild, the Innocent & the E Street Shuffle, Living in the Material World, Mind Games, Aladdin Sane, Burnin', Desperado.* Aerosmith releases its debut album in 1973. So do Queen, the New York Dolls, Lynyrd Skynyrd, the Marshall Tucker Band, and 10cc. Definitive albums pour from Steve Miller (*The Joker*), ZZ Top (*Tres Hombres*), Todd Rundgren (*A Wizard, A True Star*), Billy Joel (*Piano Man*), the Stooges (*Raw Power*), Steely Dan (*Countdown to Ecstasy*), Wings (*Band on the Run*), Emerson, Lake & Palmer (*Brain Salad Surgery*); from Hall & Oates, the Doobie Brothers, Ten Years After, Rufus, Focus, Free, and dozens more. The Roxy opens in L.A.; CBGB opens in New York. Kiss performs its first gig in kabuki *keshou,* David Bowie, his last in his Ziggy persona. Sixties diehards keep dying: The Byrds break up for the last time, Jefferson Airplane crashes. Meanwhile, live rock gentrifies into the "rock concert," from loss leader to big business. Nightly grosses climb into five and six figures. At Watkins Glen, New York, a festival featuring the Allman Brothers and Grateful Dead draws six hundred thousand to Woodstock's four hundred thousand—take *that,* 1969.

Every act cited above is on the road somewhere in North America during 1973. So are Rod Stewart and the Faces, Frank Zappa, Jeff Beck, Chicago, Jackson Browne, Linda Ronstadt, James Taylor, Carole King, Simon and Garfunkel, Steve Miller, Leon Russell, Santana, Yes, Mott the Hoople, Foghat, Slade, Thin Lizzy, Traffic, Three Dog Night, Fleetwood Mac, Johnny Winter, Edgar Winter, Savoy Brown, Mountain, Ted Nugent,

King Crimson, Grand Funk, Black Sabbath, the James Gang, Deep Purple, Spooky Tooth, Uriah Heep, Humble Pie, Peter Frampton, REO Speedwagon, Elvin Bishop, Styx, Montrose, the J. Geils Band, Genesis, Bob Seger, Bob Marley, Jethro Tull, Wishbone Ash . . . It is impossible to apprehend in today's wan marketplace a culture detonating with such vast and chaotic talent on record and in concert in a single year—let alone filling arenas every night and moving millions of albums. But that's 1973. "Everybody was like the 1927 Yankees," John Fogerty, leader of Creedence Clearwater Revival, later recalled. "You had to be like that to even be considered in the game."

Three tours and three albums by three bands in this most definitive year stand out as exemplars for the times, and for the impact that 1973 wreaks on rock, its audiences, and the musicians themselves. For the bands, fans, promoters, groupies, record companies, and drug dealers involved, life will never be the same.

Led Zeppelin's 1973 tour kicks off with back-to-back sellouts in Atlanta and Tampa—the 56,800 tickets sold at the latter break the attendance record set by the Beatles' 1965 Shea Stadium concert. Immediately, it is clear this tour will dwarf Zeppelin's previous outings. The sheer size and exuberance of the crowds are matched by the band's disorienting ascension to near superstardom: *Houses of the Holy,* which jettisons the last vestiges of Zeppelin's blooze-rock underpinnings for Page's blossoming eclecticism, reaches number one soon after the band arrives in America. Once there, they set about redefining how rich rock and rollers ought to comport themselves while reinventing how rock is stage-managed and promoted.

For most of the tour Zeppelin travel via the *Starship,* a former United Airlines Boeing 720B converted into "a fucking flying gin palace," in the words of Zeppelin's notorious road manager, Richard Cole. (The plane's comforts include a private bedroom, faux fireplace, and full-length bar equipped with an electric organ.) Where the band previously hit the boards in woolly beards and hippie mufti, Page now affects satin suits with appliqués of dragons and glyphs, his androgyne's mane precisely tousled. The once unadorned Zeppelin stage rages with pyrotechnics and clouds of dry ice. The shows are the longest and most demanding of the band's career; the encores alone occupy half an hour or more. By the time the band staggers into Madison Square for the finale, the tour grosses $4 million—$20 million, adjusted for inflation—with a top ticket price of just six dollars. Exhausted and disoriented, Zeppelin is never the same.

"When I came back from that 1973 tour I didn't know where I was," Jimmy Page later recalled. "We were playing sets for three hours solid . . . We ended up in New York and the only thing that I could relate to was the instrument on stage." Added Zeppelin's singer, Robert Plant: "I remember that tour rather like . . . a flash. Really fast. Lots of battles and conquests. And the din of the hordes. So much happened in such a short time. It was phenomenal—there were no brakes. We couldn't stop what was happening. We had no idea what it even *was*."

The Who begin the North American leg of their '73 world tour at San Francisco's Cow Palace on the wings of *Quadrophenia*'s release. The double album is Who guitarist Pete Townshend's second—and vastly more ambitious—full-length rock opera, following 1969's *Tommy*, and it quickly becomes the band's highest-charting album, vaulting to number two in the United States. When not blasting Zeppelin's "The Ocean" or Alice Cooper's "Elected," the Trans-Ams and Camaros of America's suburban youth reverberate with *Quadrophenia*'s pummeling "The Real Me." Townshend later declared that *Quadrophenia* is "the best music I've ever written, I think, and it's the best album that I will ever write."

But the prevailing analogue technology isn't up to the task of synching the album's prerecorded sound effects with live performance; plus, Townshend insists on introducing the opera's songs with lengthy mise-en-scènes that try the patience of head-banging audiences in Dallas and St. Louis. The tour gets off to an inauspicious start when, midway into the Cow Palace premiere, Moon passes out face-first into his kit and is carried offstage. (An audience member fills in.) "That actually happened on two or three other occasions," Peter Rudge, the band's co-manager in 1973, says today. "Just another day at the office."

The anarchic opening night sets the tone for the rest of the tour. Alternating incandescent performances and shows sandbagged by technical snafus, the band is jailed for several hours in Montreal after trashing a suite at the Hotel Bonaventure, causing the near cancellation of the next night's sold-out gig at the Boston Garden. The Alice Cooper entourage checks in to the hotel after the Who check out and profess shock at the vandalism. (A week later Cooper's drummer and roadies trash a Ramada Inn in Utica, New York.) The Who limp home after a final gig in Largo, Maryland.

Alice Cooper's marathon 1973 tour—sixty-five concerts in sixty-one cities in one hundred days—is unprecedented in its ambition. In the years since the band's apprenticeship with Frank Zappa in hippie-dippie 1969, Alice notices that now "every teenager wanted more stereos, sports cars, telephones, and TVs. I knew seventeen-year-old kids in Bel Air with their own Rolls-Royces and drivers." And so, in early 1973, the band launches an album and stage show about "overindulgence and affluence." The unstated subtext is that the album and tour will further enrich the musicians and their management. "We wanted to blitz the public with a tour and album of such overwhelming proportions we could retire afterwards," Alice recalled. "The basic plan was to release the *Billion Dollar Babies* album followed by a swift, hard tour across the country, playing as many dates in the largest halls in as short a time as possible."

The tour's $250,000 Busby Berkeley–style stage, built around simulated necrophilia and Alice's bloody "beheading," is loaded into two semitrailer trucks. The logistics are staggering: forty tons of equipment and supplies including a giant dentist's drill, six whips and hatchets, three hundred baby dolls and fifty-nine mannequins for Alice to ritualistically hack to death and dismember, plus twenty live mice weekly to feed a boa constrictor and 140 cases of Seagram's VO, most of it swilled by Alice. The band travel in *AC-1*, a chartered F-27 Lockheed Electra with a snake in the shape of dollar sign painted on the tail. The cabin sports a blackjack table, the walls papered with centerfolds, the cocktail napkins emblazoned FLY ME, I'M ALICE. All of this whimsy is in the service of a deadly serious objective: propel *Billion Dollar Babies* to number one and gross $6 million on the tour. Incredibly, they pull it off—the concerts sell out, *Billion Dollar Babies* hits number one. But the triumph is largely lost on the band as the tour grinds relentlessly away. "You've got the number one album," Alice says today. "You can't explain why you're so successful, so you just close your eyes. You just say, Let's ride this wave as long as we can."

The tour and album, the culmination of everything the band has strived for since they formed as high school students in Phoenix, instead tear them apart. "In the end," Alice acknowledged, the '73 tour "wrecked us all." The show's brutal theatrics and itinerary drive Alice, already a heavy drinker, into alcoholic comas. The blithe nihilism seems to embolden the audience; in Chicago, drummer Neal Smith is harpooned by a dart thrown from the cheap seats; in Toledo, the band is pelted with debris and fireworks and flees the stage after only two songs. In Evansville, Indiana, the boa constrictor wraps itself around Alice and nearly suffocates him before his bodyguard—another nod to the growing buffer between rock star and audience—cuts it off with a pocketknife. Alice insists that a towel be placed by his hotel bedside because every morning he wakes up vomiting. "I'm just trying to get through this tour alive," he said.

The band by then are isolated by their management in a feedback loop of limos, private planes, and twenty-four-hour room service under the theory that individuals treated like stars will interact with the public like stars and so further the cause. It works all too well. Poisoned by their success, the band begins having "the exact same fights we had when we were poor, except 'That's my tomato you're eating' turned into 'That's my Rolls, get your ass out of it,'" Alice said. At the tour's finale at Madison Square Garden, Alice goes onstage with six broken ribs, a broken wrist, and a fractured elbow. "I fought my way through that tour like it was a war," he said. "And it was."

Alice Cooper's '73 tour literally and figuratively outgrosses the Led Zeppelin and Who tours, yet nets the band crumbs after the tremendous overheads are deducted. Incredibly, it is followed before year's end by recording sessions for their next album and *another*, monthlong tour. After those obligations are finally met—and a cash-grabbing tour of South America is completed—the five band members never play together again. An album and show meant to lampoon conspicuous consumption instead consumes its rich, young creators. "Billion Dollar Babies took the life out of the band," Alice said. "It killed the spark between us."

Nineteen-seventy-three distills a decade's worth of decadence into twelve awesome months and resets the clock for the rest of the seventies and all that they imply. It's a year that, by any measure, ought to be its own decade. Nearly forty years hence, '73 still burns as brightly as a bong load ripped on the bucket seat of a Mach 1.

WHAT YOU WANT IS IN THE LIMO

Chapter 1

GENTLEMEN, START YOUR EGOS

Our heroes chart a course out of the 1960s into the 1970s, Led Zeppelin defies the rock-critic elite and prospers mightily, Alice Cooper discovers the power of dead babies (and chickens), and the Who attempt to out-Tommy Tommy.

It is apparently compulsory to depict the 1960s—which is to say *the sixties,* the tie-dyed simulacrum, not the decade itself—as having ended conveniently with the thunderclap and whimper of Woodstock-then-Altamont in 1969. That's the tidy, Time-Life commemorative version, not available in stores, call now. It is likewise an article of faith that the 1970s are the inevitable, pitiful, ridiculous aftershock of the 1960s youthquake and therefore deserve to be lampooned into eternity as a theme park of wide lapels, disco, and relentless self-absorption: *That '70s Decade,* the leisure-suited pleasure dome lit by lava lamp.

There is, on the other hand, refreshing acknowledgment—if not the "agonizing reappraisal" of Hunter S. Thompson, the dope-upholstered counterculture mascot whose best work, including *Fear and Loathing in Las Vegas,* was published not in the sixties but in the seventies—that the decade is more than feckless cultural and historical throat clearing, ten years of bad endings—Nixon to Nam—and paltry beginnings. The historian Bruce J. Schulman depicts the seventies as the dawning of an actual instead of fanciful age of, if not Aquarius, then nothing less than "the end of the post World War II era." Schulman rejects the purple-hazy hype lavished on the sixties as an agency for upending the status quo and declares that it is the seventies that define "the terms of contemporary American life"—said terms being constantly, maddeningly in flux without benefit of hindsight because henceforth "the experiences of the postwar generation would offer little guidance."

That's putting it mildly. Consider 1973: Ferdinand Marcos becomes president of the Philippines; Lyndon Johnson dies; Richard Nixon is inaugurated for his benighted second term; G. Gordon Liddy and James W. McCord Jr. are convicted for their part in the Watergate break-in; the Supreme Court overturns state laws prohibiting abortion in *Roe v. Wade;* the Paris Peace Accords are signed "ending" the war in Vietnam. And that's just *January.* Before 1973 is finished, the World Trade Center and Sydney Opera House open; the DEA is founded; the ATM is patented; Spiro Agnew resigns; Steve Jobs drops out of Reed College; Federal Express ships its first packages; the Arab oil embargo commences. The director Ang Lee later notes that, while shooting the film adaptation of *The Ice Storm,* Rick Moody's novel chronicling the sexual revolution limping belatedly into suburban Connecticut, "My producers and I often joked that 1973 was America's most 'embarrassing' year—with Nixon, polyester, the admitting of defeat in Vietnam, stagflation, the energy crisis. But embarrassment can be a profound and enlightening experience."

It is probably most realistic to consider the sixties and seventies a cultural continuum in which business begun in the sixties is concluded, however unsatisfactorily, in the seventies. And therein comes a moment when, by sheer momentum, the cultural detritus of the sixties—the peace and love and hash pipes, along with what David Crosby makes a fetish of calling "the Music"—comes hurtling into the seventies and into the laps of a generational cohort too young to parse the Kennedy assassination and Beatlemania but old enough to feel the gravitational pull of the counterculture and big brother's *Disraeli Gears* and *Surrealistic Pillow* albums. This is the audience, born in the late fifties and early sixties, that at the dawn of the seventies makes its appetites and buying power known and in the process radically reshapes the aesthetics and commercial scope of rock and popular music in ways still evident today. They do it by wishing only to continue the sixties hootenanny of which they are given a tantalizing glimpse, blissfully ignoring the fact that not all the bullets they dodge by arriving too late for Kent State are metaphorical: The hems of their faded Levi's breaking fastidiously across caramel Acme cowboy boots as they saunter into high schools trailing pot smoke and wan entitlement, they are the first of the postwar generation not to have to register for the draft.

The annus mirabilis of these children of both the sixties and seventies—their shimmering summer of '42—is 1973. At high schools with indulgent open-campus policies, they are allowed to design their own class schedules, come and go with near complete impunity, and smoke cigarettes and whatever else strikes their fancy in parking lots clotted with 442s and 'Cudas leaking bluish clouds from the interiors. They no longer play the hardcore sixties music that they'd worshipped from afar during their Wonder Years, the Byrds, Buffalo Springfield, the Doors, Jefferson Airplane, even—especially?—the Beatles, being one gear too retro (the Rolling Stones and the Who, having released the pan-generational *Exile on Main Street* and *Who's Next* in the two years before, are exempt). The hunger among males of the cohort for rock—*hard* rock, rock as libidinous and priapic as they are—soon supercharges the record business but appalls the nascent rock-critical elite; in the real world of record sales, it is another story. Untold millions of suburban high schoolers from Shaker Heights to Syosset, Sherman Oaks to Barrington Hills, reach deep into the pockets of their fly-button 501s and commence buying stacks, cartons, shiploads of albums, pushing sales of recorded music to $47 million in 1973. And the band the rock-crit elite hate them the most for loving is Led Zeppelin.

"In 1973, in the collective mind of the critical clique, Led Zeppelin was not only not cool, they were distinctly uncool," the record executive Danny Goldberg, the band's press officer in 1973, would later recall. The freshly minted "rock critics" toiling at *Rolling Stone* are ten years older than the average Zeppelin fans, whose sheer number and buying power render irrelevant whatever reservations self-anointed cultural gatekeepers have about the band. *Rolling Stone's* Jon Landau, dean of the rock-crit elite and later Bruce Springsteen's manager, recalled: "Zeppelin forced a revival of the distinction between popularity and quality. As long as the bands most admired aesthetically were also the bands most successful commercially (Cream, for instance) the distinction was irrelevant. But Zeppelin's enormous commercial success, in spite of critical opposition, revealed the deep division in what was once thought to be a homogeneous audience." Or, as Goldberg observed, "Led Zeppelin was the first big group to make that slice of baby boomers feel mortal." As a nonplussed rock writer bleated to Goldberg at Max's Kansas City—the Elaine's for the 1970s New York rock-crit elite—after seeing Zeppelin in concert, "Their audience is so *young*."

It is the same story in Britain, where Led Zeppelin formed in 1968 from the ashes of the Yardbirds, one of the more adventuresome of the British Invasion groups. Zeppelin's preposterous name, already as passé and metaphorically plodding as Iron Butterfly, does the band no favors with the rock press. "Led Zeppelin" is a portmanteau coined after a 1966 session for a Jeff Beck track, "Beck's Bolero," with Beck and Jimmy Page, boyhood friends and later bandmates in the Yardbirds, on guitars; a journeyman British studio arranger named John Paul Jones, né John Baldwin, on bass; Nicky Hopkins, a top London session pianist; and the Who's peripatetic Keith Moon on drums. The session went so well—after almost disappearing as the B-side to a Beck single, "Beck's Bolero" fetched up on Beck's first solo album and became one of the most influential hard-rock songs ever recorded—there was talk among the musicians of forming a band. The irrepressible Moon, who sneaked into the session in disguise to avoid the wrath of Pete Townshend, predicted the band would go over like a lead balloon—"a lead *zeppelin*," corrected the Who's bassist, John Entwistle, who was considering joining in lieu of John Paul Jones. Nothing came of the band—entreaties to the Small Faces' Steve Marriott to join as singer were aggressively rebuffed by his management. But the ambitious premise for the song—a rock interpretation of Ravel's "Bolero" filigreed with sonorous, distorted lead guitar and dramatic contrasts in tempo and dynamics—prefigured the style

Page would soon perfect with his next band. "That would have been Zeppelin, I guess, had we had a vocalist," Beck later acknowledged.

In the meantime, Page presided over the disintegration of the Yardbirds, who made their bones as blues purists—Eric Clapton was their original lead guitarist—before turning to irresistible pop hits like "For Your Love" that showcased howling guitar solos. When Clapton quit, he recommended Page, then London's most in-demand session guitarist, who instead recommended his old friend Beck. With Beck on lead guitar, the Yardbirds unleashed a string of revolutionary singles including "Heart Full of Soul" and "Shapes of Things." Weary of toiling as an anonymous session man, Page joined the group in 1966. Starting on bass, he later switched to guitar, upsetting the power balance within the band and testing Beck's fragile ego. "There was this slightly out of control egomaniac"—Beck—"and this guy who had spent years doing sessions for Burt Bacharach," the Yardbirds' Chris Dreja would recall. "Jimmy knew exactly where he was going. Very disciplined, very controlled."

Beset by volcanic mood swings, Beck abruptly departed the group during a Dick Clark package tour of America, leaving the band in Page's hands. Exhausted and broke, the Yardbirds broke up for good in 1968. Page and the band's manager, an outrageous, swashbuckling former wrestler named Peter Grant, were left with the Yardbirds name and a string of Scandinavian tour dates. The idea was floated to form a band under the name the New Yardbirds to fulfill the obligations. John Paul Jones, from the "Beck's Bolero" session, joined on bass and keyboards; Terry Reid turned down an offer for lead singer and suggested Robert Plant, an unknown toiling in Britain's West Midlands, who in turn suggested his friend John Bonham as drummer. The quartet met in London, jammed to the Yardbirds' "Train Kept a-Rollin'," and immediately gelled. After the Scandinavian tour, Grant discovered club owners and record labels in Britain had feeble interest in a band called the New Yardbirds. Undaunted, Grant took what piddling gigs he could secure and, with Page, financed the recording of what would become the first Led Zeppelin album for the now legendary £1,782, including the album cover art. The album took just thirty-six hours to record and mix. Realizing the

Yardbirds name was a millstone, Grant revived the Lead Zeppelin moniker; in an early display of the acumen that would help earn the group several fortunes, he banished the *a* in *lead* so that American deejays unacquainted with British colloquialisms wouldn't mispronounce the group's name.

The band played its first shows as Led Zeppelin in London in October 1968. The response was not encouraging; the few writers that Grant could drag to the gigs complained that the playing was too loud, the material—blues covers and a few originals from the still unreleased album—too derivative and discursive. Grant, having just toured America with the Jeff Beck Group, knew better. He'd seen the new generation of young American fans in action, not just in cities like New York but in the wretched provincial hamlets of the Midwest where the appetite for earsplitting blues-rock and guitar heroics was palpable. The Beck tour gave Grant "the opportunity to observe how young, principally male audiences, many of whom were strung out on 'downer' drugs like Quaaludes, lapped up . . . loud, frenzied blues rock," recalled Chris Welch, Grant's biographer.

While the British dithered, Grant closed a deal with Atlantic Records' Ahmet Ertegun and Jerry Wexler, who on the strength of Page's reputation listened to the unreleased tracks and signed the band to a five-year contract with a $200,000 advance. The boomer rock-crit elite seized upon the huge sum as a club to beat the band for being a "hype," in the argot of the day; in an irresistible but probably unwise rejoinder, Grant and Page responded by naming the concern publishing Zeppelin's songs Superhype Music. It was the beginning of poisonous relations with the rock establishment that would plague the band throughout its career. Grant meanwhile saw to it that Atlantic Records plied the emerging American "underground" FM rock stations with white-label copies of the album, where it received heavy airplay. The strategy bypassed the self-righteous rock press, forever after muting its influence on record sales. "When rock radio came along, the role of the rock critics was tremendously diminished," Goldberg would recall. "Zeppelin's first album was one of the first albums in the United States to break big over the airwaves rather than in the music press." *Led Zeppelin* was released on

January 12, 1969. *Rolling Stone* weighed in with a devastating review that acknowledged Page's guitar prowess but excoriated him as "a writer of weak, unimaginative songs" and flayed "prissy" Robert Plant for his "howled vocals." The band and material were deemed "strained," "unconvincing," "foppish," "redundant," "monotonous," and "very dull." The musicians were stunned. "We had appalling press at the time," John Paul Jones later recalled. "In our naïveté we thought we'd done a good album, and then this venom comes flying out. After that we were very wary of the press."

The band kicked off its first U.S. tour in Denver on December 26, 1968. The itinerary targeted the new, dedicated rock auditoriums like Bill Graham's Fillmores East and West, which along with FM radio were opening new and lucrative markets for rock. (In Los Angeles, Zeppelin shared the bill at the Whisky A Go Go with a fledgling band of young misfits with the vexing name Alice Cooper.) There was no single aimed at top-forty radio released ahead of the album, part of Page and Grant's strategy to educate audiences that Zeppelin was a serious proposition— which not coincidentally forced fans to buy seven-dollar albums instead of ninety-nine-cent 45s. (A belatedly released single, "Good Times, Bad Times," barely scraped the Billboard Hot 100.) The response in America was a repeat of Grant's experience with Jeff Beck, only more so. At a make-or-break gig at the Fillmore West, at the bottom of a three-act bill behind Country Joe and the Fish, of all absurdities, Led Zeppelin took off for good. "It felt like a vacuum and we'd arrived to fill it," Page would recall. "First this row, then that row . . . it was like a tornado and it went rolling across the country." Two months after its release, *Led Zeppelin* cracked the Billboard Top Ten and went on to sell eight million copies.

Scarcely ten months later, *Led Zeppelin II*, written and recorded on the run during the first U.S. tour, was released to marginally better reviews and stellar sales—it quickly shot to number one in the U.S. and U.K. and became an instant, genre-setting classic with bulletproof material like "Whole Lotta Love," "Heartbreaker," "Ramble On," and "Moby Dick," the latter showcasing a monumental John Bonham drum solo that unfortunately would inspire leagues of lesser drummers to likewise indulge. The album consolidated the band's success and portended the coming hordes of "heavy" bands playing pummeling, blues-based material minus the psychedelic whimsy of earlier guitar rock. The album's huge success was goosed by a format the band officially forsook: a hit single. " 'Whole Lotta Love' was getting tremendous FM play at night," Jerry Greenberg, then head of promotion at Atlantic Records, says, "and a couple top-forty stations call me up and go, 'You know, Jerry, we're getting calls for that 'Whole Lotta Love' but we can't play a five-minute, forty-second version.' " Greenberg proposed releasing an edited version and was flatly turned down—"We're not a singles band, yadda, yadda"—then took matters into his own hands. "I literally dropped the needle and I'm watching the clock," he says. "It hits 2:40 and they go into the chorus: *Wanna whole lotta love, ca-cha, ca-cha.* I took the volume dial and faded them out at 3:05—no edit, no big deal in the studio." Grant allowed Greenberg to prepare a single with the 3:05 version on one side and the full 5:05 album cut on the other and send it to top-forty stations. "Well, now it goes crazy," Greenberg says. "Stations like WLS in Chicago, WABC in New York, KHJ in Los Angeles, they're playing the three-minute version in the morning but the nighttime jock can play the five-minute version. Peter calls and says, 'Jimmy wants to know why the single's not on the charts.' I go, 'Peter, the only way you can get it on the charts is to let me release it.' " Grant relented a second time and the 3:05 version of "Whole Lotta Love," backed with "Living Loving Maid (She's Just a Woman)," the band's least favorite song on the album, hit number four on the Billboard Hot 100 and became Zeppelin's only top-ten hit single.

Led Zeppelin III followed in 1970, influenced by Crosby, Stills & Nash and the maturing folk-rock scene in L.A.'s Laurel Canyon, with which Plant was especially besotted. Where the first two Zeppelin albums were pilloried for unrelenting assault—despite the fact that, as Page would point out in exasperation, both featured at least partially acoustic numbers—*Led Zeppelin III*'s acoustic trappings were dismissed as pandering. Fed up, Page withdrew from trying to engage the rock cognoscenti. Convinced, mostly correctly, that the music press had it in for them no matter what they did, Page demanded that the next album's cover contain no reference to the band: no names, no album title, no "Led Zeppelin." It is the earnest, callow fantasy of every musician maligned by bad press to "let the music speak for itself," except that Zeppelin had the clout—and a contract giving the band absolute control over its album covers—to make good on the threat. "After all this crap we'd had with the critics, I put it to everybody that it'd be a good idea to put out something totally anonymous," Page declared, and further decreed that each band member devise a symbol for himself to be printed on the sleeve in lieu of names.

Led Zeppelin's untitled fourth album landed in stores in November 1971 and became their biggest hit commercially and, for the moment, critically. The material was the most consistent of the band's career and perfected the balance between acoustic and electric that had eluded them on *Led Zeppelin III*. Apparently vindicating Page's no-names approach, even the despised *Rolling Stone* conceded that "a band never particularly known for its tendency to understate matters has produced an album which is remarkable for its low-keyed and tasteful subtlety." The album was so dense with first-rate songs that the review didn't mention the eight-minute, two-second number that closed side one. It started with Page plucking an acoustic guitar and ended with what would become the most famous guitar solo in rock, followed by Plant's plaintive a cappella "and she's buy-uy-ing a stair-air-way . . . to hea-vunnnn . . ."

Throughout 1972 Led Zeppelin toured, triumphant, behind the album, which would eventually sell more than twenty-three million copies and become the third best-selling album ever in the United States. But it infuriated the band that, no matter how many albums they shipped or arenas they sold out, they still weren't given what they felt was their due not only from the rock press, with which they had such a tortured history, but from the mainstream media. It especially galled that the Rolling Stones' 1972 tour in support of the landmark *Exile on Main Street* preempted what should have been, at least based on sales, the Year of Zeppelin. The band was determined not to let it happen again. "Look at all the press the Stones got on their last tour!" an anguished Robert Plant berated Danny Goldberg after he was hired as the band's publicist. Plant, Goldberg concluded, "wanted mainstream fame, and while the rest of the band were not as forceful in asking for it, they certainly wouldn't mind having it, either."

It is March 1973. Led Zeppelin is about to release their fifth album, *Houses of the Holy*, and embark on a sold-out tour of America, their ninth in five years. The album is the first to comprise entirely original material—no more Willie Dixon or Memphis Minnie covers—and breaks fresh stylistic ground with nods to reggae, raga, funk, even doo-wop, along with some of Page's most labyrinthine arrangements. The tour and album are nothing less than the band's bid for respect—also true stardom. After years of actively spurning the press, they now just as actively court it. It falls to Goldberg to conjure this particular rabbit. He concludes that "other than my closest friends, I knew I would get no-where with the sixties rock critics. I could not think of anyone in the Max's clique who would have both the stature and the inclination to transform Led Zeppelin's image." As if on cue, *Rolling Stone* savages *Houses of the Holy*—one of 1973's "dullest and most confusing albums"—and blithely libels Page's masterpiece ("tripe like 'Stairway to Heaven'") while suggesting the band might more accurately call itself Limp Blimp. It's an inauspicious start to Zeppelin's image refurbishment.

The band can't know it, but what waits around the corner is some-thing far larger than cultural parity with the Rolling Stones. Stubbing out joints in high school parking lots across America, Zeppelin's true con-stituents are about to get in touch with their kingmaking mojo. They clasp Led Zeppelin, and *Houses of the Holy*, to their bosom as fiercely as their older brothers and sisters embraced *Axis: Bold as Love*. The adoles-cent fantasies of a generation are about to collide with the ambitions and pretensions of a rock band fattened by unprecedented success but starv-ing for respect and unambiguous stardom. It turns out they aren't the only ones.

By 1973 Alice Cooper is nearly as reviled as Led Zeppelin by the rock-crit establishment, not so much for the band's music, authentically grotty garage rock that elicits raves from sympathetic critics like Lester Bangs. If Led Zeppelin's audience is considered too young to be taken seriously, Alice Cooper's is embarrassingly puerile, swooning for "I'm Eighteen," the band's 1971 hit, and subsequent self-conscious "anthems" in which

Alice, in his mid-twenties, casts himself as commiserating peer to budding mallrats everywhere. "We affect the little teenage boys between the ages of twelve and fifteen more than anybody," Alice would recall. "They consider us the heroes of our time for some reason."

The rock-crit animus derives mainly from the Alice Cooper stage show. Baroque and theatrical, it trades in simulated violence and gore without any obvious compensating ironic distance. The band does nothing to refute rumors that it bites off the heads of chickens and drinks the blood, hatched early in its career when a live chicken was tossed onstage and Alice, innocently believing chickens can fly, heaved it into the front rows—the audience, not Alice, tore it apart. Each tour debuts a new gimmick with which to "execute" Alice—in the 1972 show he was hanged from a gallows after dismembering a baby doll, with Lizzie Borden hatchet and fake blood, while singing "Dead Babies" with convincing psychotic glee. The calculation behind the group's morbid image—minutely orchestrated by its manager, Shep Gordon—insulted and impressed rock insiders who knew that the band, especially Alice, bore no resemblance to pansexual necrophiles and were in fact resolutely heterosexual former track-and-field lettermen from Cortez High in Phoenix. Alice, né Vincent Furnier, is the son of a Baptist minister.

During their early days in Los Angeles as lesser protégés of Frank Zappa, the band cultivated a dramatic, confrontational stage presence and became infamous for clearing entire ballrooms with their repertoire, which included the theme from *The Patty Duke Show*. "Even hippies hated us," Alice later recalled. "And it's hard to get a hippie to hate anything." The biggest bands of the early seventies, Led Zeppelin included, still performed on bare stages in street clothes, a holdover from the Woodstock ethic in which generational solidarity supposedly trumped the divide between audience and performer (both sides ignored the fact that the performer arrived and departed by limo). Alice Cooper refused to perpetuate this charade. Even when they were nobodies, the band hit the boards in chrome pants, sequin-encrusted vests, smudged mascara, and torn fishnets, demanding homage be paid to their "stardom" and empty awesomeness. The Cooper shows—replete with costume changes, props, and the suggestion of a libretto underlying the mayhem—were the first to fully integrate a theatrical sensibility into rock performance. "We did it before Bowie," Alice recalled, "before Kiss. Before anybody."

The band at first dabbled in feckless psychedelia while Alice suffered from stage fright to the extent that he sang with his back to the audience. The same stagecraft was practiced for entirely different purposes by the brooding singer of another L.A. band, who adopted Alice as one of his manifold drinking buddies. (After the Doors' Jim Morrison died in Paris in 1971, Alice Cooper recorded "Desperado" in tribute to their fallen friend.) In the meantime Alice was still Vince, and the band—guitarists Michael Bruce and Glen Buxton, bassist Dennis Dunaway, and drummer Neal Smith—was called the Nazz until it was discovered Todd Rundgren already used the name. They rechristened themselves—for reasons never adequately explained—Alice Cooper. "Alice came up with the name," Dunaway recalled. "It shocked me when he first suggested it, but when I ran it by my parents and saw their mouths drop open I knew it was the name for us." (Alice later said he chose it so that "people would expect a blond folk singer—instead, they get these monsters.")

Meanwhile, Alice adopted a sinister persona that captivated audiences, or at least seemed to repel them less, and the band started writing songs tailored to it. Thus was born Alice Cooper, the semi-transvestite Wicked Wretch of the West, dripping mascara and attitude. Alice's aggressive makeup and drag were the handiwork of the GTOs (Girls Together Outrageously) groupie clique that befriended the band at Zappa's compound in Laurel Canyon, where they were signed after a legendary 6:30 A.M. audition when they mistook GTO Miss Christine's instructions to arrive at 6:30 P.M. "They were all pretty square then—Alice was really straight," former GTO Pamela Des Barres said. "Miss Christine made up Alice there for the first time"—demented Emmett Kelly eyes with the suggestion of fangs around his lips—"and helped him dress. The rest of the band followed suit."

After nearly sinking into oblivion after two failed albums on Zappa's Straight Records, Alice Cooper recorded *Love It to Death* with Bob Ezrin, a young Canadian producer with whom they delivered the hit "I'm Eighteen" in 1971. The Ezrin-produced *Killer* followed ten months later, featuring the calculated outrage of "Dead Babies"—a song not about infanticide but child neglect, although few bothered to scrutinize the lyrics after the dolls' heads started rolling, part of Gordon's master plan to deliberately contrive and then exploit negative publicity. The band meanwhile steadily improved; *Killer* was hailed by Lester Bangs as "one of the finest rock and roll records released in 1971."

By 1972 the band was fresh off *School's Out*, which reached number two on the wings of its title song, an international top-ten hit. Thanks to the steady drip of furor in the press over the blood-soaked stage show, Alice Cooper had achieved what the mighty Led Zeppelin still dreamed of: They were household names. Or at least Alice was. The rest of the band watched with growing alarm as Alice, a natural celebrity, usurped the group's identity by the sheer force of his personality and the fact that the band shared its name with its lead singer. By now they had been together nonstop for five years and moved from Los Angeles to a farmhouse outside Pontiac, Michigan, and, finally, to a rented mansion in Greenwich, Connecticut, where the first tracks for *Billion Dollar Babies*, the album poised to take them over the top for good, were recorded in 1972. Despite exhaustion and portents of trouble—Buxton deteriorated so badly he was replaced by session players; Alice, under unrelenting pressure as the star, ramped up his already formidable drinking—the band embraced the challenge. "Alice and I were long-distance runners— that's how we met," said Dunaway. "So we had this keep-going-at-all-costs mentality that pulled us through." Bruce, the group's chief composer, recalled that "by this point we had really started to come into our own. We were on an upward spiral."

Billion Dollar Babies, with its themes of power, money, and decadence, would be in many ways more in sync with the times than the pseudo-mysticism that pervades Zeppelin's *Houses of the Holy*. "I always said that Alice Cooper was the *National Enquirer* of rock and roll—we were not *The New York Times*," says Alice. "Half of the guys in the band were journalists in school, and we understood the fact that BOY BORN WITH DOG'S HEAD was infinitely more exciting than TAX CUTS INEVITABLE. So we wrote about things that we thought were exciting. We wrote about the fact that we were not into rock and roll for peace and love. We were in it for Ferraris, and blondes and switchblades. We were actually more honest than anybody else." Alice worked just as hard at being a star as Robert Plant, but unlike Plant, professed to find the prospect of his stardom ludicrous. "The Billion Dollar Babies concept was simply making fun of ourselves," Alice recalled. "Here was a band nobody would touch three years ago and now we're the biggest band in the world." David Libert, the band's road manager, says Alice "never took himself seriously. He took what he did seriously, I suppose, but he did not take *himself* seriously. It was almost like a joke to him, but he was okay to be around because of that." Nevertheless, Alice was not at all conflicted about embracing the full measure of his stardom. "As soon as the announcer says, Alice Cooper!—the moment I step on that stage—boom! From that point on I *own* that stage and nobody better get on it. It's *mine*. I don't care if there's a hundred thousand people, a million people, or twelve people, it's *my* stage. It's a surge of power that goes right through your body."

There was symmetry behind Alice Cooper's flaunting their unlikely success at an audience coming of age amid simultaneous recession and inflation, rationed gasoline, and a U.S. president circling the drain of his impeachment. "Elected," a reworked "Reflected" from the band's long-lost first album, was released ahead of *Billion Dollar Babies* to coincide with the bitter 1972 U.S. presidential election and promoted with a short film featuring Alice, Budweiser in hand and a chimp as his campaign manager, canvassing for votes. In the song, Alice promises that he's a "top prime cut of meat, I'm your choice" and "we're gonna win this one, take the country by storm, you and me together, young and strong!" For a generation now old enough to appreciate the implications of a protracted crisis in the federal government's executive branch, the idea of Alice Cooper running for president seemed perversely logical. The unrelenting political tempest encouraged compensating pop cultural froth—it's no accident that glam, a school of rock focused on glib, facile songs and male performers who gave off fuzzy sexual vibes, thrived in the early seventies, thanks in no small part to Alice Cooper making it palatable for both musicians and audiences outside the New York–London–Los Angeles triangle of hip. "Alice was an early glam pioneer," says the guitarist Mick Mashbir, a friend of the band from Phoenix hired to cover for the faltering Buxton on the album and tour. "Those of us who were into glam in Arizona in 1970 were a bit at risk of violence in the street." (Three years later, at the end of the Billion Dollar Babies tour, Mashbir shared an elevator in New York with Greg Allman of the Allman Brothers, and beheld "the good ol' denim-wearing Southern boy wearing a satin suit and platform boots. The change had definitely come.")

As the release of *Billion Dollar Babies* neared, Alice Cooper, reveling in and lampooning their success, believed they could have it both ways. The album, Alice recalled, "was reflecting the decadence of a time when we were living from limousine to penthouse to the finest of everything. We couldn't believe people were paying us to do this. We would have done it for free, because we were just a garage band who happened to be at the right place at the right time." But the calculus beyond the band's music that led them to this pinnacle—the relentless promotion and deft massaging of the media so that unflattering stories were spun into assets, dead babies turned into billion-dollar ones—was hardly happenstance. "Billion Dollar Babies was the first time that we had a little bit of money, a little bit of power," Gordon says today. "There were absolutely no rules at all at that time. And we had nothing to lose." Shortly after the '73 tour ended, Gordon reflected, "It was the best thing for their careers—I don't think there's any doubt about that. Whether it was the best thing for them as human beings—well, I'm not so sure about that. I'm afraid that they're going to find out, in the end, that they've paid a very high price for their success."

While Alice Cooper and Led Zeppelin in 1973 suffer at the hands of the rock-crit elite, the Who has the opposite problem. As one of the last British Invasion bands still standing, the four members are already under a bell jar in rock's permanent collection: Townshend, rock's thinking man but also of the windmilling power chords and smashed guitars; Roger Daltrey in fringed buckskin twirling the microphone like a lasso; Keith Moon flaying the drums with loony intensity; and John Entwistle, stolid and oxlike, holding the center with his bass. The band enjoys tremendous goodwill with critics and by the time *Quadrophenia,* their ninth and most anticipated album, is released, are coming off two watersheds that comprise their finest work: *Tommy*—the first full-length rock opera, released in 1969—and *Who's Next,* a massive hit from 1971 with pummeling guitars that endear the band for the first time to large numbers of the adolescent Zeppelin / Alice Cooper constituency. At black-lit parties across the land, the boys and occasional girls take extralong gurgling bong hits in preparation for the climax of "Won't Get Fooled Again" and Daltrey's window-shattering *"EE-YEEEEAAAAHHHHHhhhhh!!!"*

As a consequence, expectations run impossibly high for *Quadrophenia,* made more so by the album's ambition: another opera, this one a paean to the Who's early days as the house band for the Mods, the smart-dressing, scooter-riding, pill-popping young Brits at perpetual war with the fearsome, antifashion Rockers. Townshend conflates the protagonist, Jimmy, a Mod in the throes of a four-way identity crisis (schizophrenia squared, hence quadrophenia), from the personalities of the four members of the Who. The album took nearly a year to write and record and was beset by technical snafus, field recordings of crashing waves and whistling locomotives, and rising tensions within the band to the point that Daltrey knocked Townshend unconscious during rehearsals for the North American tour. In the end Townshend jettisoned lengthy stretches of the opera's story to accommodate the time constraints of even a double album and vacillated between elation about the material and dreadful premonition. "I was keyed up, at the time *Quadrophenia* was ready to be released, for total failure," he would recall.

Instead, *Quadrophenia* is neither triumph nor disaster—although the Who's ever-younger fan base plays it as incessantly as *Who's Next,* and it gains in stature every year and is eventually lionized, along with *Tommy,* as one of the twentieth century's pop-cultural masterpieces. It shoots to number two on the U.S. charts, but next to the unstoppable *Who's Next* and even *Tommy,* to which it is inevitably compared, it fails to connect on a visceral level outside of its hits, the pummeling "The Real Me" and "Love, Reign O'er Me," which open and close the opera's story. Rock critics in thrall to Townshend's wit, the band's sheer musicianship, and the audacity of recording another opera after the genre-defining *Tommy* give *Quadrophenia* every consideration but can't help but sound a note of faint praise. *Rolling Stone* is typical: "Townshend has taken great pains with the record, has carried it within him for over a year, has laboriously fitted each piece of its grand scale in place," but nonetheless "fails to generate a total impact." The album's reverential publicity and austere gatefold cover—a sepia photograph of an anorak-wearing Mod astride a Vespa scooter—set the expectation that *Quadrophenia* should be admired first and enjoyed second, a deadly combination for rock and completely out of keeping with the Who's reputation for high-minded anarchy. "It was almost like there was too much good press about it, which, instead of letting people just make what they could of it, was hammered down their throats," Daltrey would later recall.

Townshend and the Who hadn't set out to become the keepers of the sixties rock and roll grail—that mantle and burden was foisted upon them by besotted critics. But by 1973, with the Beatles lost forever to a dispiriting, attenuated breakup and the Rolling Stones seemingly off their game with the weakly received *Exile on Main Street* (like *Quadrophenia,* an album that would reveal its genius in the fullness of time), it fell to the Who to distill whatever made sixties rock essential into a form palatable enough to survive the seventies. Of the handful of bands at their rarefied level, the Who are by far the most transparent with the media, airing their foibles and internecine battles with refreshing candor, and the most obviously and sincerely invested in their audience. As Townshend would recall, "We wanted to play because we were into the music and into the fact that the only reality that existed was in losing yourself in people's reaction to you."

Like many of their contemporaries, the Who came together via the sixties' uncanny facility for triangulating serendipity, talent, and burning ambition. Townshend was raised in Shepherd's Bush, a working-class London neighborhood also home to the young Entwistle and Daltrey. Townshend's parents were professional musicians—his father played saxophone in a dance band—and their son traveled with them frequently to gigs around Britain. Showing signs of the multi-instrumentalist he would become in the Who, he taught himself to play guitar and banjo and joined Entwistle in a Dixieland "trad" band. After a chance meeting, Daltrey invited Entwistle to join his R&B band, the Detours, and switched

from guitar to lead vocals after Townshend joined at Entwistle's suggestion. The band changed its name to the Who in 1964, then the High
Numbers at the behest of a transient manager, then back to the Who
when Keith Moon, the drummer for a surf band called the Beachcomb-
ers, was hired after a drunken audition in which, foreshadowing the
group's future, he played so aggressively that he destroyed the kick drum
pedal.

Kit Lambert and Chris Stamp, former filmmakers, took over management as the band consolidated its hold over the Mods, adopting the
motto "Maximum R&B" as they pounded out sweaty James Brown and
Motown covers at increasingly chaotic shows. The sheer volume the Who
suddenly mustered through enhancements in amplification would have
lasting implications, not all of them positive. Townshend prevailed upon
the London music shop owner and electronics whiz James Marshall—he
toured with Townshend's father in the forties—to build him a 100-watt
amplifier, the better to drown out the sound of the audience and John
Entwistle's bass. Townshend placed the amp atop two Marshall speaker
cabinets, forming an imposing and aesthetically pleasing tower. Thus
was born the Marshall stack, soon to loom behind guitar heroes from
Jimi Hendrix to Jimmy Page. "It was such a big jump," Townshend marveled. "It meant people like us could go play really dangerous places,
because the power of the instruments was conferred back on us. We used
to challenge audiences with our machismo—you know, we were four
weedy guys." As Townshend and a generation of young guitarists across
Britain soon discovered, "me and my guitar and my amplifier were om-
nipotent in ways that me, my bike and my cricket bat were not."

A side effect of high-powered speakers placed in proximity to the
electric guitar is feedback—more so when the guitar is a semi-hollow-
body Rickenbacker, which Townshend played in emulation of John Lennon's and George Harrison's guitars in the early Beatles. Said Townshend
later, "There were a lot of brilliant young players around, Clapton and
various other people. I was very frustrated because I couldn't do all that
flash stuff. So I just started getting into feedback and expressed myself
physically." In September 1964, Townshend accidentally poked the neck
of his guitar into the ceiling of a London club and snapped it off. As the

audience sniggered, he tabulated his options and concluded that "I had no other recourse but to make it look like I had meant to do it. So I smashed the guitar and jumped all over the bits then carried on as though nothing had happened. And the next day the place was packed." Soon the Who's live shows climaxed with Townshend wrecking his guitar, accompanied by Moon upending his drums. The Mods, in their porkpie hats and smart two-button suits, reveled in the implied rebellion. "These little pilled-up Mods would come up to me and stutter, 'Y-you gotta do *more*, P-Pete, b-because it's *right*, man,'" Townshend would recall.

The Who commenced a run of landmark U.K. singles composed by Townshend—"I Can't Explain," "My Generation," "Anyway, Anyhow, Anywhere," "The Kids Are Alright." The band's artistic ambitions were confirmed by their second album's nine-minute mini-opera, "A Quick One While He's Away," but broad acceptance in the U.S. would elude them despite their scraping the top forty with "Happy Jack." Singles about gender confusion ("I'm a Boy") and masturbation ("Pictures of Lilly") had predictable consequences for U.S. airplay and record sales despite the band's well-received set at the Monterey Pop Festival in 1967. By then the Who were ruinously in debt and Townshend counted on "I Can See for Miles," which he'd written a year earlier and held in reserve, as their salvation. "It's like when your wife is hysterical and everyone including the milkman is screaming for their dough and then you say, 'Ah, but I have this *other* account.'" "I Can See for Miles" became the Who's first and only U.S. top-ten hit but didn't sell, and the band was presented with an enormous bill from Inland Revenue for unpaid tax. "When 'I Can See for Miles' bombed I thought, 'What the hell am I gonna do now?'" Townshend recalled. "The pressures were really on me and I had to come up with something very quick."

Amid the chaos, Townshend's fixation with merging rock and opera had only deepened—another mini-opera, "Rael," closes their third album, *The Who Sell Out*. On tour in the U.S., Townshend filled pages with dialogue between "Father" and "Son," and on stationery cadged from the Holiday Inn in Rolling Hills, Illinois, recorded in his small, neat hand: "See me. Feel me. Touch me. Heal me." After a year and £15,000, at

the time the most costly album ever produced, *Tommy* was drop-kicked
into the marketplace on May 23, 1969. The story of a boy struck deaf,
dumb, and blind after witnessing his father murder his mother's lover
and later mistaken for a messiah, the album was a massive creative and
commercial risk. The band was all too aware that their future hung in the
balance. The Who performed *Tommy* in public for the first time at a
London showcase for music journalists, and the reaction was mostly ecstatic, although some harrumphed that a rock opera was at the very least
pretentious, to which Townshend responded, "dead bloody right, it is."
Tommy became an international smash, floating four singles including
the eternal "Pinball Wizard," and hit number four in the U.S. and number two in the U.K. It also elevated the Who to the highest stratum of the
rock firmament and carved out a space in popular culture that is the
province of no other rock band. "What I feel is very important about
Tommy is that as a band it was our first conscious departure out of the
adolescent area," Townshend would say. "It was our first attempt at something that wasn't the same old pilled-up adolescent brand of music." Performing *Tommy* to raves from *The New York Times* to *The New Yorker* at
the Fillmores West and East and the Metropolitan Opera, where the
band received a fourteen-minute standing ovation, the Who were at last
acknowledged as something greater than the sum of the guitars Townshend smashed. It was equity—artistic and mercantile—that Townshend
intended to spend.

The result was the stillborn *Lifehouse,* which baffled everyone, it seems,
except Townshend. A spiritual and science fiction high concept—at once
a film, opera, and piece of performance art—the story centered on creating a musical vibration so pure and irresistible that everyday life is tran-
scended and reality becomes subjective. The project went off the rails
when Townshend became obsessed with actually creating the phenomenon using the new music synthesizers before a handpicked audience
and filming their reactions. The upside of the experiment was that Townshend wrote a slate of some of his finest songs, salvaged on *Who's Next*
after the project was abandoned. "*Lifehouse* was an incredibly ambitious
project but it got entirely out of hand," he later admitted.

Having come to despair trying to push the sprawling *Lifehouse* to fruition only to endure the irony of its best songs being remaindered as one of the Who's most commercially successful albums, Townshend dreaded complacency and feared for the Who's relevance. *Quadrophenia* was to be Townshend's bid to continue to push the boundaries of what, exactly, rock could stand for as the seventies bore down. As the band prepared for the 1973 North American tour, where for the first time they'd come face-to-face with an audience ten years removed from the one that stuttered along to "My Generation," they couldn't have known that *Quadrophenia* would in fact be the Who's last concept album, their last conscious stab at greatness, and the last where the band's ambitions and sense of purpose would test the conventional wisdom of what the rock audience would and would not accept. Forty years later, Townshend acknowledged as much. "I've always felt that *Quadrophenia* was the last definitive Who album," he declared. "It's an epochal record—the last great album by the Who."

Chapter 2

HOPE I GET OLD BEFORE I DIE

The epic, angst-filled, rain-and-cognac-drenched writing and recording of Quadrophenia, *wherein Pete Townshend channels his inner Mod to deliver the Who from their adolescent past and gets his clock cleaned by Roger Daltrey for his trouble.*

The Who commence recording *Quadrophenia* in May 1973, at their new Ramport Studio, still under construction. It has been nearly two years since the release of *Who's Next*, which sold more than a million copies and radically recalibrated the band's commercial and critical status in Britain and especially in America. "We'd had such a fabulous couple of years," Townshend later said. "We were described by all the rock critics of the day as being the best band in the world. And you have to cast this against what was going on around us. There were bands like Crosby, Stills and Nash, the Band, Neil Young's Crazy Horse, Jimi Hendrix, Cream—big, big, big fantastic huge-drawing bands. And we were the leading band of the day, no question."

Where the Who rode their first wave of broad-based success in 1969 with *Tommy, Who's Next* belonged to the young Zeppelin, Black Sabbath, and Grand Funk headbangers—another Friday-night party album. As the stems and seeds of suburban primo were sifted in gatefold album covers, they keened along with Townshend's falsetto—"it's own-leee teeeeen-age waste-land"—thinking he sang to them in their red-eyed self-congratulation, never guessing nor caring that "Baba O'Reilly" was Townshend's paean to Meher Baba, the spiritual master who turned him away from the drug culture. During the *Who's Next* tour, Townshend for the first time looked into fist-pumping, lighter-waving hordes who didn't know exactly what to make of "I Can't Explain" or "Substitute," the band's traditional one-two opening punch from the post–Maximum R&B days. "I'm constantly thinking about age, always watching the audience change over the years," Townshend said in 1974. "There's people that grew up with the Who, then there's the second wave"—the *Tommy* converts— "and there's the third wave." The last made an impression. "In Los Angeles, that third wave stretched from maybe fifteen years old back to thirteen," Townshend marveled. "In the whole of our career, that's the youngest our audience has ever been."

The Who's record labels would have been far happier had Townshend served up a stylistic sequel to *Who's Next*. Yet despite *Who's Next*'s rapturous reception, the Who as a whole and Townshend in particular could only summon for it faint praise—"the Who's first ordinary album," Townshend said when it was released; "we'd lost one bollock," Daltrey added. (Townshend later reconsidered and included *Who's Next* among the band's best work.) Following up *Who's Next* with more of the same would have required cynicism Townshend was incapable of embracing; he was also a remarkably prolific composer at a time when "artists churned out new records like shells from a howitzer." Where his fellow British rock stars aggressively shunned journalists, Townshend just as actively courted them as sounding boards on which his raw ideas could be shaped and sharpened; halfway through recording *Tommy*, he spent the better part of three hours trying to explain the opera's plot to Jann Wenner, *Rolling Stone*'s editor, who published the resulting transcript verbatim.

"I began to depend on having brainstorms in the presence of intelligent journalists," Townshend would recall. "Speaking to journalists was for me a combination of therapy and tutorial. It worked so well for me that I started to regard it as part of my creative process." Notwithstanding the goodwill he earned by treating rock writers as something other than supplicating cretins, Townshend shrewdly apprehended that journalists are "exposed to everything that is happening at a given time," while musicians of the Who's exalted status "become stratified by the celebrity machine that separates performers from audience." Having ratified the Who's creative license with the unambiguous commercial success of *Tommy*, recording an album of unrelated songs—another *Who's Next*, in other words—was to Townshend unthinkable. He concluded that "the Who would from then on always need audacious conceptual work; I believed it was expected of us to take chances, even to fail as we had done with *Lifehouse*. I felt I needed to produce rock operas (or something equally impudent) almost as often as I had once produced singles in our early days."

Townshend gathered the threads that became *Quadrophenia* during late 1972. The Who's burgeoning popularity demanded they play vast arenas, and he sought a replacement, in ambition and length, for the *Tommy* segment of the performances, of which both band and audience had grown weary. *Who's Next* provided "a couple of wonderful songs"— "Baba O'Reilly" and "Won't Get Fooled Again"—but didn't "provide us with a show. We needed an hour of music to fill the gap." Says Peter Rudge, who co-managed the band in 1973 as Townshend's relationship with Kit Lambert and Chris Stamp unraveled: "*Tommy* morphed into one of the great stage shows of our time. It was the forerunner of [Pink Floyd's] *The Wall* in terms of taking a piece of music and turning it into a really cohesive piece of theatrics on stage." Townshend was already enmeshed in an array of side projects, including rehabilitating Eric Clapton—who had withdrawn to Hurtwood, his aptly named country estate, to snort heroin nonstop—with a one-off concert at London's Rainbow Theatre; meanwhile Entwistle and Daltrey recorded solo albums. When Townshend found time to reflect, he decided he wanted to create "a project that would clearly demonstrate to our audience, our critics and ourselves, what the contract actually was between the Who and their fans. I thought it would be nice to have an album that encapsulated everything the Who had ever done, with a big sort of flourish, so we could really start afresh." Says Rudge, "Pete knew that he had to do it. The Who had to move on as they'd just become a one-trick pony. And it was just kind of an interesting transitional period of them coming out of *Tommy* with a new piece of work which had to find its own identity."

The band starts recording the autobiographical *Rock Is Dead, Long Live Rock* with producer Glyn Johns, but after assessing the results, including the title track and two that will end up on *Quadrophenia,* "Is It in My Head" and "Love, Reign O'er Me," Townshend laments that "it sounded like a shadow, if this is possible, of *Who's Next,*" and the album is scrapped. He commissions Nik Cohn, one of the journalist sounding boards he'd assiduously courted, to write a film treatment, *Rock Is Dead (Rock Lives).* Cohn conceives four movies, each based on a member of the band; a boy character, Tommy—a composite of the four childhood psyches of the Who—reacts to each member's life as the story advances. The treatment was never filmed, and Townshend largely forgot about it until forty years later while preparing archival materials for a *Quadrophenia* boxed set, when he realized Cohn's treatment was the probable inspiration for *Quadrophenia's* four-faceted motif, and that Cohn's Tommy character was a forerunner of Townshend's *Quadrophenia* protagonist, Jimmy. "I read it and I thought bloody hell, this is kind of it," Townshend said. "This is what gave me the idea to create a four-faceted, four-musical-themes-based rock opera."

By the winter of 1972 Townshend had written half of the songs that would comprise *Quadrophenia* but had yet to crack the opera's thematic core. During a rainy night in a drafty outbuilding at his newly purchased property in Goring-on-Thames, he had a vivid flashback to 1964 and huddling under the pier at Brighton with his art-school girlfriend, coming down from purple hearts and a day and night of fighting the Rockers. "The feeling came flooding back—of ailing, depressed, tragic, lost and hopeless." Townshend seized a notebook and scribbled a Salingeresque sketch that would later appear on *Quadrophenia*'s sleeve. It begins: "I had to go to this psychiatrist every week. He never really knew what was wrong with me . . . My dad put it another way. He said I changed like the weather . . . Schizophrenic, he called it." Thus is born Jimmy—Townshend's "young Mod, hopeless, stranded on a rock in the rain, wondering if he might find redemption through the recounting of his pathetic life thus far"—and with him the missing link to *Quadrophenia*.

As he composes the opera, Townshend resists suggestions that it follow a conventional structure, instead trusting the inchoate voice—both his and, by extension, the Who's—that first drew the Mods to the Who like a magnet. "My first audience in the Mod days commissioned me to write what they felt disinclined or unable to say. Our fans found themselves in those lyrics—they each came and told me their own story." It's a crucial distinction that separates rock's narrative from other popular culture, and Townshend, alone among his contemporaries, recognizes it as such. "Rock and pop fans don't want to identify with a story or be granted the right to feel as though they are in it or to feel like the characters in it. They want to be the story." He implicitly trusts this "deliberately unstructured and accessible narrative" that has served the Who so well, and deploys it to full effect on *Quadrophenia*, with which Townshend, by returning to and investigating the band's birth, seeks to free the Who from its past and clear a path for the future as the seventies bear down.

Townshend's timing is auspicious. After the headlong cultural tumult of the sixties, the early seventies invite a moment of reflection and reappraisal. It is, briefly, an era of revivals: Thrift-shop art deco and moderne furnishings replace macramé and concrete-block-and-board shelves in the boomers' first real homes; the vanguard of America's young filmmakers establish their bona fides with films whose stories refurbish and gentrify the recent past: *The Godfather* (New York in the forties), *Chinatown* (L.A. in the thirties), and George Lucas's *American Graffiti*, set in 1962 in the sort of stultifying small town from which thousands of boomers fled screaming. Coincidental with *Quadrophenia*'s release, David Bowie issues *Pin Ups*, his valentine to mid-sixties Brit pop and rock; it's a measure of the Who's long shadow that Bowie covers not one but two of the band's songs—"I Can't Explain" and "Anyway, Anyhow,

Anywhere." Townshend, meanwhile, fretted that rock was in danger of regressing to its pre-Beatles doldrums. "I mean, if someone like Bowie, who's only been a big star for eighteen months or so, feels the need to start talking about his past influences, then obviously the roots are getting lost. The meat and potatoes—the reasons why people first pick up guitars—are getting forgotten." *Quadrophenia* is meant to be part of the soul-searching solution. But where *Pin Ups* is pure homage—the album hit number one in the U.K. and, ironically, prevented *Quadrophenia* from rising higher than number two—*Quadrophenia* is a work of retrospection. Far from the Mod throwback that some expect, the album is explicitly written and performed to be state-of-the-art progressive rock, a genre the Who helped invent with *Tommy*. The album abounds with synthesizers, which Townshend mastered on *Who's Next*, itself a prog-rock landmark. Until Townshend concludes the technology isn't up to the task, *Quadrophenia* was to be recorded in the then cutting-edge quadrophonic sound format.

Townshend also hopes the album will restore the band's collective inner compass, still whirling after two years of endless touring and thundering financial success. "When it came to *Quadrophenia* I felt we were lost—I thought we'd lost contact with our audience, we'd lost contact with our concept." As Townshend fell ever deeper in thrall to Meher Baba, "Keith Moon was buying a Rolls-Royce every week that he couldn't pay for; John Entwistle had so many brass instruments and toys in his life that he could barely move; and Roger Daltrey, with his long hair and his rippling muscles, was fighting beautiful women off left, right and center. We all four of us were nuts. And so the importance of this album, to get it down and to make it work." Despite Townshend's foreboding, the nearly two years the band had spent on the road flogging *Tommy* and *Who's Next* sharpened their musicianship to a fearful edge and instilled in each man a near-telepathic empathy when they play. During the recording of *Quadrophenia*, Townshend recalled, "Keith Moon showed up with a different girl every day but when you asked him to go 1-2-3-4 and play the drums he did a great job. I mean, his drumming on that album is spectacular. John Entwistle was at the height of his powers, an incredibly powerful, loquacious bass player. Roger's singing is just off the map—he was just a giant on that record. And my writing, I think, has never been better."

Townshend deliberately gives the hero of his new opera the unheroic name Jimmy—"I'm thinking of calling my next hero Bobby," he later quipped—and casts him as a grasping Mod aspirant and therefore a Who fan. "He feels a failure because he thinks these Ace Faces, these Mods he admired who were the best dancers and fighters, had the bike, the bird, the most up-to-the-minute clothes, were really demigods because they had the things he wished he had." Townshend imbues Jimmy with four personalities—"Schizophrenic? I'm bleeding quadrophenic!"—each with its own musical theme heard wafting over the crashing waves on the album's opening track, "I Am the Sea." The themes nominally coincide with corresponding personalities of the Who: "Bell Boy" (Moon), "Is It Me?" (Entwistle), "Helpless Dancer" (Daltrey), and "Love, Reign O'er Me" (Townshend). At least that's the impression. "There was a bit of confusion in the idea that Jimmy was made up of four facets that were made up of the members of the Who," Townshend later clarified. "It wasn't quite like that. It was that Jimmy as a boy looked to the four members of the Who, who were all very different, and saw himself in them." The opera is essentially a long flashback in which Jimmy, having rowed himself to a rock off the coast of Brighton—the holiday resort where the Mods, in a prehistoric flash mob, convene to scarf purple hearts and rumble with the Rockers—contemplates the implications of a crushing few days in which he sparred with his psychiatrist and mother, was sacked from his job, questioned his allegiance to the Mods, considered suicide, and finally, surrounded by the sea in the pouring rain, transcends his insecurities and embraces a new life unshackled from his past. "What the story is about and the reason why the story is important is that he loses everything," Townshend said. "He becomes the Everyman of the teenage world in which he then has to ask the big questions, which are who am I and where do I want to go?"

Townshend makes no secret that Jimmy's freak-out and catharsis are a parable for the Who's odyssey from house band for the Mods to somewhat bemused rock stars. *Quadrophenia* portends what Townshend hopes will be the band's clean break with its legacy, as he despairs that they already are becoming dangerously disingenuous. "Even if one can get away with it, hypocrisy is not tolerable in something as intrinsically honest as rock and roll," he said. "It's very hypocritical for a band like the Who to stand onstage and pretend they're adolescents when all they're really doing is reliving their adolescence." Attempting to jettison a now wildly successful band's nearly ten-year legacy carries considerable risk, but Townshend presses on regardless. "What I think will hurt me about *Quadrophenia* when I'm old," he speculated shortly after the album's release, "is its deliberate self-consciousness. But I felt it was time for the Who to be self-conscious." *Quadrophenia*, then, is to be the repudiation of the band's "adolescent obsession, the teenage frustration thing." The seething protopunk who penned "hope I die before I get old" when he was nineteen comes to understand, at age twenty-eight, that his Mod manifesto is also an albatross, and he wants the Who rid of it once and for all.

Meanwhile, Townshend divines the first stirrings of a coming distraction that will prove far more disruptive than he or anyone else can imagine. "In '73, what we had was Electric Light Orchestra with a spaceship onstage, Pink Floyd doing this big stuff, the Who with their lasers, Peter Gabriel's walking around dressed as a flowerpot," he recalled "Two years later, we had punk." With startling clairvoyance, Townshend writes for *Quadrophenia* "The Punk and the Godfather," in which Jimmy attends a Who concert and has an imaginary conversation with the Godfather, "your average mindless rock star," as Townshend characterizes him, whom Jimmy lectures, "your axe belongs to a dying nation/they don't know that we own you." The song presages with eerie accuracy the 1970s punks' sputtering rejection of preening rock stars and the increasingly naked contempt for the audiences making them rich. The song also addresses the fact, seldom discussed in 1973, that rock fans can also choose *not* to buy the albums and concert tickets. As Jimmy sneers at the Godfather: "You only became what we made you . . . you only earned what we gave you."

The Who ultimately weather the punk revolution far better than their contemporaries—Led Zeppelin never entirely recover from it—because the band's smashed-guitars legacy is sufficient to inoculate them from the punks' outright contempt but also because Townshend sees in them, and they in him, a kindred. Alone among his contemporaries in the backstage-buffet-and-limousine caste, Townshend sees the outlines of the future clearly enough to write about it. "I kind of knew punk was coming," he recalled. "There was a musical revolution coming but I obviously didn't know what shape it was." He sees *Quadrophenia* as the last, best chance to keep the Who one step ahead of the zeitgeist. "I wanted to get the band back not only to its roots but also to kind of abandon, if you like, this move towards progressive rock." Exhibiting the practical streak that throughout the Who's career has contradicted his flights of righteousness, Townshend accepts as inevitable that "at the same time, I knew we had to make a progressive rock album because that's where the market was. So it was kind of a double bind."

Quadrophenia is nevertheless as ambitious as the aborted *Lifehouse* is fatally impractical. Townshend proposes to overlay an opera's libretto onto what is in effect a documentary of the Who's early milieu and capture every nuance in loving and accurate detail. It's a tall order, not least because the Mod scene is ten years gone by 1973—an eternity in the context of the trend-vaulting 1960s and '70s. It also is largely a mystery to American audiences, whereas the themes behind *Tommy*—comprising adultery, murder, and messiah-seeking gone wrong—had been familiar and universal. "In the U.S., you know, people never knew much about the Mods," Townshend acknowledged. "But the Mods were a real movement. It cut across all class lines but it was working-class London"—like Townshend and the rest of the Who. "It only lasted a couple of years, really. In '66 it got very locked into this television program called *Ready Steady Go!,* where the producers just got the Ace Faces, the trendsetters, to go on television. It was a network show, so Mod fashions spread all through England overnight." Townshend himself—a perennial awkward outsider pathologically self-conscious about his beaklike nose—found solace in the Mods, and the memory warms him even as he sits astride worldwide stardom. "I've often said I was moved emotionally by Mods, and a lot of people think it's stupid to be hung up on fashion and hair-cuts, but it was the one thing that held me together, gave me a feeling of belonging. I always felt alienated by the Woodstock Generation."

By the time he fetches up on the *Quadrophenia* sessions, Ron Nevison, an expat American recording engineer, had been mixing live sound for Traffic, Derek and the Dominos, and the Jefferson Airplane and is a staff engineer at Island Studios in London. In 1972 Ronnie Lane, the impish bassist of the Faces, took delivery of a silver Airstream trailer and, with Lane's close friend Townshend and Nevison supervising, tricked it out with an eight-track recorder and mixing console. Nevison is dispatched along with the Airstream to recording dates and is on board as engineer when the mobile arrives at Ramport. "Pete called up Ronnie Lane and said, 'Can we use your mobile studio until our studio is ready?'" says Nevison. "So I got the job kind of by default because I built it and who better to run it than me? Of course if I didn't do a good job I would've been out of there in a couple of days, I'm sure."

As it happens, Nevison is kept on throughout recording and scores his first credit on a major album. Townshend's preparation and clearheaded-ness about the material manifests wherever Nevison turns. Working at his home studio in Goring-on-Thames, Townshend created meticulous demos for *Quadrophenia*'s songs. Wishing to capture an authentic cello sound, he bought a cello and taught himself to play "adequately enough to lay down a small section," an astonished associate told Richie Unter-berger. "He's just a phenomenal musician." He also mastered the fa-mously temperamental ARP 2500 music synthesizer so completely that the company put his photo on the cover of an instruction manual. Hav-ing used the synthesizer to devastating effect on *Who's Next*—the indel-ible central riff to "Won't Get Fooled Again" is created by routing notes from an ordinary home organ through a primitive synthesizer—Townshend conjures for *Quadrophenia* sweeping soundscapes and gor-geous filigree, like the strings that form the lilting waltz-time motif to "Love, Reign O'er Me." None of this comes easily, as Nevison discovers.

Where a digital synthesizer today stores data as simply as closing a document on a personal computer, in 1973 "you couldn't just push a save button and go back to it," he says. "You had to constantly tune it up and fiddle with it. Pete didn't want to waste band time doing that."

Townshend creates a click track and then plays, one by one, all the basic instruments—drums, bass, guitar—and turns the tape over to Nevison as a guide to record the actual parts with Moon and Entwistle. Showing his regard for the delicate alchemy underpinning the Who's sound, Townshend "played very, very simple parts" on the demos "because he didn't want Keith or John following his lead," Nevison says. "He wanted them to do their own thing." Entwistle's volcanic bass on "The Real Me"—captured as a first take when the bassist thinks he's merely warming up—is one stunning result of the strategy. Daltrey and Entwistle also have home studios; using Townshend's demos, Entwistle creates the multiple brass parts that become *Quadrophenia*'s signature, particularly on "The Real Me" and "5:15." Recalled Daltrey, "I had my own studio at the time and I was running the songs down in the studio at home before I got to the studio with the Who. That helped a lot on the record— I think vocally on that album I do some vocal acrobatics."

Townshend is for the first time working without Kit Lambert, his once trusted producer and creative confidant. It was Lambert—along with Daltrey, who was far less diplomatic—who kept Townshend's muse anchored. "They were strange bedfellows, and they rubbed each other up the wrong way," says Rudge. "But underlying that there was a real respect between them." After the success of *Tommy* and *Who's Next*, Lambert drifted into booze-and-heroin-induced ineffectualness, infuriating Townshend, who shoulders *Quadrophenia* almost entirely on his own. "I was extremely fond of Kit and he was starting to come apart," Townshend lamented. "Lambert pretended to be the album's producer for the first week, showing up smashed, usually extremely late . . . the second week I sacked him, coming very close to punching him. For weeks after, we were visited by heroin dealers trying to find him."

The practicalities, or lack thereof, of recording at Ramport, a studio that is itself a work in progress, reveal themselves soon enough. With the musicians sequestered in the recording room and Nevison in the mobile parked outside, communication is via intercom and a closed video feed. "All the time we were recording we were surrounded by anxious builders watching to see their labors appreciated," Townshend would recall. "Whenever we stopped working they would start again, putting air conditioning in." Nevertheless, "a lot of love, or 'vibes' they would say, went into the place and you can feel it." Says Cy Langston, a road manager and later sound man for the Who's live shows who played guitar on Entwistle's first solo album, "The one thing everyone said about Ramport was that it had great, great, great karma. Everything in central London was like walking into a hospital. Ramport had this incredible vibe about it, with the oak-paneled walls. It was like being in a mansion." Sunlight pours through the windows, the Who's framed gold albums line the walls, and a road case with full bar—including Townshend's Rémy Martin, which he quaffs from a pewter beer mug—beckons by the entrance to the vocal booth.

One of the first tracks recorded for *Quadrophenia* is "Drowned," in which Jimmy contemplates suicide—"I wanna drown . . . in cold water"—an otherwise upbeat number with rollicking gospel-style piano played by Chris Stainton, of Joe Cocker's Grease Band. "Just as we were about to start it off I remember that I'd written it as a kind of tribute to something Meher Baba had said—something like God is like the ocean and individuals are like drops of water," Townshend recalled. "I was thinking about that and then we started to play and it started to rain outside, and then it started to thunder. And Chris Stainton's in the piano booth playing away. And we finished off the number and I could hear the piano kind of deteriorating in quality." Nevison says, "Picture me outside Ramport in this Airstream. It's raining really hard and all of a sudden I see red flashing lights and I glance out the window and there's the fire brigade that's just pulled up. What happened was that the water built up on the roof and went pouring down the air-conditioning duct and started filling up the piano booth where Chris Stainton was playing." Stainton, who performed with Cocker at Woodstock minutes before an epic thunderstorm turned the festival into a sea of mud, soldiers on as the water

rises around him. "They were really starting to boogie," Townshend recalled, "and Chris ends up shouting from the piano booth, 'It's fucking
full of water!' And as he opens the door it flows out. This is our studio we
just built. Everywhere water. And I thought it was just great, and that
take was so good."

Complicating an already formidable recording is the array of sound
effects that serve as a Greek chorus for the opera's story. "In *Quadrophenia* virtually every track cross-fades into another one rather than just a
straight cut," Nevison points out. The cumulative effect is to give the
album the flow of the movie it would eventually become. Nevison wades
into the field with a Nagra tape recorder or, as with the crashing waves
the engineer captures in Cornwall that open and close the album, the
entire mobile at his disposal. (Nevison plugs the studio into an outlet at
a public toilet—"I'm amazed it didn't blow it up," Townshend marveled.)
He has his girlfriend request a Sousa march from a brass band playing in
London's Regent's Park, which he surreptitiously records. "In Hyde Park
there's this place called the Speaker's Corner, a famous place for people
getting up on soapboxes," Nevison says. "We wanted the sound of kind
of like workers rioting"—a bridge between "The Dirty Jobs" and "Helpless Dancer"—"so I took a Nagra there and got busted by the police. They
took me off the property and questioned me and then let me go."

While Nevison braces the constabulary and spends a weekend recording the rain in Wales ("got lots of rain hoping for thunder, but never
did—you can't just ask for thunder, especially in Wales"), Townshend's
driver bribes a British Railways engineer to blow his locomotive whistle
inside Waterloo Station for "5:15," Jimmy's impulsive journey to Brighton wrecked on purple hearts ("out of my brain on the train"). Poignantly,
a snatch of the Who's winsome early hit "The Kids Are Alright" is heard
from Jimmy's point of view between the despairing "Helpless Dancer"
and "Is It in My Head?" The sessions at Ramport end July 17, 1973, when,
in a finale worthy of a Who concert, cartloads of percussion are presented to Moon with instructions to attack all of them on cue. "Keith was
out in the middle of the studio hitting everything he could, and at the
end he pushed everything over—he just went nuts," says Nevison. "I'm
glad it was on tape because a lot of that percussion didn't survive."

•   •   •

Townshend and Nevison take the completed master tapes to Townshend's home studio for mixing. During the sessions at Ramport, Townshend commuted via a chauffeured Mercedes Pullman 600 limousine "with two big JBLs in the back," notes an impressed Nevison. Now Townshend ferries Nevison from the engineer's lodgings at a local pub, sometimes by boat. For the next three weeks, it's the two of them and hundreds of feet of two-inch tape. "We didn't have enough tracks for everything, but that didn't stop us," Nevison says. "We recorded a lot of the sound effects on two-track. And when we mixed, we loaded them onto professional cartridge machines much like you'd find in a radio station, where you would have them in order, like for a thirty-second spot. And so Pete would have one on one side, I would have one on the other side, and when we needed thunder, I'd hit a button. We did a lot of stuff like that." "I Am the Sea," with its crashing waves and beguiling snatches of songs drifting in and out like Sirens, requires nine tape machines running simultaneously. Townshend, like a master builder, carries the plans for the entirety of *Quadrophenia* in his head and brings a writer's metaphorical flourish even to quality control. During one playback, Nevison looks up and beholds Townshend standing by the tape machine with a razor blade in his hand. "If you cut the tape it will stop because there is a light sensor, so he had his finger over the light sensor with one hand and a razor blade in the other hand, and the tape was all on the floor, and I got the message he didn't like the take."

Townshend and Nevison finish mixing *Quadrophenia* in September 1973, with the album's release scarcely a month away. The first date of the UK tour is October 28 at the Trentham Gardens in Stoke-on-Trent, followed by the U.S. premiere November 20 at the Cow Palace in San Francisco. Such a schedule is formidable for a straightforward album; it borders on sadistic given the complexity of *Quadrophenia*, especially in light of the band's eighteen-month absence from the road. ("Record companies like to put out albums at Christmas," recalled Townshend.) Despite the looming deadlines, Townshend flies to Los Angeles to supervise the mastering before the album is pressed. The final mix of *Quadro-*

phenia is a source of controversy for the next two decades. Daltrey, especially, is displeased. "It's incredibly weak," he still complained twenty years after the album's release. "I've heard what's on the tapes—it lacks the real power that I know is there from hearing it in the studio." Tellingly, he noted, "I think a lot of the vocals are very low."

Meanwhile, *Quadrophenia*'s elaborate packaging nears completion. A forty-four-page booklet with thirty-seven stark black-and-white photographs by Ethan Russell, photographer of the iconic *Who's Next* cover, depicts an approximation of the album's story. Weeks are consumed auditioning models and costumes that meet Townshend's obsessive Mod specifications; Jimmy is finally portrayed by a twenty-one-year-old commercial painter dragged from a pub by a Ramport secretary. "We ran out of models and finally said, 'Piss, let's use him'—and he was perfect," said Daltrey. *Quadrophenia*'s cover depicts Jimmy astride his bemirrored scooter in an anorak, shot at the studio of Graham Hughes, Daltrey's cousin. "Roger thought of the idea of painting the Who logo on the back of the kid's parka," Hughes said. "I still hadn't figured out where the group were going to appear when the idea of the wing mirrors suddenly dawned on me." Hughes shoots the faces of Daltrey, Entwistle, and Townshend as they mug into the scooter's mirrors (Moon's will be superimposed later).

Advance copies of the album sent to critics are accompanied by a remarkable document: an embargoed synopsis of the opera's story and recording notes compiled by Townshend. "Whether you like it, or hate it, this album is notable as a Who album because of the freedom we have had," he declares somewhat self-consciously. "Every facility was provided and with the synthesizer and John Entwistle's brass collection we managed to embrace musical areas we've never hit before." It is indicative of Townshend's pride and insecurity, up to his neck in a project with enormous personal significance upon which he has cast the future of the Who, that he deems it necessary to gently hector the critics about the album's significance and at the same time prostrate himself before them. "Learning, very much the hard way, about making albums that 'flow,'" he continues, "I have decided after listening and listening, that your first listen might be aided by a bit of preamble. It would probably be aided by a stiff drink and a comfy chair as the album is long and we want you to hear it all." Townshend's song-by-song annotation of *Quadrophenia*, deployed onstage to the indifference of audiences during the upcoming tour, is well intentioned but carries an unmistakable whiff of pedantry that he'd avoided throughout the band's career. "One of the reasons the Who have been so long-lasting is the fact that we've been careful not to preach and careful not to teach," Townshend said in 1971. Now, on the eve of the band's most important album, he seems to be doing both.

Quadrophenia is released October 19, 1973. The next day *Melody Maker* runs the banner TOWNSHEND TOPS TOMMY! and raves, "Pete Townshend's brainchild, a year in the making, sets new standards for British rock music." The more typical reviews are respectful but border on bafflement. "You get the feeling that Pete Townshend has tried to out-*Tommy Tommy* and gone sailing right over the top," sniped the *New Music Express*. *Rolling Stone* posits, "If in effect we are being placed in the mind of an adolescent, neither the texture of the music nor the album's outlook is able to rise to this challenge of portraiture. Despite the varied themes, Jimmy is only seen through Townshend's eyes, geared through Townshend's perceptions . . . the album straining to break out of its enclosed boundaries and faltering badly." The Who's vast reserves of goodwill with the music press undoubtedly keep the reviews from straying into outright provocation, as would have been the case with Led Zeppelin. As Townshend later admitted, "Obviously I was delighted to read headlines like '*Quadrophenia* Caps *Tommy*,' but I think they were written by critics who were just as relieved as we were to find that we could write and play another sustained 'concept' album."

The muted critical reaction does nothing to dampen expectations for the upcoming tours of Britain and America, which sell out in a matter of hours. The band has a ludicrously short time—less than two weeks—to prepare and face enormous technical challenges of reproducing *Quadrophenia*'s sound effects. Despite the intensity of the endeavor and occasional snafus, the recording of the album had gone relatively smoothly, which may instill a false sense of confidence that the tour will coalesce as easily. Townshend later marveled at "just how fucking efficient it was. Jesus Christ, you know, we were *on*. It was just that short period of recording followed by a short period of mixing, all very intense. And then of course once we got to the Lyceum Theater, opening night. Fucking disaster."

Chapter 3

LIVE FROM THE COOPER MANSION

Alice Cooper hole up in a Gatsbyesque estate as big as the Ritz and record Billion Dollar Babies, *their snarling ode to pop-culture trash, while they perfect rock stardom in residence even as the band begins to fall apart.*

Rock's transformation during the 1960s from teenage diversion to cultural juggernaut upended the music business so thoroughly that, for the first time in memory, the industry was taken at a tempo set by the musicians. At one of their first recording sessions, the Beatles defied George Martin, their producer, and the song he selected on their behalf and insisted that they be allowed to record one of their own—"Please Please Me" becomes their first number one. The Yardbirds recorded the dreck foisted upon them by their management through gritted teeth but fired back with salvos like "Shapes of Things," which dared, in 1966, to sport a social conscience and a Jeff Beck guitar solo on the bridge so unhinged it threatened to take the rest of the song down in flames. "Shapes of Things" hit the top ten in the United States and the U.K. and went on to influence generations of guitarists. At the suggestion of fellow session man David McCallum Sr., principal violinist of the Royal Philharmonic Orchestra, Jimmy Page dragged a bow across the strings of his amplified guitar for the first time; when paired with a jittery wah-wah pedal, the bowed guitar would feature prominently on Zeppelin's "Dazed and Confused" and become a centerpiece of the band's stage show, provoking further eye rolls from the rock-crit cognoscenti.

The Beatles and innovative young guitarists like Beck and Page—and soon Jimi Hendrix—quickly tested the limits of the sleepy facilities where music had been recorded more or less unperturbed for decades. By the time the Beatles tackled *Sgt. Pepper's Lonely Hearts Club Band* in 1967, the unprecedented, surreal soundscape was captured mostly in spite of the primitive four-track tape machines at EMI's Abbey Road studios in London, the fluorescent-lighted spaces therein as suited to creative endeavors as an embalming theater. "Every wall was painted a nauseating hospital-like pale green," recalled Geoff Emerick, who engineered *Sgt. Pepper* and most of the Beatles canon. It is a testament to the Beatles' pluck that they managed to render such felicitous music amid such unrelenting surroundings, and little wonder that Page and John Paul Jones, having logged untold hours as session players at Abbey Road and similarly grim facilities across London, leaped at the chance to join traveling rock bands. When, by the early seventies, advances in technology make it plausible to record professionally outside traditional studios, these same musicians and a generation of fellow-traveler recording geeks would rewrite the rules of how and where rock can and should be recorded.

With *Quadrophenia* completed, the Ronnie Lane mobile studio quickly becomes popular with other British bands recording off the London studio grid. Meanwhile, the Rolling Stones—weary of trucking recording equipment to and from Mick Jagger's country estate, Stargroves—had converted a menacing-looking lorry into their own mobile studio for hire. Jimmy Page used it to record parts of *Led Zeppelin III* and Zeppelin's fourth, untitled album, notably John Bonham's epic drum track on "When the Levee Breaks," captured for eternity in the foyer at Headley Grange, a former poorhouse in East Hampshire. When the Rolling Stones fled Britain in tax exile, their mobile followed them to Nellcôte, Keith Richards's villa outside Nice, where the band holed up in the basement and recorded *Exile on Main Street*.

So it's no accident that along with *Quadrophenia,* two of 1973's most compelling albums are recorded primarily outside traditional studios. Page and Led Zeppelin, with the Rolling Stones mobile in tow, decamp for Stargroves and lay down many of the tracks for *Houses of the Holy* (the album is mixed at Electric Lady, the New York studio Hendrix personally commissioned but barely used before his death in 1970); Alice Cooper, having moved into their rented mansion in Greenwich, Connecticut, record the first takes of *Billion Dollar Babies* in its cavernous ballroom. "I thought we might capture something really unique," recalled Bob Ezrin, who produced the three previous Cooper albums and had big plans for *Billion Dollar Babies*. "Some of the sounds that came out of that house are really special and would not have happened in a formal recording studio."

The tapes roll for *Billion Dollar Babies* in August 1972 with *School's Out* still high on the charts. No one wants to lose momentum, so the band steps straight out of months of grueling touring—in a show that in its latest incarnation reprised the knife fight from *West Side Story* and ends with Alice swinging from a gallows—into recording what will be the most important album of their career. "We were under pressure," recalled Dennis Dunaway, "but bringing it into our own home"—"home" being the gaudy Cooper mansion—"made it easier than working in a traditional recording studio." The success of *School's Out* is less a triumph than a reminder that the band has yet to fulfill the master plan they hatched as nobodies in 1968. "*School's Out* was number two," says Neal Smith. "We still had one more notch to get in. And that was the top of the charts."

Bob Ezrin was a nineteen-year-old classically trained musician and folksinger working for Nimbus Nine, a Toronto company headed by Jack Richardson, the producer of the Guess Who's biggest hits, when he first encountered Alice Cooper. Shep Gordon sent *Easy Action,* the band's second and last album for Zappa, to Nimbus Nine, where the staff played it to gales of laughter and derision. "We didn't know if Alice Cooper was a guy or a chick and eventually it became a standing joke around the office that if anyone messed up that week, he'd be forced to go and work with Alice Cooper," Ezrin recalled. Ezrin had no idea that Shep Gordon had deliberately targeted Richardson for reasons both whimsical and calculated. "What would be the most vaudevillian, pop-art, bizarre thing for an Alice Cooper record than for it to sound like a Guess Who record?" Gordon says. "It just seemed it was very Alice Cooper to get the most commercial guy with the least commercial band." Despite Gordon's entreaties—trying to force a meeting, he and the band traveled to Toronto and bivouacked in the Nimbus Nine reception area—Richardson was unmoved and dispatched Ezrin to get rid of the band. "Here's this guy Alice Cooper," Ezrin recalled. "His hair is stringy and down to his shoulders, his pants are so tight I can actually see his penis through the crotch. He's talking with a slight lisp . . . I just could not handle it." Ezrin fled, only to be dragooned to see the band perform at Max's Kansas City, where he had an epiphany that they could become stars. Backstage, Ezrin told them, "I think you guys can make hit records." The band, close to fainting with gratitude, summoned all of their punk bravura and responded, "That's good—we think you can, too."

Ezrin convinced a dubious Richardson to let him record the band even though Ezrin had no experience producing records. Warner Bros. reluctantly agreed to fund the recording of four songs. Unless the sessions strongly hinted at a hit single, the label made it clear it would drop them. The band was by then more than $100,000 in debt and barely subsisting in the farmhouse outside Pontiac. In December 1970 they gathered with Ezrin at RCA studios in Chicago and spent the next six weeks playing as if their lives depended on it. Ezrin was far more at sea than he let on. "I leapt into it without any knowledge of how to do it—I learned on Warner Bros.' dime." When the band played him the songs they proposed to record, he wanted to vomit. As a musician himself Ezrin knew "what a really great song [felt] like—I had played a lot of them." Amid the wreckage of the demos he thought he heard one—its chorus sounded to Ezrin like "I'm edgy," except what Alice actually snarled was "I'm *eighteen*." In the band's original arrangement, the song lasted eight meandering minutes; after Ezrin was finished, it clocked in at two minutes and thirty-eight seconds. "I knew it would be a hit from then on," he said. Warner Bros., at first refusing to believe the group was the same Alice

Cooper, the improvement was so vast, released "I'm Eighteen" as a single. After the song hit number twenty-one on the U.S. charts, the label green-lighted *Love It to Death,* the album that drove a dagger through Alice Cooper's swishy image for good and became their first gold record.

Billion Dollar Babies is conceived as the band's winking, self-consciously grandiose commentary on the Alice Cooper phenomenon, a postmodern conceit before irony and rock and roll are entirely reconciled. Recalled Alice: "We were getting voted the best band in the world over Led Zeppelin, the Rolling Stones and the Beatles. We'd look at that and laugh—I almost called up McCartney and said: 'Listen, we didn't vote on this.'" As it turns out, *Billion Dollar Babies* is so well played that the joke is lost on nearly everyone, from credulous fans who bond with the album's muscular hits to the killjoy rock crits who dismiss the album as pretentious fodder for the Cooper stage show—"tedium ranging from boredom to humdrumity," harrumphs the same *Rolling Stone* critic who kneecaps *Houses of the Holy.*

Billion Dollar Babies includes one of Michael Bruce's finest songs—the Stonesesque "No More Mr. Nice Guy"—as well as bulletproof group compositions like the title track, "Elected" (a radically reworked "Reflected" from *Pretties for You*), and "Generation Landslide," the lyrics of which Bob Dylan, of all people, praises. The unsympathetic expectation outside the Cooper entourage is that *School's Out* is surely Alice Cooper's peak. "*School's Out* was such a mega success that people thought, Well, they can't go any further than that," says Alice. "And *Billion Dollar Babies* was going to be twice as big as *School's Out*. We were just getting started." The record industry's standard demands an incredible two albums per year in an era when "recording artists" like Alice Cooper are expected to write their own material while touring nonstop. "Back then that's what you did," says Alice. "You made an album, toured, made an album, toured." Says Smith: "You always have to remember that we were either on tour or in the recording studio or in the rehearsal studio. If we did a show down in Puerto Rico and we got there a day before, that was our vacation for that year." The constant roadwork and communal living means the band kills what little free time they have barraging each other with ideas. "Michael, Dennis and myself were writing songs all the time," Smith says. "It never stopped. And so whenever there was an album that was ready to go it wasn't like we were writing for that album—there'd already be a new generation of songs." The downside to this arrangement, as Alice Cooper and innumerable acts toured to death in the seventies discover, is that after a certain point, blinded by fatigue and success, it is easy to overreach with underwhelming material. "We were like rats on a wheel," says Gordon. "We were just running to keep up."

The United States is soon to be mired in stagflation and gas shortages, but you'd never know it as the band settles into the Galesi Estate in Greenwich, former residence of Ann-Margret—the neighbors include Bette Davis and Nelson Rockefeller. Built by a Broadway boulevardier, the fifteen-thousand-square-foot mansion oozes Gatsbyesque dissipation and boasts a ballroom so vast it accommodates the immense stage for the upcoming tour. "It had, like, fifty-foot ceilings and a fireplace you could park a car in," says Smith. Ron Volz, the band's first full-time roadie, moves their belongings from their previous domicile, the freezing, ramshackle farmhouse outside Pontiac. "We pull up to these twelve-foot friggin' gates and it's like, Holy fuck! What the heck is this! Then we see the house and it's just outrageous." The next day the band arrives and divvies up the thirteen bedrooms. Alice and his longtime girlfriend Cindy Lang, a fashion model, occupy the master bedroom; in a portent of things to come, Buxton holes up by himself on the third floor. "We put the rehearsal studio and all the equipment in the dining room and the sound gear and the four-track in the library, where we recorded rehearsals," Volz says. "The ballroom held the setup for the show. It must have been sixty feet wide and ninety feet long."

The Cooper Mansion is the perfect foil for a band about to record an album whose cover is a simulacrum of a snakeskin wallet with a jacket sleeve that depicts them fondling albino rabbits and one million dollars in cash. Having spent the entirety of 1971 and 1972 playing sold-out concerts in progressively larger venues, the band for the first time cashes serious checks. Parked in the mansion's porte cochere, supplementing the limos coming and going to the Cooper management nexus in Manhattan, are Bruce's Jaguar and Smith's new Rolls-Royce Silver Shadow. Before David Libert signs on as road manager, he is summoned to the mansion to meet the boys. It makes a lasting impression. "Here they were in this enormous room—I guess it was the ballroom—and they were practicing hanging Alice with the new gallows that Warner Bros. had built for them in their prop shop," says Libert. "It was really bizarre because his parents were there watching him get hung time and time again. So that was my first encounter with them."

There is no mistaking Alice Cooper, then, for a band of selfless hippie brothers sharing a communal yurt. Long before they earned their first royalties, Gordon decided that "if I treated them like rock stars, the world will treat them like rock stars. When I signed them I went out the next day and bought a 1954 Cadillac limousine, so they'd always be getting out of a limousine. Same thing with the mansion. It was to make them look like billionaires." By the time they move into the mansion, "we had anything we wanted," Smith says. "All we had to do was just tell the people that work for us to go get it." The band pass the time feeding live rodents to Chiquita, the boa constrictor Alice drapes over his shoulders onstage, and firing ordnance out the windows from a cache that includes a .22 rifle and a .38 Special. Smith decorates his room with bloodred everything and Nazi regalia. "We tore the place up," says Bruce. "Well, actually Neal and Glen tore the place up. Neal would flick his drumsticks up and they'd stick in the copper ceilings, the handmade stuff from Italy, and Glen would shoot the statues." Dissatisfied with the aspect ratio of the porn he's watching, Buxton pokes a hole in a wall and relocates the projector to the adjoining bathroom. Alice, a media junkie before the term is coined, consumes endless hours of television—*The New Price Is Right*, Marx Brothers movies, *Mister Ed* reruns, it doesn't matter. "Offstage I'm like Ozzie Nelson," he assured. "Cookies and milk—well, cookies and beer." The traditional refreshments of high-flying rock and rollers are available at the mansion—an acquaintance of the band sends "care packages" of contraband from Phoenix—but Alice takes perverse pride in his rep as a world-class boozer, not doper. He is never without a can of Budweiser during the day or a bottle of VO after sundown, the daytime whiskey embargo a concession to Gordon, who strongly suggests—in a prehistoric intervention—that Alice lay off the booze because it is destroying his personality.

The band are only sporadically in residence at the mansion as they tour heavily throughout 1972 in support of *School's Out*. When they return to Connecticut to begin rehearsals for *Billion Dollar Babies,* Glen Buxton—an even heavier drinker than Alice—continues his decline. The band, especially Alice, love Buxton unconditionally and consider him a wayward brother. "Glen was our Holden Caulfield, our Keith Richards, our juvenile delinquent," says Alice. "He was the last remaining pillar of defiance. He didn't contribute that much to the music, but the one thing he did right was the opening riff for 'School's Out'"—the song that kicked Alice Cooper into the big leagues—"which was one of the greatest riffs of all time."

Now Buxton vanishes into his addictions, an unreliable performer onstage and an empty chair in the studio. Ezrin is forced to deploy uncredited session guitarists to cover his parts. In the end, according to Smith, Buxton does not play a single note on *Billion Dollar Babies* (Bruce disputes this). His sole contribution may be smashing his guitar at the beginning of the solo on "Sick Things" that should have been his, overdubbed by a session man. "Sick Things" is meant to lampoon Alice Cooper's slavishly loyal fans; instead, it can just as easily describe the growing unease among five young musicians and old friends who suddenly find themselves within reach of the pinnacle they've worked toward without a break for five years.

Mick Mashbir, an affable guitarist who performs with various Coopers when the band lives in Phoenix, is en route to London in 1972 when he drops by the mansion. The suffocating atmosphere astonishes him. "There was no sense of camaraderie," Mashbir says. "Everyone just hung out in their own rooms and had little contact with each other during the day, unless they were in the practice room." Mashbir has cycled through enough bands to know trouble when he sees it. "It just didn't feel like a close group," he recalls. At this crucial moment, with their careers riding on the new album and tour, it seems to Mashbir as if "they had worked very hard for years and just wanted to get the job done." He is especially struck that "the band really led a very isolated life. They never threw one party when I was there." After two weeks, Mashbir says his good-byes and presses on to London. In the meantime, the band and Shep Gordon discuss how to finesse the situation with Buxton. A mobile twenty-four-track recording studio is due to arrive at the mansion to start laying down *Billion Dollar Babies'* basic tracks, and a European tour in support of *School's Out* looms. Complicating matters is the fact that Buxton founded the group and even taught Dennis Dunaway how to play the bass. "I mean, everyone agrees that he was the heart and soul of the band, so for him to kind of just fade away was sort of Syd Barrettish," says Smith, invoking the luminous, erratic founder of Pink Floyd who degenerated into full-blown schizophrenia. "We had a lot of conversations between Dennis, Mike, Alice and me about what we were going to do. And what they did in Pink Floyd is they put Syd Barrett on the payroll and got another guitar player."

As the band's competence and confidence grew with each album and tour, Buxton fell further behind. Before *Love It to Death* was recorded in 1971, Bruce woodshedded for months and emerged a gifted rock and roll composer. Although the band collaborates incestuously and often shares writing credit, Bruce more often than not brings the germ of a song or completely finished compositions lock, stock, and chorus. Alice rewrites Bruce's lyrics to suit the themes of the latest album and stage show; Bruce's first verse of "No More Mr. Nice Guy"—"I used to be such a sweet, sweet thing, but that was just a burn / You used to break my back just to kiss your ass and you got nothing in return"—becomes, after Alice's rewrite, "I used to be such a sweet, sweet thing till they got a hold of me / I opened doors for little old ladies, I helped the blind to see." It's a fruitful collaboration, and increasingly those songs are hits. "Michael's songwriting was what made the band," recalled Dunaway.

Bruce's blossoming talent and work ethic inspire the rest of the band but diminish Buxton, who withdraws in stages as the power balance shifts to the group's other guitarist. Says Bruce, "I felt bad for Glen that he didn't see how unique the time was and I did, I just poured myself into it, to the point where I didn't have a girlfriend and I was all about the music. I didn't want it to be over but everybody knows that it'll be over sooner or later. And I tried to get the most out of it I could at that time." The sophistication of Bruce's compositions demanded that Buxton raise his musicianship; instead, he refused, with growing sullenness, literally to play along. "Things would come up that were difficult to play and Glen wasn't quite up to the task," recalled Ezrin. "I think he ran away from situations where he felt embarrassed, and he was becoming more and more embarrassed as time went on." Says Bruce, "As the band started becoming successful he got worse because now the pressure is on. Bob Ezrin is a very intelligent, talented guy and he is trying to work with Glen but on the side is pulling his hair out." Listening to the playback of one of Buxton's parts, "Ezrin goes, 'What is that sound I hear? It sounds like metal,'" says Bruce. "It was [Buxton's] jewelry rattling. We had to do it all over again. It was just one thing after another."

Alice's bond with Buxton, marinated in a thousand and one lost weekends, is perhaps deepest. But even as Alice himself spends large swaths of 1972 in "a VO coma," his ambition and survivor's instincts never waver; Buxton has no such resolve. "Glen was my best friend and I just watched him disintegrate," Alice recalled. "All of us talked to him about his drinking and drug use but we just could not pull him out. Glen would say, Yeah, yeah, you're right, you're right, but he couldn't stop. He only felt comfortable when he was trying to get away with something. Everyone knew we had a career to protect so we faked it as long as we could." Says Gordon, "We all, I think, share in a little bit of guilt on that."

As Buxton retreats from Alice Cooper's inner circle, it falls to Ezrin, as producer and uncredited collaborator, to preserve the band's integrity on record. He and Alice Cooper form a demented version of the famous symbiosis between the Beatles and their producer. "Bob was our George Martin," Alice says. "He saw there was something really exciting about what we did. He said, If I can get your songs to be as exciting, we're gonna have something unbelievable here." It is Ezrin who, as Beatles biographer Philip Norman characterized Martin's role, "happened to be of the rare breed who are content to use their talents in improving other people's work." Like Martin, Ezrin is "the editor that all creative promise strikes it if is lucky." Ezrin also actively participates in shaping the Alice

Cooper image. "He got it really early on," says Smith. "He not only got it, but he helped enhance everything that we were trying to do. He was the sixth member of the band."

Prior to *Love It to Death,* Alice Cooper's chief source of outrage is their feigned transsexualism and femme stage personae, already paying diminishing dividends as the sexual revolution matures. "I made people feel uncomfortable because I looked and acted strange but I hadn't yet made them feel I was dangerous," Alice recalled. "Ezrin especially enjoyed the dangerous element in me and helped nurture it. He and I both felt it urgent for Alice not only to be strange, but this time to be scary." This crucial tweak of the Alice character—from pouting, bitchy drag queen to ghoulish pseudo-psychotic—marks the beginning of the band's march to superstardom. It also serves to make Alice, once and for all, the cynosure of the band; from here out, the albums increasingly hew to an implicit story line—mirrored in the theatrical stage show—in which Alice is the protagonist and the band play supporting characters. It is an arrangement fraught with implications for the other four members that, as Alice's personal stardom surges in 1972, they begin to appreciate fully.

Mick Mashbir is sleeping on the floor of his basement flat in London three months after his visit to the Cooper mansion when a telegram arrives from Shep Gordon summoning him to Connecticut to play on *Billion Dollar Babies.* In the first-class cabin of a 747 he reflects that he has just been given "an express elevator ride to the rock and roll penthouse" and also that "Glen was a lead guitar player and so was I." He wonders how Buxton feels about him parachuting in at the eleventh hour to work on the album. It doesn't take long to find out. When Mashbir arrives, he finds that the ennui among the band has deepened since his visit. Unable to bring themselves to fire Buxton, they are also incapable of acknowledging that it's what needs to be done. Mashbir is hired as an ad hoc— and uncredited—sideman until a permanent solution can be finessed. "Mick was an amazing guitar player," says Smith. "He was fresh, nobody really knew him, and he was great for what we needed." Mashbir isn't debriefed beyond Gordon's telegram and sizes up the situation at the mansion by degrees of deduction—Alice, Buxton's best friend, greets him coolly, he notices. "When I arrived I knew something was amiss—I wasn't sure what was going on and we were friends so I needed to find out how [Buxton] felt about my arrival." When Buxton answers his bedroom door and beholds Mashbir, he blurts, "Mick! What are you doing here?" It falls to Mashbir to break the news to Buxton that he will, in effect, replace him on the record. Buxton responds: "Cool. Do you want to see my fish?"—a blue oscar he keeps in his bathtub.

The next day Buxton refuses to leave his room to rehearse. When he skips the next rehearsal and the other Coopers carry on without comment, Mashbir wonders, but "I was new there and it wasn't my place to ask." It becomes obvious to him that Buxton "had become persona non grata." Buxton's slow-motion self-destruction, passive-aggressive withdrawal, and the band's hiring a temporary lead guitarist in response defers a potentially explosive situation but does not defuse it. Alice, Smith, Bruce, Dunaway, and Buxton have lived under the same roof for five years and have consummated deep personal bonds—Smith's sister, Cindy, lives with Dunaway and sews the band's stage costumes. They are also bound by a management agreement in which all five jointly own the Alice Cooper name. Kicking Buxton out of the band on the eve of their biggest album and tour is not only emotionally unimaginable—from a business and public-relations standpoint, it is out of the question. "I think we just looked at it this way: There was a dilemma, and we've solved it," Smith says. "[Buxton's] problems didn't stop but at least he was still there with us." On the other hand, "when you're headlining Madison Square Garden and having gold and platinum albums, it starts to get very serious and professional. And at that time we were stuck: We had to make hit records and we had to do the tour. So we brought in Mick."

The importance of Bob Ezrin cannot be overstated. "He pulled the melody out of songs and strengthened them," Alice recalled. "He invented riffs and bridges and hooks. He ironed out the songs note by note, giving them coloring. We never played so well or sounded so good." Ezrin teaches his charges the importance of what to leave out—"the discipline of recording, rehearsing material and jettisoning stuff that was unnecessary. These were things that they had never thought about." Before recording starts on *Billion Dollar Babies,* Ezrin as always pores over the raw material. "Basically I was the arbiter, but everybody got to express themselves." Dennis Dunaway—far from the stereotypical retiring bassist and, like Alice, a former art student—supplies a platform-booted kick in the pants to material he deems insufficiently adventuresome. "I was always the crusader for the avant-garde. Anything that we would come up with that sounded like anyone else, I was always there to change it." It is Dunaway who "forced a stick of dynamite" under the album's title track, which, as cowritten by Reggie Vincent, a friend of Buxton's, is an inchoate countryish ballad until Dunaway leaps up at rehearsal and improvises the song's brutal main riff on the spot. But Ezrin is also a relentless taskmaster. Obsessed with timekeeping, he taps an ashtray with a pencil as a metronome through the band's headphones as they cut the basic tracks. He is also direct to the point of cruelty. "Ezrin had the unfortunate style of making fun of you if you fucked up," says Mashbir. "It was supposed to be jokey but it didn't really serve a positive purpose. It took me a while to get used to it."

Hanging over the *Billion Dollar Babies* sessions is the pregnant absence of Buxton. "Now, Glen could play as good as anybody," says Alice. "Nobody wanted to see Glen fall behind. But when we finally got into rehearsals, he was way behind. He'd put a little riff here, work on this, work on that. And then it got to the point where we actually had to get somebody to play for him." Ezrin had called in session players to cover Buxton's parts in the past—notably Dick Wagner for the solo on *School's Out's* daunting "My Stars"—but never before has the band attempted to record entirely without their friend, and certainly not while he sulks in his tent like a rock and roll Achilles.

After a week of rehearsals with Mashbir subbing for Buxton, Ezrin and the mobile recording studio arrive to capture the basic tracks. "Things didn't go well for a number of reasons," Mashbir says. "For one there was a lack of songs to choose from—I don't know if it was from laziness or complacency but having to write and arrange in the studio really didn't help the flow. Then there was the pressure to follow up *School's Out* without Glen." Affairs reach such an ebb that, according to Mashbir, Ezrin considers pulling the plug on the sessions. There are also

intrigues, unspoken, amid the band's power base. Michael Bruce champions the hiring of Mashbir, as well as a guest pianist, Bob Dolan, which
coincidentally serves to dilute the influence of the Alice-Ezrin axis in the
band as Ezrin delegates Buxton's lead guitar parts to top-flight session
players like Wagner and Steve Hunter. "Most of the ideas for those albums came from me anyway," Alice recalled. This is not a state of affairs
to warm the heart of the group's chief songwriter—Bruce is already ex-
quisitely aware that Alice's stardom is rapidly overshadowing the rest of
the group. "Bob brought in the element of world-class musicianship and
that is like playing poker, it raised the stakes for everybody," says Bruce.
"You could not ignore it. And Alice got a free pass. At least for Alice,
nobody is going to replace him singing. But when [Ezrin] invites all the
killer guitarists around, we're like Oh, God, I need to try to hang in there.
I realized later that all I have to do is write a really good song."

The sessions at the mansion start each afternoon at two as the instrumentalists wander downstairs; Alice, whose vocals are recorded later,
huddles with Ezrin in the mobile's control truck parked outside. The
ballroom is especially suited to capturing a capacious drum sound, so
Smith finds himself perched along with his twenty-one-piece drum set
on scaffolding high above the dance floor where he pounds out the dirgelike opening to "Sick Things." For "No More Mr. Nice Guy," Bruce plays
in an adjoining antechamber while Mashbir occupies a five-by-seven-
foot coat closet with his 1959 Stratocaster and Fender Deluxe amp. "In
between tracks we would go out to the mobile truck and have a listen
and get critiqued," Mashbir says. Ezrin selects the strongest performances from five or six takes and splices them together on the fly. "A
very effective time-saver," Mashbir observes. "Cherry-pick the best intro,
verses, chorus and bridge and ending and voilà—a great basic track."

The songs are keyed to the Cooper stage show as never before. Opening the album—and every show on the Billion Dollar Babies tour—is
"Hello Hooray," an obscurity Ezrin unearths from a 1968 Judy Collins
album, written by Rolf Kempf, a "crippled guy from Canada," as Alice
noted, which for a curtain raiser conveniently starts, "Let the show begin,
I've been ready!" Alice adds lyrics about circus freaks, hula hoops, "the
American dream and its recruits," and turns what had been a wistful hip-

pieish contemplation into a strutting rock star's manifesto—"God . . . I . . . feel . . . so . . . *strong!*" Ezrin trowels on strings, woodwinds, an aeolian choir, pinball-machine bells, and, during the fade, timed artillery fire à la the *1812 Overture*. (Smith is particularly taken with this touch, except that "I wanted the cannons to be a *lot* louder.") "Unfinished Suite" springs from Alice's desire to inflict the superamplified sound of a dentist's drill on an arena audience. The song imagines a nitrous-soaked dream of espionage to the combined themes of *I Spy*, *The Man from U.N.C.L.E.*, and James Bond movies—in the stage show, Alice attacks a dancing tooth (played by Cindy Smith) with a giant toothbrush. The subtext of previous Cooper shows—Alice "misbehaves" and is punished for his "crimes"—culminates on *Billion Dollar Babies* with "I Love the Dead," written by Alice, Ezrin, and Wagner, who overdubs the song's monumental solo. Alice contributes lyrics—"one of the most poetic songs I ever wrote . . . an Edgar Allan Poe kind of thing"—that declare his love for the deceased "before they are cold, their bluing flesh for me to hold." Onstage, Alice ruts with the dismembered body parts of several female mannequins and is led to the guillotine. The song is the album's most blatant affront to conventional taste, to the point that Alice later concedes its creepiness is "a little out of place" amid *Billion Dollar Babies'* bubbly odes to money, power, decadence, and pop-cultural trash.

As the band plows through the basic tracks, they get glimpses of greatness lurking on the tapes. Dunaway recalled cutting the bed track for "Elected" at the mansion and realizing that "when it got to that tail end where the bass does the cascading, descending riff, I knew it was a hit. I can't say the same thing, for example, about 'I'm Eighteen'—I had no idea that was going to be a hit." In the end the band captures the basic tracks for "Billion Dollar Babies," "Raped and Freezin'," "No More Mr. Nice Guy," "Hello Hooray," and "Unfinished Sweet" before the European tour commitment cuts the sessions short. They are resumed at Morgan Studios in London during a break from an uproarious string of European dates where the sudden and dramatic improvement in the quality of groupies is casual evidence that Alice Cooper's stardom is no longer conjecture, as is the endorsement of London's gadabouting rock stars including Keith Moon, Marc Bolan, and Harry Nilsson, who drop by the studio to pay their respects and—the ultimate compliment—to jam. At Morgan, Bruce adds a crucial rondo segment to "Billion Dollar Babies" sung in duet with Alice and Donovan Leitch, who records in the next-door studio. It is at this late juncture that Buxton suddenly decides, unannounced, to assert himself. "So we're doing this stuff and I'm trying not to step on anybody's ego and Glen comes walking in," says Bruce. "He sits down. He's got his little table there with his cigarettes, ashtray. He gets a guitar amp and he's moving it by the microphone. Everyone's just kind of ignoring him because of what we're doing in the control room. He finally comes and pounds on the window and goes out and sits down and says, 'I'm ready to do my parts.' And here we were doing vocals with all these people. He didn't check in, he didn't even come into the control room to see what was going on." It's a telling moment in Buxton's increasing self-inflicted isolation from his old friends. There will be others.

The band don matching white satin suits at the photo session for the album sleeve at the studio of David Bailey—the court photographer of Swinging London—amid one million dollars in cash delivered under guard. Alice clutches a sobbing naked baby—its eyes painted with Alice's trademark psycho-clown mascara—and leers at the camera with malevolent glee. When they are about to return to Connecticut, Ezrin informs the band that they are still one song short. Exhausted, they decamp to the Canary Islands, where Gordon installs them in a resort hotel under construction and informs them they aren't leaving until they write one more song. "Usually, Dennis brings an idea, Michael has an idea, or I bring an idea, and then we put something together," Smith says. "But this was like, 'Okay, let's write a song.' We weren't really coming up with a lot." Smith breaks the creative dam when he plays a staccato drum riff reminiscent of the groove for "Sympathy for the Devil." "Michael started strumming the chords and the song"—"Generation Landslide"—"came together in like fifteen, twenty minutes," Smith says. Alice spends the song on a stream-of-consciousness jag that culminates in a prophetic couplet that name checks the album: "And I laughed to myself at the men and the ladies, who never conceived of us Billion Dollar Babies." For Bruce, writing the song under the gun is one of the band's proudest moments. "It was just the five of us and our road manager. There was no-body else and it's one of the best songs on the album. And in a pinch, this band was able to pull large furniture out of our asses and come off smelling like a rose. We had a band moment and it was just the band, and that is what I liked about it. We can still write good music without the Wagners, the Hunters and everybody else. We were still able to do it, which was refreshing to know."

A final round of recording awaits at the Record Plant in New York, but *Billion Dollar Babies,* for all practical purposes, is in the can. A year that begins with the band touring behind its breakthrough hit ends with a new album that in nearly all respects is even better. *Billion Dollar Babies* is Alice Cooper's most fully realized work—the album they've been building toward since Zappa signed them as a novelty act—and they know it. "When we heard the album back, we looked at each other and said, 'Boy, I hope this is a hit,'" Alice recalled. "But in our heads, we were already thinking, This is going to be a hit." Says Bruce, "I was amazed—the album really grew on me more than I even anticipated. I didn't really get it totally until I was out on the road. We were well into the tour, there were some people in my room, and I was listening to it and I'm just ear-to-ear smiles." A listening party is held at the Record Plant partly to placate the studio's beleaguered staff, whom Ezrin drives to distraction—at one point during the sessions he arranges for a live guitar amplifier to be hurled down an elevator shaft so he can record the crash.

It is January 1973; the album's release is two months away. Opening night for the tour that will change the band's lives as thoroughly as *Billion Dollar Babies* is scheduled for March 8 in Philadelphia. Having briefly congratulated themselves, Alice Cooper turn to rehearsing a stage show several magnitudes more brazen and outrageous than the album that inspires it.

Chapter 4

DANCING DAYS

Led Zeppelin let their hair down at Mick Jagger's country house and emerge with Houses of the Holy, *which wins the hearts and loins of America's post-Woodstock youth starving for rock—and rock stars—they can call their own.*

Jimmy Page came to understand the limits of recording technology—and the humorless middle-aged men wielding it—as a London session player in the mid-sixties. A disciple of the revolutionary recording techniques developed in the 1950s by Les Paul, the guitarist and inventor whose signature Gibson guitar would soon become indelibly associated with Page, he despaired as session after session was conducted as if it were 1953 and the musicians were backing Rosemary Clooney. Recording engineers at the time made little accommodation for the leap in volume and dynamics of rock performance, rendering listenable the early singles on which Page played uncredited—including the Who's first hit, "I Can't Explain"—only in the context of low-fidelity, high-energy artifacts. Page noticed that microphones were always placed directly in front of the bass drum. "The drummers would then play like crazy but it would always sound like they were playing on cardboard boxes," he would recall.

It's one of many revelations Page tucked away for the day he and Led

Zeppelin walked into Olympic Studios in October 1968, fresh off their Scandinavian tour as the New Yardbirds. The chaotic Yardbirds gave Page plenty of latitude to experiment with guitar technique but also to consider what, exactly, he wanted to achieve when he got his slender hands on his own band. The experimentation by Jimi Hendrix and others that propelled rock to unprecedented sophistication just as the sixties ended and Led Zeppelin began was not lost on its founder. "Look at the Beatles," Page recalled. "Here was a band that went from 'Please Mr. Postman' to 'I Am the Walrus' in a few short years."

The contract Peter Grant secured with Atlantic Records gave Page total artistic control over Led Zeppelin—as did the fact that he and Grant financed the recording of Zeppelin's first album themselves. Page had no one to answer to except himself: no meddling record company, no pop producer like Mickie Most angling for the next hit single. He decreed Led Zeppelin would be "a marriage of blues, hard rock and rock with heavy choruses." Considering the abuse Page was about to take from the rock-crit cabal for these and subsequent ambitions, history ultimately endorsed his vision. The *New Yorker* music critic Alex Ross remarked approvingly in 2007 that "Dylan and the Beatles may have won the plaudits of intellectuals, but Led Zeppelin launched a no less ambitious raid on music history, commandeering rock, folk music, Delta blues, Indian and other non-Western music, and smatterings of classical tradition."

As it turned out, Page's vision for Zeppelin would, in the space of two albums and one year, set the standard for all commercially successful rock for the next two decades. "He knew his way around a studio like he knew his way around an old bookshop in Manhattan," says Michael Des Barres, who led the glam band Silverhead and later signed with Zeppelin's Swan Song vanity label. "He created what became the template for every rock and roll band since." The guitarist's crystalline clarity as he harnessed his bandmates' potential is striking even decades after the fact. "I wanted artistic control in a vise grip because I knew exactly what I wanted to do with these fellows," Page said. "I knew exactly what I wanted to do in every respect. I knew where all the guitars were going to go and how it was going to sound—everything."

Page the autodidact was unencumbered by the technical dogma of his engineer on the first Zeppelin album, Glyn Johns. Page augmented John Bonham's enormous sound by placing microphones several feet from the drums—one of several techniques that imparted an air of indulgent spaciousness and made Zeppelin's albums feel alive even on the most pathetic teenage stereos. Page bowed his guitar, plugged it directly into the mixing console to get a particular flavor of distortion, alternated limpid acoustic verses with pile-driving choruses, and hired a tabla player to accompany his winding guitar étude, "Black Mountain Side." In one of several clashes with his engineer, Page wanted the echo of Plant's vocal on "You Shook Me" to precede Plant's voice—a trick Page first deployed to tart up a Yardbirds single when Mickie Most was beyond caring. Johns flatly told Page that it couldn't be done; Page showed the skeptical engineer how to turn the tape over, record the echo on a spare track, then turn it back over again. Afterward, recalled Page, Johns refused to play back the results. "Finally I had to scream, 'Push the bloody fader up!'" The effect worked perfectly. "He just couldn't believe that someone knew something that he didn't—especially a musician."

Page deployed different engineers for each of the first three albums "because I didn't want people to think that they were responsible for our sound." For *Led Zeppelin II*, Page selected Eddie Kramer, a staff producer at Olympic Studios whose engineering résumé included the Rolling Stones and all of Jimi Hendrix's albums. Kramer had first encountered Page in 1963 at a Kinks session under the aegis of the band's American producer. "When it came time for the lead guitar parts, Shel Talmy wanted the best rock guitarist on the scene, which happened to be Jimmy Page," recalled Kramer. While engineering the session for Donovan's "Hurdy Gurdy Man" at Olympic in 1967, Kramer recorded both Page and a retiring bass player with Prince Albert bangs named John Baldwin, soon to change his name to John Paul Jones.

With the more amenable Kramer aboard for the new album, Page had specific ideas for the extended bridge to "Whole Lotta Love," a galvanizing but blatant reworking of Willie Dixon's Chess Records chestnut "You Need Love." What ended up on the finished track sounded like a kitchen sink of chaos—squealing theremin, backward-tracking guitar, and Robert Plant's guttural moans—but Page plotted every last screech and howl.

Kramer's chief recollection of mixing the section is of him and Page "just flying around on a small console twiddling every knob known to man." Said Page, "I told him exactly what I wanted to achieve in the middle of 'Whole Lotta Love,' and he absolutely helped me to get it." (Grateful Zeppelin fans, particularly those given to augmenting their leisure activities with LSD, achieved shattering epiphanies listening to "Whole Lotta Love" through headphones.)

By the time the band recorded their fourth, untitled album in 1970, Page had mostly abandoned the studios, preferring to record basic tracks at Stargroves or Headley Grange with the Rolling Stones mobile. "We could relax and take our time and develop the songs in rehearsals," he said. "We didn't have to worry about wasting studio time." Page used the idiosyncrasies of location recording to achieve sounds impossible in a traditional studio—Bonham's legendary drum cannonade is captured by simply hanging two stereo microphones in Headley Grange's entry and letting the monumentally hard-hitting drummer and the stone walls do the rest. The technique revived the fortunes of at least one song, "When the Levee Breaks," thought to have been unrecordable. "We tried 'Levee' in an ordinary studio and it sounded really labored," Page said. "But once we got Bonzo's kit set up in the hall at Headley Grange and heard the result, I said, 'Hold on! Let's try this one again!' And it worked."

So it's no surprise that Page turns to Stargroves to record *Houses of the Holy*. Page is adamant that Zeppelin not repeat itself. "The key to Zeppelin's longevity has been change," he said in 1975. "We put out our first LP, then a second one that was nothing like the first, then a third LP totally different from them, and on it went." Even so, *Houses of the Holy* is a radical stylistic departure from the preceding fourth album as well as the rest of the canon. The blues base that perfumes Zeppelin's earlier work vanishes completely; Page's solos are fleeting or are incorporated directly into the structure of the songs, particularly "The Song Remains the Same," originally a galloping instrumental in several movements before Plant added globe-trotting lyrics—"California sunshine, sweet Calcutta rain." Built around a slurred minor chord from Page and lush strings from John Paul Jones's Mellotron, "The Rain Song" is partly a rebuttal to George Harrison's unsolicited advice to Bonham that the problem with Zeppelin is that they don't do any ballads—this despite the slow-dance national anthem and soon-to-be most-requested ballad in history, "Stairway to Heaven." (Perhaps the ex-Beatle had channeled Frank Sinatra's infelicity that Harrison's "Something," from *Abbey Road,* was the greatest Lennon-McCartney song ever written.) In a friendly intramural dig, Page's opening chords of "The Rain Song" unquestionably quote "Something."

Elsewhere on *Houses of the Holy* is experimentation that goes completely off the rails but with results so compelling it hardly matters— "D'yer Mak'er," a bizarre conflation of Ricky Nelson's "Poor Little Fool" tattooed with Bonham's sledgehammer drumming and Page's incongruous reggae riffing, ends up getting the most airplay in America. Michael Des Barres visited Bonham's house while the band was rehearsing material for the album and noticed that Bonham's jukebox was stocked exclusively with James Brown records. "That's all, nothing else. Bonzo would do flows that were so unpredictable and come right back into the groove. He combined the discipline of [Brown's] Famous Flames with the sound of thunder." While at Bonham's, Des Barres watched, fascinated, as the band wrote and broke down "D'yer Mak'er" with scarcely a word among them. "To see them interact, there was no language, there was no, 'Let's go to the E minor.' They had an intuitive, instinctive relationship."

The band's creative telepathy results in "The Crunge," an impromptu jam that derives from a James Brown–style funk groove played by Page and Jones with irregular timekeeping to keep the cover bands guessing. "Bonzo started the groove on 'The Crunge,'" Page recalled, "then Jonesy started playing that descending bass line and I just came in on the rhythm." Ever the perfectionist, Page swaps out his beloved 1959 Les Paul on the track for a Fender Stratocaster for its impudent, trebly tone. In her academic study *Houses of the Holy: Led Zeppelin and the Power of Music,* the musicologist Susan Fast points out that the one aspect of the album that ought to appeal to critics but never does is the sly, self-deprecating humor baked into songs like "The Crunge," which closes with Plant calling for the band, Godfather of Soul style, to "take it to the bridge" in a song that doesn't have one. On "D'yer Mak'er"—the title itself a play on *Jamaica*—Fast notes that "the lumbering sound of Bonham's characteristically heavy drumming and Plant's 1950s-inspired lyric and crooner-style singing largely [undermine] what should be an airy reggae groove: it's funny because they sound incompetent." The deliberate, jarring changes that interrupt the flow of "The Crunge" "makes it sound as though the band doesn't quite understand how to work the groove . . . in both 'D'yer Mak'er' and 'The Crunge' the band's presumed rhythmic ineptitude makes fun of their whiteness."

The album also reflects Page's growing appetite for exotic tunings and patterns—he taps Middle Eastern modalities for "Dancing Days," upon which he builds layer upon layer of guitars, and perfects Zeppelin's acoustic-electric typology on "Over the Hills and Far Away." Closing the album is one of his most infectious riffs and Bonham's mightiest backbeats, "The Ocean," Plant's metaphor for the sea of fans that spreads before him nightly in concert. Page blithely includes Bonham's sea-chanty count-off—"We got four already but now we're steady . . ."—a nonchalance that belies the song's sophistication; "The Ocean" whipsaws between 15/8 and 7/8 time before wrapping with a swinging coda and guitar solo played in the style of Scotty Moore, guitarist on Elvis Presley's "Baby, Let's Play House," the song that inspired the twelve-year-old Page to pick up a guitar.

Houses of the Holy does little to refurbish Led Zeppelin's reputation with rock critics, who pile on after *Rolling Stone*'s "Limp Blimp" grenade. Even the band's fan base are frankly mystified by "Dy'er Mak'er" and "The Crunge," which swerve into alien cultural territory—which is to say the still-ungentrified terra incognita of dub and soul that discomfit white American male suburban youth for whom the blues, as interpreted by bands like Led Zeppelin, is about as ethnic as it gets. Otherwise, the album aligns perfectly with the cohort's aesthetic; compared to the occluded intensity of the fourth album, *Houses of the Holy* fairly bounces with the exuberance and optimism that only a sixteen-year-old American—or English rock star—can muster unironically in the face of gas shortages and historic inflation. Plant's lyrics may grate on critics predisposed to hate them, but with summer around the corner when the album arrives in the U.S. in March 1973, it's hard not to be lulled by Plant's daffy promise that "dancing days are here again," especially if one isn't mortified to sing along with the next line, "I've got my flower, I've got my power, I've got a woman who knows." To millions of credulous ears, Plant's words and Page's music on *Houses of the Holy* seem as fresh and potent as their own teenage awesomeness. The band, wishing only to please themselves, confer their high spirits onto the record and directly into their core audience's hearts and minds. "You can really hear the fun we were having on *Houses*," Page said after the album sold seven million copies.

At the same time, Page and the rest of Led Zeppelin are deadly earnest about the band, its image and the music they write, record, and perform— never more so than on the eve of the tour and album through which they seek to reach cultural parity with the Rolling Stones. It is precisely this sullen vanity that plays a large part in their ever-tightening bond with their core audience while further poisoning their relations with the rock press. One of Zeppelin's few champions is a prodigy rock writer named Cameron Crowe, only sixteen when he first covers the band for the *Los Angeles Times* in 1973. It's a telling example of the split in the supposedly monolithic baby boom generation that an actual sixteen-year-old is necessary to apprehend Zeppelin's appeal and interpret it for a mainstream audience. Part of the resentment toward the band among boomer rock critics stems from fresh memories of bands as broadly popular as the Beatles at least acknowledging the counterculture in songs like "Revolution." But by 1973, "the heroes of the new decade, from Grand Funk Railroad to Led Zeppelin, were selling nothing more significant than their own stardom," points out the pop-culture historian Peter Doggett. Zeppelin's fatal error, then, is to take themselves as seriously as their fans do.

The sessions for *Houses of the Holy* began in January 1972—with breaks for tours of North America, Europe, and the Far East—and wrapped in August. The band did not explicitly set out to record their next album. "We had no set ideas," Page said. "We just recorded the ideas each one of us had at that particular time." Nevertheless, six songs destined to comprise the heart of *Houses of the Holy* were captured: "The Ocean," "D'yer Mak'er," "Dancing Days," "Over the Hills and Far Away," "The Song Remains the Same," and "The Rain Song." To engineer the album, Page summoned Eddie Kramer, who'd impressed on *Led Zeppelin II* with his willingness to experiment and a work ethic that matched Page's uncompromising standards. Kramer arrived at Stargroves to find the band in supreme spirits and at the top of their game. "The lads were really happy there, recording with the amazing acoustics of the old mansion and frolicking around in the parklike setting. They were so confident and so happy with what was going on. The general feeling was excellent." The output was of such quality and quantity that several songs were held back to be parsed among subsequent albums.

As had been their practice on previous albums, Zeppelin recorded *Houses of the Holy* at multiple locations as the band slotted in time between tours of Australia, Holland, Belgium, North America, Japan, Switzerland, and the U.K. In addition to Stargroves and Headley Grange, the band recorded at Electric Lady and London's Island and Olympic studios. But *Houses of the Holy*'s buoyant sonic landscape traced primarily to the weeks Kramer and the band holed up inside and outside the stone walls at Stargroves in the spring of 1972. One sun-splashed afternoon, Kramer set up microphones and stools on the mansion's manicured lawn "to try to get a completely neutral acoustic environment devoid of any reverberation." Page and John Paul Jones strummed their acoustic Martin guitars as birds tweeted poignantly. For the first playback of "Dancing Days," Kramer opened the doors to the mobile and blasted the song into the blue Berkshire sky. In those days Kramer documented his sessions with a Nikon and snapped the musicians—even the reticent Page "wearing a V-necked cardigan and looking like the perfect English schoolboy"—dancing in geeky triumph as their creation echoed across the estate. Their exuberance and, even at this late date, innocence is oddly touching, especially in the context of their public personae as barbarians bludgeoning with guitars instead of cudgels.

Kramer meanwhile marveled at the power of Bonham's playing—he and his Ludwig Green Sparkle model drum kit were sequestered in Stargroves's conservatory. "The recording setup for Bonham was simple," the engineer said. "One could almost put any kind of mic on his drums and it would sound like Bonzo. He was to my mind the finest hard-rock drummer of all time." Bonham's other nickname within the Zeppelin entourage, the Beast, suggested a man scarcely in control—a surly drunk, he was prone to mood swings and sudden violence. But once settled behind his drums, he was a focused and uncompromising talent. "One of the marvelous things about John Bonham which made things very easy," said Page, "was the fact that he really knew how to tune his drums, and I tell you what, that was pretty rare in drummers in those days. He really knew how to make the instrument sing, and because of that, he could just get so much volume out of it by just playing with his wrists. It was just an astonishing technique." Bonham's thunderous introductions to "D'yer Mak'er" and "The Crunge" and rock-steady timekeeping on the slippery, meter-shifting "Dancing Days," "The Ocean," and "The Song Remains the Same" gave *Houses of the Holy* an unshakable foundation that supported whatever flights Page fancied.

The Stargroves sessions were completed with such dispatch that Led Zeppelin was on the road for nearly a year before the album was finally mastered and released. In an unusual move that betrayed their confidence in the material, the band added songs from *Houses of the Holy* to their set lists during their 1972 world tour that was ostensibly promoting the fourth album and its masterpiece, "Stairway to Heaven." At a June 25 concert at L.A.'s Forum, they performed no fewer than three—"Dancing Days," "Over the Hills and Far Away," and "The Ocean"—plus a snippet of "The Crunge" during the middle section of "Whole Lotta Love," which in concert had devolved into a protracted jam session.

Just before embarking on the tour the band met with Hipgnosis, a London graphic arts studio with a reputation for designing enigmatic album covers with the psychedelic intensity of Fillmore posters smudged with droll seventies attitude. (Within the year Hipgnosis would produce the iconic pyramids-and-prism cover for Pink Floyd's *The Dark Side of the Moon*.) The first meeting did not go well. According to Page, Hipgnosis's cofounder, Storm Thorgerson, arrived "carrying this picture of an electric green tennis court with a tennis racquet on it. I said, 'What the hell does this have to do with anything?' And he said, 'Racket—don't you get it?' I said, 'Are you trying to imply that our music is a racket?'" Hipgnosis later successfully pitched photographing a family, painted silver and gold, climbing the rocks at sunrise at the Giant's Causeway in Northern Ireland. (Try to imagine for a moment, in an age of artless digital downloads, a band lavishing such Cecil B. DeMillean attention on an album cover.) As on the fourth album, there is no printed mention of the band or the title; instead, the cover is wrapped with a paper sash, inscribed HOUSES OF THE HOLY, which conveniently covers the naked bottoms of the children, allowing Atlantic Records—which must hew to the total-artistic-control in Zeppelin's contract—to exhale. But not before the album's release was pushed back from January to March due to problems printing the cover's iridescent colors; Peter Grant finally demanded Atlantic Records fly the Hipgnosis partners to New York to oversee production. "There was always a situation when it came to the covers," says Atlantic's Jerry Greenberg. "Always."

Greenberg is struck by how much the band, especially Page, trusted Grant to look after its business interests. "Just like Mick [Jagger] ran the show for the Stones, Jimmy ran the show for Zeppelin as far as the records were concerned," he says. "Jimmy was a stickler for mastering—he would come over and sit with the guy and make sure everything was right. As far as the marketing was concerned, he left that to Peter, and Peter would be the guy who would sit with me and say, 'Let's do this, let's do that.'"

When *Houses of the Holy* is finally released, Greenberg says, "there is definitely a sense that everybody felt like this could be one of their biggest." Atlantic launches a print and radio ad campaign—the latter leaning heavily on a snippet from "D'yer Mak'er"—that runs in the music press and on syndicated rock radio shows like *The King Biscuit Flower Hour*. Per Led Zeppelin's custom, there is no advance single; "Over the Hills and Far Away" is finally released as a 45 in May, followed by "Dy'er Mak'er" in September, but are largely superfluous as the album hits number one in the U.S. five weeks after its release, displacing *Aloha from Hawaii via Satellite* by Elvis Presley, whom Plant idolizes.

Indicative of the chaotically catholic tastes in the spring of 1973, the top ten that week comprises, besides Zeppelin and Elvis (Elvis!), Alice Cooper's *Billion Dollar Babies* (number one three weeks earlier), Bread, Pink Floyd (*The Dark Side of the Moon*, beginning its record-setting 741-

week chart run), and Gladys Knight and the Pips. The excruciating "Tie a Yellow Ribbon Round the Ole Oak Tree" tops the singles chart, followed closely by the bubble-gum glam throwaway "Little Willy" by the Sweet, but the rest of the top ten is studded with classics in waiting: "You Are the Sunshine of My Life" (Stevie Wonder), "Drift Away" (Dobie Gray), "Daniel" (Elton John), "Stuck in the Middle with You" (Stealers Wheel), "The Night the Lights Went Out in Georgia" (Vicki Lawrence, an early country-pop crossover hit); on the lower rungs are "Walk on the Wild Side" (Lou Reed), "Right Place, Wrong Time" (Dr. John), "Killing Me Softly with His Song" (Roberta Flack), and the debut hits for Bette Midler, Focus, Edgar Winter, and the Electric Light Orchestra.

"Those were great days," Greenberg says. "The great days of music, great days for Zeppelin and great days for Atlantic. That whole magnitude of magic doesn't exist today." In a departure from lionizing the 1960s as a lost Arcadia, Greenberg invokes the 1970s and the generations born afterward who can only experience the moment through the proxy of recordings. "It's unfortunate that people missed that '73 *Houses of the Holy* era," says Greenberg. "Because that was spectacular."

Chapter 5

"WE KNOW HOW TO MAKE THE MONEY"

How Peter Grant put the Led in Led Zeppelin, Shep Gordon put Alice Cooper in paper panties, and Peter Rudge got the Who (and the Stones) out of jail and to the show on time.

The men who managed rock and roll in the fifties for the most part had no affinity for the music or musicians beyond the cash it generated. Colonel Tom Parker, a carny sharp and convicted con man who immigrated illegally to America from Holland, outflanked several more plausible managers and seized complete control of Elvis Presley's career in 1956. Shrewd enough to grasp the potential of a white singer making "race records" palatable to the vast white teenage American audience of the 1950s, shameless enough to keep his boy Elvis from lucrative European performances for fear of deportation, Parker tended to Elvis's interests with single-minded zeal. (Compulsively seeking the edge in every transaction no matter how trifling, he ordered about Pullman porters while brandishing a wad of bills, replaced by coins after the bags were stowed.) Twice Presley's age, the Colonel controlled every aspect of the King's life and career, aggressively licensed his name and likeness no matter how cheap or vulgar the product, steered him into appalling movies, and eventually claimed up to 50 percent of his income.

Rock's second coming in the mid-sixties introduced several new flavors of manager, few particularly savory. Given that British Invasion bands and their hits were driving the business, British managers were suddenly thrust into shepherding the careers of their charges not only in Britain but in America, where some were hopelessly out of their depth. Brian Epstein, the Beatles' manager, was punctilious, polite, and thorough; he looked after "the lads" with paternal care and reshaped their image from leather-jacketed rough boys into the besuited Fab Four who ended their historic performance on *The Ed Sullivan Show* with meticulous bows. But Epstein was a fatally inexperienced show businessman and so underestimated the group's merchandising potential—the streetwise Colonel Parker cashiered $20 million worth on Elvis's behalf in 1956 alone—that he signed away a breathtaking 90 percent share of the income in the U.S. to a third-party outfit named Seltaeb (*Beatles* spelled backward). Though Epstein renegotiated a still embarrassing 49 percent cut when he realized his mistake, in the litigation that followed, American chain stores canceled their merchandising contracts. The fiasco ultimately cost the Beatles an estimated $100 million. As Paul McCartney later lamented, Epstein "looked to his dad for business advice, and his dad really knew how to run a furniture store in Liverpool."

As the sixties progressed, an altogether different breed of manager asserted itself in Britain. The most notorious was Don Arden, a former tummler who combined Colonel Parker's opportunism with a ruthlessness that earned him the sobriquet "the Al Capone of Pop." As recounted in *Starmakers and Svengalis,* a history of British rock management by Johnny Rogan, Arden's break came via Jimi Hendrix's future co-manager, Michael Jeffery, which Arden parlayed into managing the Nashville Teens, cresting on their hit version of John D. Loudermilk's "Tobacco Road." Arden kept the band on the road, where they earned decent money but seldom saw much of it. When the Teens' pianist, John Hawken, demanded to be paid in full, Arden lifted him by the throat, pinned him against a wall, and bellowed, "I have the strength of ten men in these hands!" then dragged the terrified pianist to an open second-story window. Hawken managed to flee before finding out whether Arden was bluffing. Perhaps not. Having added the Small Faces to his stable, Arden discovered that an associate of Robert Stigwood, later to manage Eric Clapton, had made overtures to the group. According to Rogan, Arden and four intimidating wingmen descended on Stigwood's London office, where Arden dangled him by his legs four stories above the street. Arden later recalled that the incident was merely a bit of theater meant to "nail [Stigwood] to his chair with fright." This he presumably accomplished; Stigwood's company never signed the Small Faces.

To cover his sprawling bookings, Arden employed an outsize former bouncer as his point man and enforcer. His name was Peter Grant, the same Peter Grant who, under the aegis of Led Zeppelin, would soon usurp from Arden the mantle of Her Majesty's Scariest Rock Manager. From Arden, Grant learned that absolute control and trust were essential when large sums of cash were involved, as well as projecting an intimidating facade that left no question that, as Arden informed a rival, "suicide might be better than causing trouble for me." Michael Des Barres, future glam star and Zeppelin confidant, had no illusions about the provenance of the rock business he saw as a young Londoner. "The British gangsterism of the late fifties and early sixties informed rock and roll to a degree most people are unaware of," he says. "The rhyming slang that was invented by criminals in the working class in London—to 'suss' somebody out—became the adopted language of rock and roll." So did the Arden-tested school of window dangling favored by the underworld. "Peter Grant was with Don Arden and Don Arden was a gangster," says Des Barres. "Don Arden held [the Small Faces'] Steve Marriott out the fucking window and said, 'Let's talk about your publishing.'" Arden taught Grant the extremes a manager must at least imply he is willing to invoke in the rock and roll wilderness, where a handshake and a menacing demeanor have the force of signed contracts. "They say there's honor among thieves," says Cy Langston, the Who's early road manager. "Don't get me wrong. But you get the vibe that what's said is said. It's a done deal."

Grant was a natural antiauthoritarian, and his genius lay in challenging show business traditions that rock and roll—and especially Led Zeppelin—would soon render obsolete. He single-handedly rewrote the rules of engagement that record companies and promoters had to follow when dealing with Zeppelin, which were quickly adopted by grateful fellow managers and became industry standards. In exchange for co-financing the recording of Zeppelin's first album, Grant secured not only total artistic control for Jimmy Page but an upper hand in business affairs. As the band became a top concert draw, Grant slashed promoters' percentages from 40 percent to 10 percent on the premise that no "promotion" was required beyond announcing the concerts and watching them instantly sell out. Substantial income that would have gone to middlemen now flowed directly into the band's bank account, enabling Grant to purchase a sprawling country estate accessible by a drawbridge spanning a moat rumored to be stocked with alligators.

Grant's roughneck background was suited to the nascent rock business of the mid-sixties, where men with little formal education—Grant left school at thirteen—but quick wits and a nose for cash carried the day. He worked a variety of odd jobs—stagehand, waiter, Fleet Street runner—and as a professional wrestler and movie double for Robert Morley. Having tasted show business, Grant bought two minivans and hired out as a driver for early rock and roll acts and later road-managed Little Richard, the Everly Brothers, and Chuck Berry on their first tours of Britain. Eager to seize the opportunities presented by the wide-open rock and roll business, Grant established a management company with Mickie Most, the Yardbirds' producer, and struck pay dirt with the New Vaudeville Band, whose novelty song "Winchester Cathedral" hit number one in the U.S. in 1966. When the band was about to leave for an American tour, they recommended that Grant hire as roadie one Richard Cole. It was here that, as in a movie, the opening riff to "Whole Lotta Love" should fade up ominously, for the meeting of Grant and Cole—former boxer, scaffolder, and budding rock buccaneer—would have lasting consequences for the business of touring rock and roll. Other bands of the early seventies had sold-out tours, but few earned as much as Zeppelin, nor traveled amid an entourage as aggressive, paranoid, or ganglike. "The common denominator in the operation that Peter Grant and Richard Cole ran was fear," says Danny Markus, an executive at Atlantic

Records who traveled extensively with the band. "They were thugs, and they ran it like thugs." But all of that lay in the future; Grant appraised the sloe-eyed specimen demanding thirty pounds a week to road-manage the ludicrous New Vaudeville Band and hired him on the spot.

In 1967, Grant took over the faltering Yardbirds from their latest manager, Simon Napier-Bell. By then Jeff Beck had departed the group—soon to release his first solo album—and Jimmy Page was struggling to keep the band together, though by then, flayed by endless tours, incompetent management, and no real money despite their fame, they were exhausted and apathetic. When Grant took them on, he and Page—the two newcomers—formed an immediate if unlikely bond: the giant, uncouth former wrestler simmering with resentment and potential violence, and the wan, weedy guitarist genius who abandoned touring for the studios after contracting mononucleosis from the stress of the road. It is the beginning of a relationship that will sustain and enrich both men for the next thirteen years. "Jimmy loved Peter and Peter loved Jimmy," says Des Barres. "They were absolutely loyal and faithful to one another, like Elvis and the Colonel. They were inseparable psychically and Peter realized that, and gave a very loving place in which to protect Jimmy. Jimmy was very frail—which belied his veracity as a guitar player—and Peter was his absolute bodyguard and spiritual protector."

With Grant in charge, the Yardbirds were booked for what would become their final tour of America, in 1968. With Beck gone and Keith Relf, never a strong leader, retrogressing as front man, the power in the Yardbirds shifted entirely to Page, who divined in the tatters of the band the outlines of Led Zeppelin. Even then the Yardbirds performed a version of what would become "Dazed and Confused," the signature spooky dirge and highlight of the first Led Zeppelin album, lifted uncredited from a song by the New York folksinger Jake Holmes (presaging Zeppelin's attribution troubles with "Whole Lotta Love," among others). The Yardbirds broke up for good when the band returned to Britain. In the aftermath, Grant secured for Page the rights to the Yardbirds name; meanwhile the unfulfilled Scandinavian dates loomed and Page set about recruiting what was billed as the New Yardbirds but what was, once John

Paul Jones, Robert Plant, and John Bonham signed on, Led Zeppelin in all but name. Having had in America a firsthand look at the vast potential for the right kind of rock band, Grant waited as Page put one together. Despite his profane, preemptive style, Grant meddled not at all in the creative side, trusting Page and his handpicked bandmates to take care of the music; Page and the band implicitly trusted Grant's business instincts. It was a mark of maturity and confidence on both sides that served them tremendously at a time when drug-fueled egos ruined the prospects of many promising bands. Grant already had a reputation for laying down his life for his charges; that he did so when none of them earned him any serious money was a credit to his character. With Led Zeppelin, he finally had musicians in his wheelhouse whose talent was commensurate with his instincts for taking care of business. As Grant soon made abundantly clear, he did not stand on ceremony or honor business as usual if it remotely contradicted Zeppelin's agenda. "Peter Grant cared solely about his artists," Danny Goldberg recalled. "Everyone else could fuck themselves."

When Grant signed Zeppelin to Atlantic, Jerry Greenberg invited the manager to his home in Connecticut for dinner. It was a gesture that Grant, in the last days before the band broke and he was still struggling to make his mark, never forgot. Says Greenberg: "I think all of a sudden it was like, 'Well, wait a minute, this man has a nice family, he took me into his home . . .'" (Grant made an impression on the Greenberg household. "After he left, I remember my kids said to me, 'Daddy, is he, like, a clown?'—because he had all these scarves on and was such a big guy.") When the first Led Zeppelin album was released and commenced its rocketing ride to the top ten, Greenberg was included in the band's inner circle, admittance to which was tightly controlled by Grant, with expulsion possible at any moment for the most capricious of reasons. Grant, says Greenberg, "kept everybody away." Lisa Robinson—besides Cameron Crowe one of the few journalists willing to file positive stories about the band—"was one of the inside people. Steve Weiss, his attorney. And obviously Richard Cole. But outside of that I don't think there's many other people you could name."

Neal Preston, a Los Angeles–based photographer, would shoot the band in 1973 and thereafter tour with them extensively as their court photographer. "They had a very, very, very small inner circle," says Preston. "You look at the Stones—the Stones must have had easily ten times the staff that Led Zeppelin had. They were very careful about who they trusted. Peter was very of the street—he came from that rough, British hooligan background. He was very representative of that era of manager and that style of doing business." Grant told a friend of Preston's that "his nose could tell if someone was good people or not. 'The nose does not lie.' It was not even that he had to size you up or anything, he just had a feeling about you. Peter, for whatever reason, trusted me and decided to welcome me with open arms into the fold." Danny Markus also made the cut, thanks to his capacity to absorb the band's casual abuse while doing their bidding. "I never let them see me sweat," Markus says. "Somehow I got over the wall. There were so many perimeters, you didn't get inside. Nobody did." Says Preston: "When you worked for Led Zeppelin, obviously you had to do your job well." In addition to Grant's perfectionist work ethic, he says, "there were other considerations and questions. Which were: 'Do you know how to keep your mouth shut?' 'Is your ego bigger than any of the members of the band?' 'Do you want to be treated like the fifth member of Led Zeppelin?' The answers are obvious, but those were the litmus test that you absolutely had to pass." Grant would make sure that Markus was never entirely secure in his position. "I'm sort of like in on a pass: I don't play any instruments. I'm not in charge of royalties. I'm just here to help him get through this experience in America. He just had a way about pulling the rug out from under you and making you sort of fearful. He never, ever showed his wrath to me. But he was scary; he was very scary *looking*. I mean, he was like six five and weighed three hundred pounds and he wore these gigantic Hawaiian shirts and Navajo jewelry, and he loped when he walked."

Marsa Hightower, a publicist colleague of Danny Goldberg's at the PR firm Solters & Roskin, becomes friendly with Grant while working the second half of Zeppelin's '73 tour. "If you were inner circle you were treated quite well. If not, you were fair game for abasement—no respect for those lovely little ladies, fawning photographers, or record company execs." Burned into Hightower's memory is the fate of the Los Angeles photographer Richard Creamer, "a paparazzo to be sure but a gentle soul and childlike in demeanor." Hoping to make entry into the Zeppelin fold, he enlarges and frames one of his photos of the band and brings it to the Riot House—né the Continental Hyatt House, Zeppelin's notorious base camp on the Sunset Strip—"no doubt dreaming of making a connection and getting some appreciation from the bad boys of rock," Hightower recalls. Instead, Bonham sits Creamer down and, as in a Tex Avery cartoon, smashes the photo down over Creamer's head, leaving the frame dangling around his neck. Hightower later gives the photographer an exclusive with Paul and Linda McCartney to atone for Zeppelin's abuse.

If life is rough around Grant within the cloistered circle, it is memorably so outside the perimeter. Pat O'Day co-founded Concerts West, one of the first national promoters of rock concerts and thus instrumental in Grant's plan to circumvent local promoters and their fees; starting in 1973, Grant partners with Concerts West for the band's North American tours. O'Day witnesses Grant's singular style of roadwork and is both impressed and appalled. "Peter's intentions were to be protective, efficient, cautious and professional in all matters concerning the group," O'Day would recall. "Unfortunately, he had a cocaine habit of proportions bigger than his own, and it left him argumentative, volatile and dangerous. Loving and caring one moment, paranoid and devoid of compassion the next, he was about as much fun to be around as a Cuisinart full of nitroglycerine. Thirty days on the road with Led Zeppelin was like one year with any other group due to the tension."

There is one man in rock and roll at the time who can see and raise Grant for sheer hardscrabble backstory and chutzpah. Bill Graham (né Wolodia Grajonca), founder of the Fillmore concert halls in New York and San Francisco, was spirited out of Germany ahead of the Nazis as a boy and studied Method acting in New York before turning himself into a rock and roll dance promoter in San Francisco's Haight-Ashbury. It was at Graham's Fillmore West that Led Zeppelin had their breakthrough performance on the crucial first tour in 1968–1969. From the start, Graham and Grant seemed destined for some epic clash of ego. Recalled Graham: "What I didn't like about Led Zeppelin was that they came with force . . . I didn't care for their image and I didn't care for what came back toward the stage while Led Zeppelin was playing: pushing, shoving, climbing over one another with complete disregard for personal safety. Naked aggression." The feeling was apparently mutual. "I do remember when we first arrived to play the Fillmore, we came to get the gear in and [Graham] told us all to go and fuck off because he was in the middle of playing some handball game on the floor of the Fillmore," recalled Robert Plant. "And we stood and watched him and said, 'Well. Who *is* this asshole?'" The animosity between the camps—what Plant later characterized as "egos and territories and domains and kingdoms and pecking orders"—would eventually boil over in 1977 during a Graham-promoted concert at the Oakland Coliseum in which Grant, in collusion with Bonham and Richard Cole, beat one of Graham's employees so badly he ended up in the hospital and criminal charges were filed. But for now, however much he disapproves of Grant and his methods, Graham is happy to collect the 10 percent of Led Zeppelin that would otherwise go to a competitor.

Zeppelin's reputation had preceded them in America from 1968 onward. But as Des Barres points out, "When you get to the mythic reputation of bands, it's usually the people that are around them that create the myth and mythology. The artists themselves are so isolated that their myths are created for them by the sycophants whiling away their hours in the outer sanctum—Richard Cole and a couple other guys who worked for Peter on those notorious tours, who had sprung from the loins of gangsterism in the East End of London." The British rock journalist Nick Kent, who covered Led Zeppelin in the early seventies, pointed out that "Cole was the real barbarian in Led Zeppelin's court—most of the deeply lurid tales of wanton cruelty associated with them actually stem from incidents initiated by him." Grant, on the other hand, was capable of generating mythology entirely on his own. "Peter Grant was like a Gypsy king in the forest of rock and roll," says Des Barres. "He sat at the end of a banquet table that was laden with eggs Benedict and cocaine. He wore jewelry around his neck that weighed more than I did. He was a massive man. In every respect."

Shep Gordon arrived in Los Angeles in 1968 with Joe Greenberg, his business partner and fraternity brother. After graduating with a degree in sociology from State University of New York, Buffalo, Gordon worked in Manhattan's garment district at Devine Garments, which manufactured clothes for the deceased, before heading west. "I decided I was going to go to California and save the world," he says. Gordon worked for exactly one day as a probation officer at Los Padrinos Juvenile Hall in Los Angeles before reconsidering. That night, he checked in to room 224 of the Landmark in Hollywood, not realizing it was one of L.A.'s early rock and roll hotels. "I heard someone screaming by the pool—I had just come from a jail, so I thought of violence—and separated these two people. They were fucking and the girl punched me. It was Janis Joplin. And she introduced me to Jimi Hendrix and the Chambers Brothers." Gordon and Greenberg set up camp at the Landmark and printed business cards using the hotel's address. As to the nature of their "business," Gordon says, "I was doing a couple of illegal things." His customers were his new musician friends at the hotel. "They said to me, 'What do you really do for a living other than, you know, selling us some things?' And I said, 'I don't know.' And Hendrix said, 'Are you Jewish?' And I said, 'Yeah.' And he said, 'You should be a manager.'"

One afternoon Gordon and Greenberg, biding their copious spare time, wandered into the Inside/Outside boutique on Wilshire Boulevard. When the store's pretty blond seamstress heard them tell a salesman that they were rock and roll managers, she asked, "Who do you guys manage?" The truthful answer was nobody, but they confidently answered, "The Left Banke," pulling from the air the New York band whose only hit, "Walk Away Renee," was two years in the past. ("I had a friend from college who managed the Left Banke," Gordon says. "That was sort of my cover.") Cindy Smith sized up the young hustlers and hustled them back; she told them her brother was in a band and that

Frank Zappa wanted to sign them but they needed a manager to close the deal. In addition to not managing the Left Banke, Greenberg and Gordon had no idea who Frank Zappa was and demurred until Smith added, "They're getting a six-thousand-dollar cash advance." The putative managers suddenly discovered a hole in their busy schedule and drove thirty miles west to Topanga Canyon, where Smith's brother, Neal, lived in a rented bungalow with his bandmates Michael Bruce, Glen Buxton, Dennis Dunaway, and Alice Cooper, who had taken to sleeping in a homemade coffin.

When Zappa agreed to sign Alice Cooper after their legendary 6:30 A.M. audition at his Laurel Canyon log cabin, he turned them over to his manager, Herbie Cohen, who offered a six-thousand-dollar advance for three albums on Zappa's Straight and Bizarre record labels. One of the conditions was that Cohen manage the band, an obvious conflict of interest the desperate musicians were willing to overlook but which Merry Cornwall, who booked the band into their first gigs at the Cheetah, a discotheque on a Santa Monica pier formerly the setting for *The Lawrence Welk Show*, advised them to decline. "We were stumped," Alice recalled. "We had to find a manager before signing the deal, and we had to sign the deal while Zappa still wanted us." Says Neal Smith: "Zappa wanted us to sign with Herbie and we said, 'Uh-uh, man, that's not gonna happen.' And then we met Shep Gordon. The timing was absolutely perfect." Gordon and Greenberg agreed to attend the band's performance at the Cheetah's Lenny Bruce birthday celebration while the Coopers stalled Zappa. The night of the show, the band wasn't halfway through its opening number when the heckling started. This was nothing new; opening for Led Zeppelin at the Whisky in 1969 the night he coincidentally lost his virginity in his coffin in Topanga Canyon, Alice hit the stage dressed in pink pajamas and a garbage can. Part of the band's appeal, if it could be called that, lay in bullying audiences with their outré femme stage presence and turning abuse back on hecklers. That willingness to transcend their meager musical talent with what amounted to belligerent performance art was what attracted Zappa to the band in the first place. "We never went onstage with the attitude of, Gosh, I hope you like us tonight," Alice says. "We'd take them by the throat and shake them and never, ever give them a chance to breathe." But that night at the Cheetah the audience reaction was particularly dire. Recalled Alice: "When the audience screamed 'Get off!' I screamed back, 'I'm a star!' I spit at them. I shoved my hand down the front of my pants and yelled, 'Eat me, you cowards!'"

By the time Merry Cornwall gave them the hook fifteen minutes into the show, the three-thousand-strong capacity audience had fled. Greenberg was aghast but Gordon, according to Alice, was "clapping like a seal. 'You cleared the auditorium in fifteen minutes!'" he marveled. "'Three thousand people in fifteen minutes . . . I don't care if they fucking hated you. It's mass movement. There's power and money in that. Jesus! Three thousand people!'" After *Billion Dollar Babies* hit number one, Gordon reflected, "I had never seen such a strong negative reaction. People hated Alice, and I knew that anyone who could generate such strong negative energy had the potential to be a star, if the handling of the situation was right." (Forty years later, Gordon admits: "I mean, that was the story I told the press. Whether that was really what I thought . . ." Gordon laughs. "You do what you gotta do.")

The next day, the band and their nascent managers met at the Landmark. "I'll get into this for one thing," Gordon told them. "I want to make a million dollars. Then we'll get out. I don't care what you sound like or what you look like. I think you can do it. If you want to make a million bucks you'll have to stick with it for as long as it takes and as hard as it gets. Okay?" The band agreed. In their first act as managers of Alice Cooper, Gordon and Greenberg moved the band into a five-bedroom house with a swimming pool above the Sunset Strip, the $350 rent to be paid out of the $6,000 advance from Zappa. But the musicians still hadn't signed the contract, and now Zappa demanded that the musicians' parents cosign because Alice was only twenty. When the parents arrived from Phoenix, beheld the rented mansion, and were informed their sons were under the guidance of managers from New York named Gordon and Greenberg, they refused to sign until they met them. The twenty-two-year-old Gordon got right to the point. "All right, I'm a Jew," he announced to the skeptical parents, including Alice's minister father. "What should you care? We know how to make the money." There followed, Alice recalled, a "terrible silence." Then they signed.

Joe Gannon was production manager for the Kingston Trio, managed the Baja Marimba Band for Herb Alpert's A&M Records, and was Bill Cosby's road manager before he was tapped to join Zappa's fledgling record labels in 1968. "They wanted somebody who had a name in regards to record contracts, production," Gannon says. "I worked for Herbie Cohen. I was his second in command." Michael Bruce compared the operation to *The Producers*, a repository for loss leaders. "'I know! We'll start a record company! And we'll sign every rotten band in town: the GTOs, Wild Man Fischer, Captain Beefheart, the Alice Cooper group. And then, just to make sure the nail gets close to the heart, Herbie Cohen is going to manage every band.'" Soon after Gannon was hired, Cohen told him that Zappa wanted to sign a group called Alice Cooper. "Herbie said, 'Just go out there and look at them and we'll sign them, it will keep Frank happy.'" Gannon journeyed to a Cooper gig during a period when the band was performing covered in white sheets. This he reported to Cohen, who figuratively shrugged. "Herbie says to me, 'Don't worry about it. They have no management, they have no idea about signing people or BMI or ASCAP.'"

Gannon scheduled a meeting with the band. "They show up and these two guys walk into the room. They said, 'Hi, I'm Shep Gordon and I'm Joe Greenberg and we're the managers of these guys.'" Gannon ushered them into his office and closed the door. "I said, 'Listen, Joe, Shep. I got no ax to grind. I don't know how you got to manage this group and I don't have any problem with you. But when you go next door and tell this guy'"—Cohen—"'he's going to fucking rip your head off. He's going to do everything except take a fucking knife to your ass and cut you a new asshole. I'm just giving you a warning.'" Gordon and Greenberg, veteran poker players, entered Cohen's office, from which emanated the sounds of Cohen screaming at them. "It got more radical than that," says Gordon. "He broke a chair, got a sharp piece of wood and came after me.

The GTOs"—the Zappa groupie clique who'd befriended the band—"got in the middle of us and whisked me out. He was a strong guy, Herbie, and he could have killed me."

Nevertheless, Gordon and Greenberg ended up managing Alice Cooper. "Not that these guys had any idea what they were doing," says Gannon. "Frank was pissed that we went ahead with it, but that's the reason we made it out of that whole black hole, because we didn't have Herbie Cohen as our manager," says Bruce. The band finally signed to Zappa's label and cut their precious first album in November 1968. "They did the first album, *Pretties for You,* which was a piece of shit and the reason for it was Frank never even got near it," says Gannon. "The first album was recorded at Whitney Studios in Burbank," says Gordon. "We all got there at nine o'clock. Maybe an hour later Frank showed up, said hi to everybody and said, 'Listen, I got some meetings. I'll be back at five to pick up the tapes and whatever you have that's the album.' We didn't know—we thought that's how you made an album. I remember Alice saying, I guess this is the way the real guys do it."

Pretties for You bombed when it was released in 1969, and Zappa's interest in Alice Cooper, already tenuous, evaporated. "We were at the end of our rope," says Gordon. "Everybody hated us. So my job was just fighting the world and thinking of stuff crazier than the day before." Gordon decided his only hope was to exploit the band's chief asset, its awful reputation. "I came up with this ridiculous idea of getting like clear plastic clothes, getting the band onstage, calling the police and getting them arrested for indecent exposure, which we thought would really explode their careers because parents would hate it." Neal Smith's sister, Cindy, duly sewed the costumes and the band hit the boards at Thee Experience, a club on Sunset Boulevard. Gordon called the police from a pay phone backstage, outraged that "there's naked people on stage and guys with girls' names," but by the time the police arrived a design flaw in the costumes manifested itself. "The heat of their bodies had fogged up the plastic," says Gordon. "So the police walked in, looked around and just left. We literally couldn't get arrested. We left town the next day."

The only way Alice Cooper earned any money was on the road, and Gordon and Greenberg used all their wiles to keep them there. "Here's a trivia question," says Bruce. "What was the first bootleg album ever?" Bruce refers to *The Great White Wonder,* a 1969 Bob Dylan bootleg, portions of which in different form later surfaced on *The Basement Tapes.* According to Bruce, wherever the band traveled, several cartons of *The Great White Wonder* traveled with them, to be sold to local record stores under the counter to finance the roadwork. During these excursions, one of Gordon's agents got the band booked into a Toronto pop festival. Gordon's negative-word-of-mouth-equals-future-stardom thesis was sorely tested as the band's drag-and-roll stage show, a stretch even in L.A., played badly in the provinces. Innkeepers burned by the band's habit of skipping out on bills colluded to hold their equipment truck ransom for ten thousand dollars. For much of the summer of 1969 the band lived in flophouses in Detroit, where they managed to develop a small following. Then, during their performance in Toronto, someone tossed the now legendary chicken onstage. "The next day, the word spread throughout the rock business that I had killed a chicken onstage and drank the blood for an encore," Alice recalled. The incident temporarily roused Zappa, who supposedly advised, "Well, whatever you do, don't tell anyone you didn't do it." Shep Gordon heartily agreed.

The chicken incident later paid dividends for Gordon's master plan of breaking the band by cultivating a negative mystique, but in the short term it made booking Alice Cooper nearly impossible. As roadwork dried up, the band returned to Los Angeles and recorded a second dismal album, *Easy Action,* another commercial flop, and spent most of 1970 sporadically gigging in transience—Gordon scored them a cameo playing "Lay Down and Die, Goodbye" in *Diary of a Mad Housewife*— before settling in the farmhouse in Pontiac. Buxton took over the dining room and had athletic sex with his girlfriend while Bruce tried to write songs. "You just can't go, okay, I'm going to write an album here, don't mind me," Bruce says. The chaos forced Bruce into the farm's paddock, where he woodshedded for months and composed what would become several of the band's signature hits. A roadie meanwhile conjured a custom sound system. "From that point on we were consistently sounding kick-ass," says Bruce. "Without that, we probably would have broken up and gone home. But we started sounding really good and could sound the same every night, which is a really, really important step." The band was accepted into the tight, tough Detroit–Ann Arbor rock axis—the Stooges, Bob Seger, Mitch Ryder, and a band called the Frost, whose lead guitarist, Dick Wagner, would later ghost for Buxton on *Billion Dollar Babies*. Gordon delegated the band to Leo Fenn, a Detroit-based manager. "He knew all the venues and all the promoters," says Bruce, "so boom, we finally had a guy that could book the band." As momentum built, Gordon dispatched Fenn on the relentless recruitment of Jack Richardson, which yielded instead Bob Ezrin, the hit single "I'm Eighteen," and the gold album *Love It to Death*. Eighteen months after they limped into Pontiac broke and nearly broken, Gordon installed Alice Cooper at the Galesi mansion in Greenwich. The build toward *Billion Dollar Babies* had begun.

Gordon, Alice, and Ezrin collaborated on the band's stage show for 1971's *Killer*, which ratcheted up Alice's dark persona with "Dead Babies" and his humorless decapitation of the dolls, complete with stage blood. "I would write the shows to make Alice the most despicable character you could possibly imagine," says Gordon. "At every show he came out dressed in black, perpetrated these horrible crimes against society. Then the townspeople would revolt and capture him, execute him, and then he would be reborn in white." The theatrical flourishes were unprecedented. "I can't minimize how far we were able to expand what was acceptable on a rock and roll stage," Gordon says. He soon discovered that not everyone in rock and roll was impressed. "When Alice opened for Ike and Tina Turner, Bill Graham grabbed my partner by his throat and started screaming at him: 'You tell these fuckin' faggots that they either fuckin' play music or they become fuckin' actors. Nobody's doin' both on my stage.'"

For the *Killer* tour, the Warner Bros. prop department contributed a convincing gallows for the show's climax. Dunaway, dressed as a vicar, read last rites and Bruce noodled a requiem on the organ as Buxton marched Alice up the stairs, looped a noose around his neck, and pulled a lever. Piano wires attached to Alice's costume broke his fall, but the effect was convincing enough that, along with the hacked dolls, blood, and chickens, the negative word of mouth that Gordon repurposed as positive publicity was spreading. "If I did my job perfectly," Gordon says, "every single morning, every parent would say to their kid at the breakfast table, 'If you even *think* about going to see Alice Cooper, you're grounded for a month.'" Alice was questioned by police in Atlanta because it was rumored he bludgeoned kittens to death onstage with a hammer. (Confronted in his hotel room before the show, Alice responded, "It's not a bad idea, but I didn't think of it.") "Shep Gordon was very shrewd," said Dunaway. "He knew how to make negative things into positive things. So, over and over we would do things that would get negative press and use it to our advantage."

Gordon switched the game plan with 1972's *School's Out,* as the Alice persona morphed from monster to Huntz Hall, the incorrigible cutup of the *Bowery Boys* series. "We were writing to a character that we had invented, almost like writing a play," says Alice. "There was a master plan with Bob Ezrin, Shep, and I about who Alice was, what he would and wouldn't say. And then I was gonna play that guy." Gordon also started to ramrod the name of the band into the straight press by promotional jujitsu. He arranged for the sleeve of each copy of *School's Out* to ship wrapped in paper panties. This alone would probably provoke low-grade controversy, but Gordon was swinging for the fences. He devised the plan after someone told him about an obscure statute that prohibited importing flammable clothing. "I ordered a very small quantity of flammable panties and a very large quantity of nonflammable panties," says Gordon. "And when the flammable panties came in I called customs." The panties were confiscated and Gordon fed the story to a reporter at *The Washington Post,* which ran it on page one. When Warner Bros. learned of the stunt, Gordon took a frantic call from the label, outraged they'd have to recall 700,000 copies of the album, until Gordon revealed that those were wrapped in the nonflammable, legal panties. Never one to squander the band's resources, Gordon deputized Joe Gannon to drop 15,000 of the surplus panties by helicopter on a sold-out Cooper show at the Hollywood Bowl. "Everybody was screaming when those panties came down," Gannon says. "It caused a fucking riot in the streets." Says Bob Brown, the band's publicist, "Then of course the pilot gets busted for violating the Bowl's airspace, which is more publicity." Confronted with disappointing box office for a concert in London, Gordon hired a truck pulling a twenty-foot billboard of Alice posing naked with a snake and parked it in front of Buckingham Palace. When the stunt generated no coverage, Gordon had the truck driven to Piccadilly at the height of rush hour, where it mysteriously "stalled" and blocked traffic for two hours; the next day, every newspaper in London carried a photo of Alice and his snake. The concert sold out.

Within the entourage, Gordon—though only twenty-six and soft-spoken to the point of somnolence—was a formidable authority figure. Linda Bischoff joined the Cooper organization after the Billion Dollar Babies tour as an assistant and subsequently toured with Alice as costume manager. "Everybody was just scared of Shep," Bischoff says. "Shep would sit there, very calmly, very pensively, reflectively. He had this little habit—his left hand would come around and stroke the front of his bald patch, go from the front to the back, and he'd look at you, and he'd hear you out, and then he'd say, 'Okay, just get it done.' 'But, Shep—' 'Just. Get it. Done.' He didn't take no for an answer. This is what he wanted done, and you were just gonna have to find a way to do it. He never yelled, never raised his voice." David Libert recalled a Cooper gig at Detroit's Cobo Hall that devolved into a riot after the band decided not to play an encore. "I remember standing next to Shep onstage looking at it," Libert says. "The audience was going nuts, throwing chairs and everything. And as calm as can be, because Shep was a very calm guy, he turned to me and he said"—Libert affects a stoned-FM-disc-jockey monotone—"'Look, Libert. Full-scale riot.'"

For *Billion Dollar Babies,* Gordon reprised his paper-panties tour de force with a sleeve photograph depicting the band surrounded by a million dollars in cash. Just as the cover is about to go to press, the Secret Service supposedly intervenes, invoking a seldom-enforced prohibition against publishing photos of actual currency. ("They may have to do it over with Monopoly bills," fretted a typical wire service story.) As to whether Gordon planned the entire "crisis" in advance, Brown says puckishly, "I'm not telling. I'm just saying this probably crossed his mind." Gordon never showed his hand during this incredible spree of calculation, which his colleagues dismissed as sheer luck. As he confides to Bob Greene, a young *Chicago Sun-Times* columnist who traveled with the band in 1973: "If all the things that were used to build up Alice's name were made public, we'd be dead in five seconds. Because the magic would be gone. The fans don't want to hear that kind of thing—they want to believe Alice is everything his image seems to be. And as long as people are willing to believe that it just kind of happened, then I want them to go on believing that."

Though the members of Alice Cooper not named Alice Cooper bridle at the suggestion that it was Gordon's Florenz Ziegfeld–like promotion, instead of their hard-won musicianship, that carried the day, to a man they acknowledged that without the triangulation of Shep Gordon, Bob Ezrin, and their own mulish persistence, they might have ended their career emptying clubs on the pier in Santa Monica. "We were certainly rough," says Bruce. "The thing was, we were quick learners and would try anything, and so we adapted very quickly. I look back and we did four albums in two years, and that's what propelled us—the good recordings and Shep's savvy management. I mean, in '69 we opened for Led Zeppelin at the Whisky and now fast-forward to '73 and we are getting off the plane and Led Zeppelin is getting on the plane. So, we were hanging in there with the best of them. When you look at the people that were charting in '73 it was a Who's Who of music, and we were at the top of the pile. So that's not too shabby."

Led Zeppelin and Alice Cooper reach 1973 guided by the same driven men who joined them in their professional infancies and staked their own careers on their mutual success. Peter Grant knows what he needs to triumph in America in 1969 and does everything except sign a blood oath with Jimmy Page to get it. Shep Gordon, Alice Cooper, and Bob Ezrin are equally and mutually incompetent when they blunder across each other but relentlessly raise their game until the band has the number one album in the U.S. and a sold-out North American tour. "It's not like Alice could become a doctor or I could become a teacher," says Gordon. "We had to make it work. We had no choice."

The Who's trajectory was never as tidy, linear, or sure-footed; chaos

stalked the band from Townshend's first smashed guitar. Where Grant
exploited an extant rock-music infrastructure and Page's reputation
when weighing anchor with Zeppelin, the Who launched amid the anarchy of Beatlemania in the prehistory of 1964, when Townshend played a
one-minute-thirty-second version of "I Can't Explain" to Shel Talmy
over the telephone, desperate to prove to the producer of the Kinks that
his band was just as recordable. It's worth noting that the Who signed
with Talmy directly, whose production company financed the recording
of their landmark early singles, including "My Generation." While Talmy
deserved recompense for taking the risk and producing the records, the
bifurcation of the Who's business interests between an independent
producer and Decca Records—with whom they signed for a miserly
royalty—was precisely the sort of contractual swamp that swallowed the
money and careers of untold sixties rock bands. Alice Cooper narrowly
avoided it by signing not with Frank Zappa's manager but with Gordon,
who despite his total ignorance of the record business grasped that what
was best for the band was best for him and Joe Greenberg. By the time
the Who release *Quadrophenia* in 1973, they have been through four
managers and are breaking in their fifth and sixth in the persons of Bill
Curbishley, who managed Daltrey's solo career, and Peter Rudge, a
quick-witted Cambridge graduate who spent 1972 skippering the Rolling Stones on their soon-to-be-legendary tour of North America.

The Who's first manager, Helmut Gorden, was soon joined by Peter
Meaden, "a pill-popping publicist with so many ideas in his unnaturally
active mind that he couldn't always spot the right one," recalled the British rock journalist John Pidgeon. Meaden's campaign to align the Who
with the Mods was one of his better ones—in a stroke it gave them an
influential, fashionable constituency and a marketable look; changing
the band's name to the High Numbers and having them record a pandering single, "I'm the Face," that bombed with the Mod audience it sought
to flatter turned out to be singularly bad ideas that left Meaden vulnera-
ble to usurpers should anyone else have wanted a piece of a band with a
dynamic stage presence but few tangible assets. But just as Gordon and
Greenberg became rock managers when happenstance demanded it, the
Who soon encountered a pair of young comers who would perform a

similar reinvention when circumstances suggested that the band could be more than a diversion for amphetamine-addled Mods.

Kit Lambert and Chris Stamp were filmmakers and flat-mates. Like many partnerships formed during the stirrings of Swinging London, they were from utterly different stations: Lambert was the son of the composer Constant Lambert, attended Oxford, and moved through life with blithe self-possession and entitlement. Stamp, the son of an East London tugboat captain, was comically working-class by comparison. Lambert was the visionary, Stamp the street; together they set about looking for their main chance. It was Lambert who suggested that they direct a film built around one of the rock bands suddenly swarming London and soon found himself at a High Numbers gig at the same club where Townshend smashed his first guitar. Lambert and Stamp convinced the hapless Meaden to accept a buyout, installed themselves as managers, changed the band's name back to the Who, and set about finishing the job with the Mods that Meaden had started. "Kit was the ultimate Barnum and Bailey con man in a lot of ways," recalled Bill Curbishley. "He would bluster his way through things—he had a lot of front and courage that way."

Seizing control of the band from Shel Talmy proved more problematic, as Talmy single-handedly shaped the group's sound, delivered them a string of hits, and had a contract to back it up. As Talmy later told Richie Unterberger, "My problems with the Who were with Kit Lambert, who was out of his fucking mind—I think he was certifiably insane, if he hadn't been in the music business, he would have been locked up. The problem with him was his giant-sized ego plus paranoia. He felt I was usurping his authority because I was producing these recordings." Recalled Stamp, "Very early on Kit and I realized that if we weren't in control of the recording, it would just be hopeless and we would lose this gigantic piece of what the destiny of the Who was. And so we had to get out of that contract." In the end, Lambert and Stamp prevailed, but not before settling the lawsuit Talmy filed against the Who in 1966. To be rid of their producer, the band agreed to pay Talmy a 5 percent royalty on all of their recordings through 1971, which, to Talmy's everlasting good fortune included *Tommy* and *Who's Next*. With Talmy out of the way, Lambert assumed the mantle of the Who's producer as well as co-manager, and here his instincts began to yield results.

Lambert and Stamp formed Track Records to record the band, creating in effect a classic vertically integrated business in which they controlled each step of the Who's career, from recording to manufacturing the albums and singles. (They also had the wits to sign an unknown American guitarist being squired around London by Chas Chandler, former bass player of the Animals—his name was Jimi Hendrix.) Lambert's greatest contribution to the Who was as Townshend's muse and sounding board; whatever he lacked in practicality, he was unquestionably the right man to enable Townshend's ideas, which were growing increasingly quixotic. From the start of their relationship, Lambert informed Townshend's creative foment, giving him a crash course in classical music from the stores of knowledge absorbed from his father. When Townshend began chafing at having to crank out hit singles, intimating that it might be necessary to leave the band, Lambert encouraged him to write more challenging material—1967's "I Can See for Miles," the Who's only top-ten American hit, is a stunning example. Lambert also didn't bat an eye when Townshend pushed for even more ambitious material. "I would say to Kit, I really want to write a fucking opera," recalled Townshend. "I don't want to write rock songs all the time. And he constantly encouraged me on the basis of his background." Says Rudge, "Kit Lambert to me was a genius. He was personally undisciplined and he obviously had tremendous problems, but I maintain to this day that without him there was no Who. Kit was the guy who pushed Pete."

Lambert was indispensable during the writing and recording of *Tommy,* as producer of the record but also as Townshend's editor and muse. When Townshend's brilliant but inchoate ideas for the opera's story threatened to overwhelm, Lambert took it upon himself to write a script that straightened the opera's spine and put the project back on track. It was Lambert who realized early on that *Tommy* couldn't be contained on a single record and green-lighted a double album, with the attendant expense and risk. When presented with Mike McInnerney's surreal album-cover artwork, it was Lambert who insisted the four faces of the Who be incorporated into the design. Ironically, *Tommy*'s success and the Who's subsequent two-year marathon of touring distanced Lambert from the band and especially from Townshend. The tremendous income the album generated allowed Lambert to indulge in high living, both metaphorically—he bought a palazzo in Venice—and literally: He and Stamp become heavy cocaine users, with Lambert devolving into a heroin addict. Having abdicated his creative consultancy with the band, Lambert began to fail them in a fiduciary capacity, allegedly dipping into their royalties to pay for his drug habits and lavish lifestyle.

By now the day-to-day operations of Track Records—and, by extension, the management of the Who—were being handled by Bill Curbishley, a friend of Stamp's brought aboard in 1971, and Rudge, who presided over the band's American affairs from New York. Rudge recalls the cluelessness that still pervaded mainstream record labels desperately trying to keep up with rock's artistic foment. "When I came to America in 1970 with *Tommy* under my sleeve and took it in to MCA"—the Who's American label—"I was told 'Great, this is great. We're really good at these operas—we just released *Camelot* with Richard Harris.'" Both Rudge and Curbishley increasingly supplied the due diligence that Lambert and Stamp now either delegated or ignored. "Kit was brilliant—he saw the rock and roll business more clearly than anyone I'd met at the time," says Rudge. "But what [Lambert and Stamp] weren't good in was executing and implementing because Kit was a heroin addict. You couldn't rely on him."

In the end, Daltrey, asserting himself in the face of Townshend's creative monopoly and deeply wounded by the managers' rejection of his solo album, agitated most forcefully for Lambert and Stamp's dismissal. Townshend resisted, reluctant to cut the cord with Lambert after years of creative intimacy. Matters finally came to a head during the building of Ramport studios and Lambert's drug-enhanced noninvolvement during the recording of *Quadrophenia*. "He left me holding the baby for the production, which was bloody difficult," Townshend fumed. According to Richard Barnes's *The Who: Maximum R&B*, when Curbishley informed Lambert and Stamp that the group were owed nearly eighty thousand pounds that they needed to finance construction, Lambert wrote a check for half the amount and departed for his palazzo, but before leaving put a stop on the check. Townshend was also infuriated to learn that large portions of his songwriting royalties from America had disappeared. Daltrey demanded that Lambert and Stamp be fired, or he would leave the band; Townshend finally acceded, though the partnership wasn't officially dissolved until the inevitable lawsuit was adjudicated several years later.

With Curbishley and Rudge nominally in control, the Who finish *Quadrophenia* and gird themselves for the British and American 1973 tours. Rudge's experience on the Stones' American tour the year before— where he herded the band and a small army of hangers-on including Truman Capote and Princess Lee Radziwill, along with transient drug dealers and a groupie who was chastely sleeping her way through the entourage in order to finally bed Mick Jagger—had honed his skills to a fearful edge. Observing Rudge in his Beverly Hills hotel suite, phone in one hand, cigarette in the other, going toe-to-toe with Bill Graham at the beginning of the tour, journalist Robert Greenfield noted that Rudge was a "beefy, hawk-nosed twenty-five-year-old Englishman with hair nearly down to his shoulders who spins off sentences like a rugby player breaking away from the field." Rudge, raised working-class in Wolverhampton, in fact played rugby at Fitzwilliam College at Cambridge. According to his friend, the music journalist Chris Charlesworth, Rudge was "fast talking, street wise" and could "handle himself well if things became physical"—in other words, the holy trinity of the rock manager's skill set. He quickly became adept at parsing the evolving rock ecosystem. "The rock star came out of that era," Rudge says today. "Some guys played it well, like Mick and Bowie. And some guys didn't play that game, like Pete." Rudge shepherded some of rock's mightiest egos under battlefield conditions, but even Keith Richards was no match for Townshend. "He was the most difficult client I ever managed," Rudge says. "He was the most difficult to read. You never knew which Pete Townshend was going to show up. He was a man of such incredible extremes. He's obsessive-compulsive, whether it's religion, drink, drugs, music, whatever. Nothing was negotiable with Pete."

Rudge got his first taste of the Who's capriciousness while at Cambridge, when he booked the Who for a 1966 college ball that the band impudently canceled with twenty-four hours' notice. "Suddenly the day before, I get this telegram: KEITH MOON ILL. WHO HAVE TO CANCEL. I said, What? You can't cancel!" Rudge journeyed to Track Records' Oxford Street offices, where he confronted Lambert and demanded the band fulfill the obligation. It made an impression—Lambert hired Rudge after he graduated, though as always with Lambert there were complications. "I walked into the office in my new Take Six jacket and everyone looked at me really strangely," Rudge says. "What I found out later was that a lot of kids used to turn up like me and say, 'Kit hired me.' And Kit being gay, he used to pick them up at clubs and promise them a job."

By 1971 Rudge was so adept at managing the Who's U.S. tours that Townshend recommended him to the Rolling Stones, which was how he found himself the chain-smoking ringmaster in charge of the Stones' traveling circus in 1972. Rudge's attention to detail was staggering—he saw to it there was a local attorney in every city to deflect the nuisance lawsuits that a cash-machine rock tour inevitably attracted. He also had a droll British wit that he unfurled like the Union Jack when the occasion arose—when Jerry Rubin phoned for tickets to a sold-out Stones concert at Madison Square Garden the afternoon of the show, Rudge responded, "Tell him to steal them."

Rudge would handle the Who's affairs from a Warhol-bedecked New York office and later branch into managing other artists, among them the opening act for the *Quadrophenia* tour, the blazing southern rock band Lynyrd Skynyrd, who had just released their first album in 1973. The Who had always taken pride in launching the careers of unknown American bands by allowing them to bask in their slipstream when they toured. "We used to find bands on the road and if we liked them, we'd take them," recalled Daltrey. "All of them made it—they all became huge bands: the James Gang from Cleveland, Lynyrd Skynyrd." It must have been daunting for the five young Floridians. "Here was this band from Jacksonville, which had never played to more than a thousand people at a time, who were now gonna step onstage in front of twenty thousand people every night to warm them up for one of the biggest bands in the world," recalled Al Kooper, the band's producer.

Rudge meanwhile girds himself for yet another assault on North

America, secure in the knowledge that there is very little the road can throw at him that he hasn't already finessed. "His stamina," *Billboard* magazine declared, "is the stuff of rock and roll legends." During the Stones' '72 tour, dressed in black velvet jacket and jeans—"the quintessential rock-biz outfit, glamour and poverty all at the same time," observed Greenfield—Rudge set the template for the mammoth tours by the Who, Zeppelin, and Alice Cooper that would follow one year later. "I think that was the tour that kind of defined, as self-serving as this may sound, what future rock and roll tours could be," says Rudge. "We controlled everything: We carried our own production, had our own advancement, had all these things that really hadn't been implemented at the level we implemented them. That Stones tour went some way to showing the way forward for how to run those tours."

Throughout the '72 tour, Rudge confronted a continuum of crises that threatened to cascade into catastrophe if not for his intervention. When the bus taking the Stones from a gig in Tuscaloosa to the airport was becalmed in traffic and the cop that Rudge beseeched responded, "Ah don't give a fuck if you make yoah plane or not," Rudge himself leaped off the bus and cleared a lane through the morass. When Jagger, Richards, and three others in the entourage were jailed in Warwick, Rhode Island, for assaulting a photographer hours before a gig in Boston, Rudge put the rest of the band on a bus, conjured a phalanx of lawyers, and got Boston mayor Kevin White on the phone, who instructed the Warwick cops to release the band and give them a police escort to the Boston Garden. Meanwhile, Rudge coughed up the bail from three thousand dollars cash he carried, dragooned two limousines, and, with police lights and sirens blazing, got his boys to their show—the concert wrapped at two in the morning. "All this," Rudge sighs at one point, "just to put a band onstage."

Chapter 6

ON THE ROAD FOR FORTY DAYS

Goin' mobile with Pete Townshend's air-conditioned gypsies; Alice Cooper's Budweiser must be in cans (brewed in the USA! No exceptions!); Robert Plant is not impressed with the stereo in his suite, with dire consequences for the stereo; and other tales from the coke-flecked, large-living rock-star road of '73.

The rock and roll road gives the music breadth and legend. No matter how fire-breathing a hit or the thousands of times it blasts from a car radio, there is nothing quite like being front and center when a rock star in full rut shreds the same song at twice the tempo and ten times the volume. As Lester Bangs reminds colleagues clutching their love beads, aghast over the music's tumescent turn in the seventies: "Rock and roll, at its core, is merely a bunch of raving shit."

As the seventies downshift away from the sixties, receding in the rearview mirror, along with the tie-dye and paisley and Timothy Learyisms, is the ad hoc, underpowered, and enfeebled live rock and roll performance. The immense sound reinforcement deployed at the Woodstock festival in 1969 shows promise—as does the Grateful Dead's pristine touring rig, designed by their patron, the acid king and electronics whiz Owsley Stanley. But these are exceptions. Within the first three years of the seventies, an infrastructure able to support live rock in an arena setting—with sound capable of reaching ships at sea and lighting as choreographed as a chorus line, along with personnel capable of moving it all from city to city without breaking a sweat—invents itself out of sheer necessity. When in place, it utterly changes the economics of touring, at once inflating expenses but also creating opportunities: nightly grosses in arenas are four and five times what can be extracted from the crumbling ballrooms and theaters that first played host to rock. The mitigation is paid for by audiences who willingly pack the amphitheaters, so in thrall to the experience they forsake their comfort and safety, which to bands watching the bottom line as never before is immaterial—they're there to play and get paid, and in any event what security is provided is there to protect them, not the audience. (During the Billion Dollar Babies tour, female audience members who breach the stage are escorted to the wings; males are hurled back into the front rows.) Buy the ticket, take the ride, seems to be the attitude, and not at all in the sense that Hunter S. Thompson intended when he coined the phrase. Before the seventies are finished, more than a dozen young Americans lose their lives at rock concerts.

Elvis Presley offered the first glimpse of the potential of large-scale live rock and roll—to tour constantly but also profitably by selling out large municipal sports arenas. "For years only Elvis could sell out fifteen thousand tickets a night, and only one of him existed," recalled Pat O'Day, who parlayed promoting local dances in Seattle in the early sixties into booking Led Zeppelin in the seventies. "No one held second place. There *was* no second place. The public was not yet accustomed to the rock and roll concert business." The Beatles' 1964 American tour was conducted in baseball stadiums, but at ticket prices so low that the tour barely covered its overheads. "It would be nearly a decade before young people had the discretionary income necessary to afford tickets priced high enough to make such events economically feasible," O'Day pointed out, and "adequate sound systems were developed capable of making such shows a valid musical experience."

•   •   •

Among other items on his lengthy CV before his affiliation with Alice Cooper, Joe Gannon cofounded and later road-managed the Kingston Trio. In the early sixties, Gannon says, "twenty-five of the biggest and the best places in all of the major eighty markets to do a concert were not anywhere near a major market," but in college towns where the concerts were booked by student committees as familiar with show business as they were with the Crab Nebula. "So, they want to have the Kingston Trio," Gannon says. "And I said, 'How much do you have?' 'Well, I think we can get like eighty-five hundred dollars.' I went, 'What do you charge?' 'We don't charge.' I said, 'Well, suppose you could charge like a dollar or two dollars. You could give us seventy-five hundred dollars and then we'll take all the cash that you rake in.' 'Oh, yeah, we have no problem with that.' 'How many people would you think?' 'Like ten, eleven thousand.' University of Maryland. I end up taking about twenty thousand dollars in three bags full of single dollar bills out of the fucking place. Un-fucking believable! I got a guarantee of a hundred percent of the gate plus seventy-five hundred dollars. I made about twenty, thirty thousand dollars that night, a Tuesday night, in Maryland." When Gannon finally stops laughing he adds, "But that's kind of like what eventually permeated, in regard to who did what in the concert format, like ten, twelve years later." Peter Grant would have loved Joe Gannon.

Before he was Alice Cooper's road manager, David Libert had a brush with fame singing with the Happenings, a vocal group in the style of the Four Seasons who scored a gold record in 1966 with the wistful "See You in September." "The rock and roll technical infrastructure didn't really exist then," says Libert. "If there was a local gig in the Northeast, we had a truck and a guy that would drive our gear. We played lots of colleges and they would provide these sound systems which were kind of a joke." Before the early seventies, bands seldom toured with their own PA systems—it was the promoter's responsibility to provide one. In addition to guaranteeing the band wouldn't be forced to play before a segregated audience, the four-page contract for the Beatles' 1964 U.S. tour stipulated: "PURCHASER [promoter] will furnish at his sole expense a hi-fidelity sound system with adequate number of speakers." In practice, promoters were given to vastly overestimating what constituted "hi-fidelity" when it was their sole expense to provide it, and the Beatles were barely audible throughout the tour. As late as 1970, says Libert, "normally even big bands, they would show up and there would be a sound system they had never seen before. But sound systems were just coming in—there were companies forming at that time."

One of them was Heil Sound, founded by a pipe organist and electronics geek with no affinity for rock but a keen appreciation for the dynamics of sound in a live environment: Bob Heil played and maintained the pipe organ at St. Louis's Fox Theater. In 1966 Heil opened a music shop in his tiny hometown of Marissa, Illinois, where he sold Hammond organs. As it happened, rock bands at the time were repurposing the Hammond B-3, a favorite of jazz and blues musicians, into a screaming lead instrument on par with the electric guitar. (Felix Cavaliere's carnivalesque organ solo on the Young Rascals' "Good Lovin'" was played on a B-3.) Entombed in fruitwood cabinetry and meant for permanent installation in churches and rec rooms, the B-3 was both fragile and heavy; few bands toured with one, which led them to Heil's Ye Olde Music Shop in Marissa. "What happened was I started renting Hammond organs to the rock groups who came through St. Louis," Heil recalled. "Nobody was doing that—Hammond organ dealers thought, 'We're not gonna rent these freaks an organ.'"

When Heil heard the pathetic sound systems bands played through, he scavenged two huge Altec A-7 speakers from the Fox Theater and paired them with radial horns, ring tweeters, and thousands of watts of amplification. When in 1970 the Grateful Dead's Owsley Stanley–designed sound system was impounded, along with Stanley, on a warrant while the band was en route from New Orleans to St. Louis, Heil took a call from a panicked Jerry Garcia backstage at the Fox Theater: "Hey, man, I heard you have a really big PA." Heil trucked his creation to the Fox and mixed sound at the concert; the next day, the Dead took Heil and his PA to New Jersey and on the rest of their tour. Word of Heil's "really big PA" spread, and soon his sound systems were traveling with ZZ Top, Jeff Beck, Peter Frampton (Heil perfected the guitar "talk box" made famous on *Frampton Comes Alive!*), and the Who—Townshend will commission from Heil the unprecedented quadrophonic sound system used on the U.K. dates of the 1973 *Quadrophenia* tour.

Meanwhile, in Dallas, two rock musicians and an audio engineer assembled a sound system for their band so superlative that other local bands clamored to rent it. "The fact that we'd built this and were musicians, we related to the music more than someone who didn't understand what the requirements were," says the band's bassist, Rusty Brutsche, cofounder of Showco, which soon rivaled Heil Sound as the dominant rock-touring sound company. Seeing the same niche in the marketplace as Heil, Brutsche and his partners designed a dedicated PA to rent to bands playing Dallas on national tours and debuted their new system at a 1969 gig for Mountain, a band notorious for playing at stupefying volumes. "When Mountain showed up they had a semi full of Sunn amplifiers, three cabinets high, that completely covered the stage," says Brutsche. "Once they started to play you couldn't hear anything out of our sound system. It was a disaster."

Showco retrenched and built an even bigger system. The first band to use it, Three Dog Night, was so impressed they leased it for the rest of their tour; another was assembled and immediately dragooned by Led Zeppelin when they passed through Dallas. Brutsche set out in a Ryder truck and spent the rest of 1970 on the road with the band. "We went all though America, then Australia, Japan, and Europe. Just me and one other guy. We did it all: drove the truck, set up the gear, tore it down and drove all night and did the same thing the next day." It was a measure of the need for competent concert sound management that Zeppelin—pathologically hostile to outsiders—entrusted Brutsche not only with setting up the gear but mixing their live performances; thereafter, he would mix sound for every Led Zeppelin concert until the band's demise in 1980. The band, says Brutsche, "were just really hard, very demanding—there was immense pressure for everything to work well. It was a high-tension gig." By 1973, Showco is providing sound for both Zeppelin's Houses of the Holy and Alice Cooper's Billion Dollar Babies tours.

With the concert business suddenly big business, promoters establish regional fiefdoms and defend their territories fiercely: Ron Delsener in New York, John Scher in New Jersey, Barry Fey in Denver, Larry Magnon in Philadelphia. (In Buffalo, brothers and concert promoters Harvey and Bob Weinstein later found Miramax Films and become the first of Hollywood's so-called mini-moguls.) "There were about a dozen flagpoles out there of major people that the acts would remember when they toured, because they were characters," recalled Tom Ross, a booking agent whose clients included Fleetwood Mac and Linda Ronstadt. "They controlled the cities—they'd get the police department to escort you from the hotel to the arena. It was real big-time show business. And everybody thought it would never end. Nobody questioned anything because everybody was making money."

The scent of fast cash attracted inexperienced promoters with financial backing outside the industry—sometimes "drug money that needed to be washed," says Ross—who would push up prices by acceding to demands from bands that went beyond aggressive business into reckless greed. It became possible for a single concert to wipe out a promoter, so that a less-than-capacity audience at a twelve-thousand-seat hall, previously a manageable loss, would represent a catastrophic fifty-thousand dollar bath. Managers quietly reduced or even waived the band's fee in such situations for the Schers and Delseners; the newer or less beloved were left to fend for themselves. Callow promoters accepted toxic dates where a triple bill featuring the resurrected Jimi Hendrix, Janis Joplin, and Jim Morrison would be a hard sell. "Friday night in Texas," Ross recalled ruefully. "Experienced promoters know that high school football owns Friday night in Texas."

As the new generation of rock managers like Shep Gordon, Peter Rudge, and especially Peter Grant entered the business, they questioned the wisdom of delegating blind trust to local promoters. By carrying their own sound and lights instead of relying on sketchy rentals, they enhanced the quality of their productions while taking a profit center away from the promoters and turning it into a recoupable expense. "We would bring our own sound and lights and charge the promoters, and the promoters would go crazy," says Libert. " 'I can get that for half the price!' and blah, blah, blah. Well, take it or leave it. This is the deal. And they grudgingly would do it." Selling out seventeen-thousand-seat arenas gave the new managers the leverage to demand transparency from notoriously opaque box office accounting. In the early sixties, according to Ross, "most artists were paid on the flat—if ticket prices were three dollars and the hall held ten thousand, the gross would be thirty thousand dollars and they'd pay the act five thousand—I remember when we got six thousand, that was a hurdle. The promoters would say, I'm losing money! But you really didn't know what the costs were."

As arena rock took off, the managers pushed back. Flat fees gave way to guarantees and percentages. Says Gannon, "The way all these holding contracts read in those days was . . . let's take a number like twenty-five thousand dollars a night, okay? Twenty-five thousand against sixty percent of the gross over whatever the break-even point was." Managers and booking agents scrutinized the expenses promoters claimed and unsurprisingly discovered "there was a lot more profit than we thought," Ross recalled. Earlier in his career, Ross booked the Olympic figure skater Peggy Fleming into municipal arenas and got to know the building managers. When rock moved into those same arenas in the early seventies, he was uniquely qualified to call bullshit on promoters who were padding their expenses. "If they said the rent was twenty percent [of the concert's gross] and I knew it was only ten percent, we started saying, Nope, we're not gonna do that. And if you don't come straight we're gonna play for somebody else." When the agents and managers looked some more, Ross said, "a lot of the costs that promoters would charge us—for catering, for limousines—were actually companies they started and owned. So they were making a profit from little ancillary businesses that they used to farm out. The parking concession used to be an area the building sometimes would throw in for free and then the promoter would say, 'Oh, we've got to pay for the parking attendants.'"

Deducing the promoter's true expenses became a black art for tour managers, who had to settle up in the hour or so after the band stepped onstage. "Usually you have a deposit," says Libert. "So you really only pick up half [the fee], plus the percentage money. You have to sit down and figure it out. Count the unsold tickets if there were any. Count the turnstile if you had one. Everybody's looking to fuck you, so you get pretty good at trying to figure it out so they can't." By the Billion Dollar Babies tour, Libert has seen it all. "They'd change the turnstiles, print extra tickets, put in extra rows in the arena that weren't on the manifest. All kinds of shit. You name it, they did it. Charging more for catering than it really was, charging more for security than it really was. The promoters felt they had to do that because the bands were charging so much, that's the only they would make money." On their '73 tour, Alice Cooper play for a guarantee against 60 percent of the gross receipts, not net, which greatly simplifies Libert's accounting. "You didn't care about expenses. A guarantee against sixty percent, whichever is greater, meant that the promoter really didn't make a dime until he sold those last two thousand seats in the arena. And I didn't have to look through every fucking bill to find out what the break point was."

Touring with the Rolling Stones the year before, Peter Rudge confronted every conceivable form of mendacity from local promoters and hall managers, the latter often political appointees. "There was this hall manager in Mobile, Buddy Clewis, and he bought a Stones date from Peter for twenty-five thousand dollars," says Patrick Stansfield, who worked with Rudge on the '72 tour and later road-managed the band himself. "And he bitched and moaned about the rider, which included breakfast, lunch, and dinner for the crew and a bucket of rose petals for Mick Jagger to throw. Buddy was there when Peter came in to count the house"—count the number of seats—"before the show. And he finds a hundred and fifty seats that aren't on the manifest. And Peter threw a fit. 'Buddy! A hundred and fifty seats! That's a king's ransom, I tell you! A king's ransom! It's completely unacceptable!' And Buddy doesn't bat an eyelash. 'Oh, Peter, for gawd's sake. We had our ladies make a nice lunch for your crew. We went to the funeral parlor to get them rose petals. Nobody's been arrested yet. Those chairs are for my directors, I got a board I gotta keep happy. That's my damned retirement, anyway. I suggest you forget about it.'" Rudge, says Stansfield, tabulated his options, shook his head, and walked away. "Nobody's been arrested—yet," laughs Stansfield. "There was innuendo dripping from that."

Chip Rachlin worked for Bill Graham at the Fillmore East before joining ICM as a booking agent in the seventies, where his clients included

America, the Eagles, and Billy Joel. "I announced I was leaving the agency business and was covering my last show date, in D.C.," Rachlin says. The promoter was Jack Boyle, whom Rachlin knew well. "Charming rogue, great guy, used to hang out with the Kennedys. He said, 'I'm going to let you ask me any question you want tonight. Just one. I'm sure you must have some.' I said, 'Yeah, show me where you cheated.'" Boyle led Rachlin to the dressing room, where the postshow catering was laid out. "Jack pretty much had the same catering, every show. At the center of the dessert section was this five-gallon tub of ice cream. You wouldn't think anything about it. He said, 'Take a spoon. Put it into the ice cream.' So you get it down about half an inch and you scoop that into the bowl. He says, 'Try and get ice cream below the half inch.' You couldn't—it was plaster of Paris. He said, 'That put three kids through college.'" Surely Boyle exaggerates. Rachlin didn't think so. "The ice cream would show up as a seventy-five-dollar charge. If you do two hundred shows a year . . . And who knew how many other cement ice creams he had around the building? I guarantee you, no tour accountant, *nobody* would catch that." (For an indoor show Rachlin covered, a Virginia-based promoter claimed two thousand dollars of rain insurance as a deductible expense. "The tour accountant said, 'What are you talking about?' And [the promoter] said, 'Well, this is a notoriously slow market. We probably do half the show as walk-ups, and if it rains, they're not coming.'")

As album sales crashed into the millions not only for Led Zeppelin and Alice Cooper but for unsung road warriors like Foghat, Bachman-Turner Overdrive, ZZ Top, and the Edgar Winter Group, the tenor of touring went large as well. "No longer is a mass audience at an auditorium, arena or outdoor bowl satisfied with five guys in T-shirts doing a medley of their hit records," declared *Billboard*. "With ducats rising toward ten dollars for posh seating in these huge venues, major rock acts are spending thousands of dollars and months of pre-tour planning to present the ultimate in visual and aural presentation." Where Elton John's first U.S. tour comprised an entourage of twelve, in 1973 he travels with fifty support personnel, which swells to twice that in 1975 and includes transport via the fabled *Starship*. It's all part of an inexorable proliferation, a kind of arms race of the demimonde, what the military calls "mission creep," in which a successful strategy is encumbered with others larger and gaudier until it becomes so unwieldy it is cast aside.

Rising in tandem with the bands and promoters and managers during the early seventies is a growth industry in rock and roll media relations. Just servicing the alternative press and the dominant music magazines—the *Creem*s and *Crawdaddy*s and *Circus*es and *Hit Parader*s as well as the mainstream-aspirant *Rolling Stone*—keeps the press departments at the record labels in a lather. When the newsweeklies and major daily newspapers begin covering rock as an ongoing cultural story and assign dedicated reporters and editors to the beat, some farsighted young publicists see opportunity. Hired first by the old-school showbiz PR firms like Solters & Roskin as "house hippies"—whence comes Danny Goldberg, soon to be subsumed into Zeppelin's inner circle, but also from the record labels themselves—these new publicists cut a wide swath through the music industry and influence the tenor and practices of public relations for years to come. They glimpse in the rock and roll circus raging around them the chance to work for and with people who like them are graduates of the 1960s counterculture in the first throes of adulthood.

"In '73 it seemed to me that the people in charge—I was twenty-six years old at the time—were us," says Carol Klenfner, a New York–based publicist. "The record company presidents and big executives were older, but we were all in this together. And it was all about music. There's nothing comparable to that now except maybe if you work at Google. Music was the lingua franca for us in that period. To be working in the music business was like our dream come true. And to have the authority . . . I was Elton John's first press agent when he came to the U.S. Every day it was Procol Harum and Jethro Tull and the Eagles. It was so much fun and so exciting to go to work. You never knew who was going to walk through the door."

Michael Ochs was director of publicity for Columbia Records and later one of rock's first archivists. "It was a great club, we all knew each other and we all turned each other on to the artists on our labels and traded favors back and forth," Ochs says. "If a writer called me looking for something new I'd say, Oh, this group on RCA is incredible." *Saturday Night Live*, with its poisonous ironic distance and suffocating generational self-congratulation, is still two long years away. For the moment, especially in Los Angeles, the cohort of young adults working in the record business have yet to shed the last of their innocence; the record labels, not yet fully under the lash of corporate overlords, meanwhile spend lavishly on "artist development," which among other endeavors means throwing really, really great parties with plenty of free booze and food and not a discouraging word to those who wish to indulge in off-the-menu refreshments sometimes provided backchannel by the hosts.

Bobbi Cowan, niece of Warren Cowan, Frank Sinatra's publicist, was den mother of the young L.A. press agents. "The record companies believed, as we all did, that spending some money to launch a new act or new album was part of the process," she recalled. Cowan and her colleagues took inspiration from Bob Regehr of Warner Bros. Records—the hippest and most free-spending of the West Coast labels. Regehr passed into legend for throwing, with Shep Gordon, the mother of all seventies record-company parties, a demented counterpoint to Truman Capote's black-and-white ball conceived when the Ambassador Hotel, in whose kitchen Bobby Kennedy was assassinated in 1968, refused to book record-company parties into its Venetian ballroom. Regehr circumvented the embargo by insisting he was booking a coming-out party for a young debutante from Pasadena. Engraved invitations in Spencerian script were mailed. The night of the ball, the hotel realized too late that the deb was in fact Alice Cooper, and the coming-out party a press event to tub-thump *Love It to Death*. "The hotel went fucking crazy," says Gordon. "They had no idea." Recalled Alice: "Guests were greeted at the door by two men dressed in gorilla suits. The Cockettes, a troupe of drag queens from San Francisco, wore full beards streaked with glitter—they were the cigarette girls and sold cigars, cigarettes and Vaseline." The highlight of the evening was an appearance by TV Mama, a three-hundred-pound entertainer who sang "I Love You Truly" topless at Gordon's request. "I said to her manager, 'Is there any way I can pay more money and get her to take her top off?' And he looked at me and said, 'Son, to you she might be TV Mama, to me she is TV dinner. That'll be five hundred.'"

Both Cowan and Klenfner work for Gibson-Stromberg, the defining seventies rock and roll press agency whose wide-lapel, dangling-coke-spoon bravado and client list are unmatched. Partners Bob Gibson and Gary Stromberg represent Crosby, Stills, Nash & Young, B. B. King, James Taylor, Steely Dan, Leon Russell, the Eagles, and dozens more. "They were *the* PR firm in the seventies," says Will Yaryan, publicist for the Who's Quadrophenia tour. "Their clients included everyone at one time or another and the people who worked there fanned out over the music scene." From their redoubt on Sunset Boulevard—the slogan TWO FLACKS NO WAITING mounted on the wall—Gibson and Stromberg hold court in offices without desks, a touch Yaryan adopts when he moves to Atlantic Records, with one crucial difference. The centerpiece of Stromberg's office is a coffee table upon which a large crystal bowl is filled at all times with a prodigious supply of cocaine.

The symbiosis between profligate record companies willing to underwrite publicity and Gibson-Stromberg's unique flair for generating it makes an impression on Bob Greene, the *Chicago Sun-Times* columnist. "It was simplicity itself," Greene recalled. "On a Friday morning, if you were bored . . . you might call Gibson-Stromberg. 'What's going on?' Gary Stromberg might say. 'What have you got this weekend?' you might ask. And he would check his list of itineraries, and by dinnertime you would be in the front cabin of a jet bound for some medium-sized city in the Northern Hemisphere, where a chauffeured limousine would be waiting for your flight, and a room on the band's floor of the best hotel in the city would be waiting for your presence. By the end of the night you would be drinking champagne with the members of the group [and] consorting with the most beautiful women in the state."

But Gibson-Stromberg weren't just good at spending their clients' money; they were geniuses at playing the media like Keith Richards plays "Tumblin' Dice." Gibson-Stromberg orchestrated the publicity juggernaut for the Rolling Stones' '72 tour that Robert Plant would bitterly invoke when Danny Goldberg is hired to secure Zeppelin mainstream coverage in '73. For the Stones tour, after landing covers and features in *Rolling Stone* and the cream of the mainstream magazines, Gibson-Stromberg made sure that writers almost as famous as the band were assigned to the stories. William S. Burroughs was briefly on board; Terry Southern took his place. *Rolling Stone* editor Jann Wenner's weakness for social climbing was fed by Truman Capote, a bit of stunt casting that resulted in no actual story for *Rolling Stone*—the magazine ultimately commissioned Andy Warhol to interview him about the tour—but endless free publicity for the band as Capote gabbed about life with the Stones on *Johnny Carson*. As Gibson summed up the strategy: "I would have liked to have seen Teddy Kennedy come along to write about the Stones. It's just as ludicrous."

When the Beatles toured in 1964, their contract for backstage amenities stipulated: "in all dressing rooms for THE BEATLES, the PURCHASER must provide four cots, mirrors, an ice cooler, portable TV set and clean towels." Minus the ice cooler and TV, that's more or less what the average county jail cell provides today. As late as the late sixties, backstage accoutrements at the average rock concert were largely an afterthought. "To say that it was marginal is an exaggeration," says Ochs. "There was nothing. Cheap bottle of wine. Maybe some cookies." The entitlement that comes to define rock stardom in the seventies—and the ostentatious luxury that embodies it—gains its first foothold in the big tours of 1973. A sample from Alice Cooper's backstage hospitality rider is typical:

> PURCHASER shall provide three (3) cases of Budweiser, three (3) cases of Michelob, one (1) gallon of apple juice, one (1) gallon of orange juice, two (2) cases of Coca-Cola, one (1) case of ginger ale, and assorted fruit. This is to be placed in a cooler with ice in ALICE COOPER'S dressing room. Additional food appropriate to the occasion is encouraged. The Michelob beer must be in bottles and the cases of Budweiser

must be in cans. In states where the sale of beer must have an alcoholic content of less than 6 percent (i.e. 3.2 beer), the beer must be imported from another state.

When the band plays Canada, Alice—who drinks beer all day, every day—refuses to drink Budweiser brewed there. "It had to be American," says Bob Brown. "If we went to Canada, on the rider, it specifically said they had to import it from America. It would cause Libert and everyone else to go crazy if we found it said 'bottled in Canada' on it." When Alice develops a phobia that he will be poisoned, promoters are instructed to provide bottles of Seagram's VO, his other drink, with the Treasury seals intact. Compared to the no-brown-M&M's backstage clauses immortalized during the 1980s, these demands seem almost trifling. (The infamous eleven-page Van Halen rider prohibiting brown M&M's also stipulates, among literally hundreds of compulsories, three fifths of Jack Daniel's Black Label, two fifths of Stolichnaya, one pint of Southern Comfort, two bottles of Blue Nun, four cases of Schlitz malt liquor, and one large tube of K-Y jelly.) But the fact that, starting in the seventies, the bands and their management cared enough to demand the very best and specify it in the contracts speaks volumes about their priorities and self-possession. From *Starship* to limo to hotel suite, when you're a 1970s rock star, all the world's a backstage. Which, as day follows night, gives rise to the backstage *pass,* ending whatever pretext of comity still exists between audience and performer.

"In the sixties it was like you were all one big family, there was no crowd control or security guards at the side entrances," says Dave Otto, a Cincinnati entrepreneur who, like Bob Heil and Rusty Brutsche, saw a gap in the market and filled it. As rock moved into arenas, Otto perfected a technique for printing on flexible rayon with an adhesive backing. Thus was born the modern backstage pass. As Otto explains: "The cloth adheres well and goes with the contour of your body"—as untold groupies discover when applying one over a swelling halter-topped breast—"and does not fall off." In short order, Otto's backstage passes become the industry standard and a potent symbol of the stratification of rock culture as the audience-performer dynamic shifts to star and supplicant. "There was a mystique about them," acknowledges Otto. "A backstage pass was more valuable than a front row seat ticket." Before long they become pseudo-currency—groupies deduce the fastest route to the backstage sanctum is through a pass proffered by a roadie rounding up talent for the postshow party or, for the brazen, in an unsolicited exchange of fee for service, the latter earning the humble passes the sobriquet "knee pads."

All of these entitlements breed an insidious contempt for the throngs herded into the arenas who buy the tickets and the albums. The rise of festival seating during the early seventies—no reserved seats and no chairs at all on the arena floor, which maximizes capacity and profits and forces audiences to stand the entire performance—is casual evidence of the cavalier attitude toward the "fans" from the backstage sanctum. Otto vividly recalls festival seating's crush at the stage-front barricades. "It was dangerous as hell," he says. "I remember one concert, middle of the crowd, this very pretty blond girl, she's got this flowing dress on. Well, she starts walking across people's *shoulders*. She wants to get backstage. And as we're watching we see guys' hands going up and you find out she didn't have any underwear on. If she goes down for the count she's liable to get raped, whatever." The lead singer motions for security to pluck her from the fray. For her troubles and random gropings, "she got what she wanted," says Otto. "Backstage." Libert rejects the suggestion that rock star perquisites inevitably diminish the rock star's audience. "I don't believe that for a minute," he says. "I mean, first of all it's a sea of faces. It's not like you can go out and shake everybody's hand. It was very important to Alice to entertain that audience; I don't think he ever took them for granted. Yeah, [the band] were isolated. But I don't think anybody disrespected the audiences, ever."

The gulf between rock star and fan depicted in *Quadrophenia*'s "The Punk and the Godfather" just as easily describes the dynamic at any arena-rock concert—including several during the Who's 1973 tour where Townshend, almost inevitably, fulfills the prophecy of the song's lyrics. This despite the fact that the Who are almost neurotically attuned to their audience; Townshend goes so far as to apologize in *Melody Maker* for the bad sightlines at one hall on the British tour for *Quadro-*

phenia. "We still want as much, maybe even more, out of a performance as the audience does," Townshend said after the third performance on the American leg of the tour. Nevertheless, Townshend on several occasions launches shocking—for him, anyway—renunciations of the audience directly from the stage when he deems the response to *Quadrophenia* inadequate. He also indulges in the worst rock-star infantilism, including helping trash the luxury hotel suite in Montreal for no real reason other than that he can. "I like getting drunk with the guys, smashing up hotel rooms," Townshend admitted after the tour ends. "I don't know why I like bawdy situations but I do dearly love them. The bawdier the better."

Bob Gruen photographs and travels with dozens of bands in the early seventies—Led Zeppelin, Alice Cooper, and the Who among them—and witnesses firsthand the creation of the rock-star mindset. "It's contempt for everybody," Gruen says. "It was just, 'We're special, we're gods, everybody adores us and we deserve whatever we want.' They were above the law. There is a sense of entitlement when you're in a band. You have twenty people traveling and supporting you, and even they feel special. There's a cockiness that goes along with that, and you have a gang to back you up. And because you have this arrogance, you kind of take over. Going through the airport with a band is much more fun than going through by yourself. Every minute is planned, there's people yelling, 'Come this way! Get in this car!' You really don't have a lot of contact with the people around you or even with the ground. You're kind of coming in from the air, you land in the town, you drive everybody crazy, and you're gone before dawn. So there is this feeling of a military operation where you come in, and you conquer, and you're gone. So that screwing a couple of girls and leaving without knowing their names, that's part of it."

On the Billion Dollar Babies tour, says Libert, "Everybody was living in this bubble. Think of it: You put your bag outside your hotel room and then the next thing you know, it's outside your hotel room in the next city. You go downstairs, you hop into a limo, it takes you to your own airplane, the airplane flies you to the next city, you hop out, you hop into another limousine, it takes you to the next hotel. You don't really touch reality and there's people to keep everybody else away. It just becomes normal." Alice, says Libert, "was never left alone, ever. There was always somebody with him. I remember there was an incident where he was going to be left alone. The limo would take him to a private jet that would take him somewhere else where somebody would be waiting for him, but he would be on his own, on a certain level. I said, 'You sure you're going to be okay, Alice?' He goes: 'Jesus Christ, Libert, I'll be okay.' He says, 'I don't need you to wipe my ass. You just make sure there's toilet paper there.'"

Gruen first encounters Led Zeppelin during the '73 tour while waiting to join them in a limo outside the band's New York hotel. "There were a few autograph fans standing on the sidewalk. And before the band walked out, Peter Grant came out with Richard Cole, and the two of them walked through and over the fans. Didn't even go so far as to push them out of the way, but acted as if they weren't even there and literally knocked the kids down like they were bowling pins. It was just pointlessly cruel to the people that supported the band. I mean, it would have been harsh if they had yelled at them or pushed them out of the way. But I didn't even see them attempt—they just banged right into them and knocked them down. Whereas the band seemed cheerful and pleasant and without a care in the world because they had these two killers watching out for them."

Shortly after Gruen's introduction to the ways and means of Zeppelin's handlers, he captures the iconic photo of the band preening in front of the *Starship* at Teterboro Airport in New Jersey—the four young lions, two with shirts open to the waist, wear the most amazing expressions, somewhere between naked smugness and equally naked pride. "Somebody said, 'Let's get a picture with our plane'—it was really kind of spur of the moment, like a snapshot," Gruen says. "Nowadays, to do something like that you'd have to meet with stylists and lawyers and all kinds of people weeks in advance. But in that case we just got out of the limo and walked in front of the plane and took some pictures." For Michael Des Barres, accomplished student of rock and roll atmosphere, the photo is "a deification . . . an absolute visual symbol of the elevated magnificence of a rock and roll band. We'd seen the Beatles getting off a plane to thousands of people screaming, but you'd never seen a shot of nobody there but the band and their fucking plane. That photograph changed everybody's perspective of what achievements a rock and roll band could garner. It's the photograph that every rock and roll band since has tried to emulate," even if, as Gruen points out, "you actually rent the plane and they paint your name on it. They didn't own it."

Gruen is struck by the immensity of Zeppelin's success and their eagerness to indulge it. "They had the plane, they're playing a stadium—that was something that I don't think the bands of the sixties would have dreamed of," he says. "Being in a band in the sixties was about having fun. Rock and roll was a way to get a free drink and meet a girl. You weren't expecting to make a lot of money, but you could have fun. After the success of Woodstock, where they saw just how big the audience was, people started wanting to cash in on that." Says Peter Rudge, "Woodstock made everybody aware of what the commercial potential was of what up until that time had been, essentially, an alternative culture and in many respects a cottage industry. From that came this business that we're in now, for better or worse. And in the early seventies, bands like the Who, the Stones, and Zeppelin were the ones who led the way." Says Rachlin: "As record sales and ticket sales increased, it attracted more of a business atmosphere. It didn't hit the record company side that hard because you still had the Ahmet Erteguns and Jerry Wexlers and Mo Ostins and Bob Krasnows and people like that who were still controlling the A&R process. What it did start to do was bring in tour accountants, business managers, and other specialized people who are only concerned about maximizing the cash."

There remain flashes of sixties-style audience care and feeding. Perhaps as penance for the debacle of 1969's Altamont festival—where Hells Angels hired as "security" went berserk and attacked the audience with pool cues and stabbed to death a gun-toting fan in front of the stage—the Rolling Stones authorized Rachlin to engage in stealth noblesse oblige on the band's behalf. "I did the ticket pulls"—complimentary house seats—"for the sponsors, the record company, the press, anybody that was on the inside." Inevitably, not all the tickets would be claimed by the day of the sold-out concert. "The instructions I had were, just before showtime, to walk the perimeter of the building looking for couples, not single guys, because a guy on a date acts differently." Rachlin would approach a ticketless couple and ask if they wanted to see the Stones. "They'd look at me and go, 'Yeah, how much?' I said, 'That's wasn't the question. *Do you wanna see the Stones?*' You had to establish that you were in control. And I'd pull out two tickets, hand them to them and say, 'Go in that gate. If I see you try to sell these tickets I will have you arrested. This is courtesy of the Rolling Stones.' Now, they didn't believe anything you were saying. And they would go to the usher, hand the tickets to him like they were radioactive . . . and off they'd go. And they were inevitably great seats."

In the meantime, there is so much money sluicing through the system that there is plenty left over for bulk cocaine purchases for the entourage and ego enhancements like the *Starship*. "Peter Grant had made such a stink in terms of cutting out the middleman that now, at last, these pampered anorexics, these velvet-clad princes, were getting paid," says Des Barres. "And that's the reason, I think, why suddenly things changed and took on a whole other excess. Once the bands started to make money, that huge money, it began." By the early seventies, for everyone from Crosby, Stills & Nash—soon to travel in a brace of Learjets and sleep on hand-embroidered pillow shams designed by Joni Mitchell—to that unlikeliest "sixties band" of all, Led Zeppelin, rock stardom becomes the prevailing rock and roll reality. The self-righteous intolerance of negative reviews, the imperious demand that every whim be met, the wild power imbalance between band and audience that manifests in teenage girls willingly prostrating themselves for whatever sexual denigration the boys fancy, form an archetype later parodied in *This Is Spinal Tap* with such devastating accuracy that Eddie Van Halen—he of the no-brown-M&M's—fails to see the humor at all. "I didn't laugh—I wept because it was so close to the truth," said U2's guitarist the Edge, who upon becoming one of the planet's mightiest rock stars would petition relentlessly to build a 12,785-square-foot mansion and four others on a pristine Malibu ridgeline. But when U2 formed in the mid-seventies as a scrappy Irish punk band, it had been in explicit rejection of vintage '73 rock stardom and all its devices. "Fifteen-minute guitar solos, fifteen-minute drum solos," the Edge lamented. "There was a huge element of self-indulgence, professional rock musicians who looked down upon their fans. Those old colors were dead, and we wanted none of it."

One of Danny Markus's first tasks when he joins Zeppelin's '73 tour is to stock the band's suites at Chicago's Ambassador East with stereo equipment. After going to some trouble to assemble audiophile-level gear, Markus stops by the hotel to check up on his charges. "So I'm up in Robert's room, I think Jimmy was there, and I guess they were sharing some marching powder and I'm looking around, 'What happened to the stereo? Did it work out?' And Robert says, 'Come here.' And we go down to one of the guest bathrooms in the suite and there it was, in the bathtub, in like a foot of water." Markus, like all who deal with the band—or those who do the bidding of any band at the Zeppelin level in 1973— takes the moment in stride. "That was his way of saying, the 'road' way of saying: 'Hey, this didn't work out.' He didn't take it out on me personally, he just thought that's where it deserved to be. And again, I never let them see me sweat. I'm like: Okay. Y'know? Not a problem."

The thousand-dollar custom stereo disappoints so it is drowned in the bathtub? *No problem.* The Budweiser in the dressing room is brewed in Calgary and has to be replaced by a case flown in from Detroit? *No problem.* I'm tired of fucking you and want to fuck your friend instead so get out of my suite even though it's three A.M. and you're wasted on Quaaludes? *No problem.* This is the mindscape—financial, philosophical, logistical, sexual—that defines rock stardom on the road in North America in the spring and summer and fall of 1973. It is light-years away, in every respect, from the attitudes and realities that shaped Led Zeppelin, the Who, and Alice Cooper when they first plugged in the electric guitars, tested the drum kit, and raised their voices as young unknowns. It's at once the end of one era and the beginning of another, not that anyone can apprehend that at the time. That will come later, with hindsight, perhaps wisdom. "The three words that defined the sixties were 'peace and love,'" Mick Mashbir, the Alice Cooper guitarist, says forty years later. "The three words that defined the seventies were 'cash and cum.'"

Chapter 7

LET THE SHOW BEGIN

Keith Moon passes out at Quadrophenia's *San Francisco premiere; Led Zeppelin sells 56,000 tickets in Tampa, become "bigger than the Beatles"; Alice Cooper loses his head as the* Billion Dollar Babies *tour launches in Philadelphia.*

Quadrophenia is scarcely finished when the Who enter Shepperton Studios on October 10, 1973, to rehearse for the upcoming U.K. and U.S. tours. The first concert, in Stoke-on-Trent, deep in Britain's West Midlands, is less than three weeks away. The material is the most challenging the Who have attempted to replicate onstage, made even more daunting by the band's noble resistance to hire sidemen out of concern that it will dilute the group's identity and disappoint the fans. "The Who had always prided themselves on being able to play songs from the albums onstage," said Entwistle. The band plays "Won't Get Fooled Again" and "Baba O'Reilly" with backing tapes on their previous tour, but those merely replicate Townshend's underlying parts. "It's one thing to play to the sort of metronomic backing track of 'Won't Get Fooled Again,'" recalled Entwistle. "But with the complex time changes of *Quadrophenia* we got crossed up too easily. We had to play it perfectly to make it work."

The backing tapes for *Quadrophenia*—replete with crashing waves, whistling locomotives, and the waltz-time synthesizer riff from "Love, Reign O'er Me" among dozens of other effects—are cut in Ronnie Lane's mobile barely two weeks before opening night. Deploying them requires unnerving precision, much of it borne by Bob Pridden, the sound engineer, from a control board on Townshend's side of the stage, and Keith Moon, who must play along in unwavering time to preset tempos. Says Cy Langston: "These days it's just little cartridges, you put in an MP3, but in the old days, it was a four-track tape machine onstage. One of the tracks is a click track, and the drummer has to wear headphones because he's gotta hear the clicks. So Keith Moon used to wear these headphones, which were duct taped so they wouldn't come off, because once he lost the click track, he couldn't get the band in time with the tape."

For all his lunacy and explosive playing style, Moon is a consummate timekeeper and adapts, but Daltrey is increasingly vocal in his distaste for the tapes. "Once you were playing with a tape, that's when it started to die for me," he recalled. "You were no longer free to do what you felt like doing. You'd be stuck into this thing. It made the sound bigger and we were still a four-piece, but it didn't work creatively for me at all."

The staging is to include projected footage of each of the Who—windmill guitar riffing, microphone twirling, drum bashing, and bass playing—which in turn has to sync with the backing tapes and the live band. It's another example of Townshend's creative vision outstripping the technology at hand—perfected twenty years later on multimedia extravaganzas like U2's Zoo TV tour—and adding yet another layer of complexity to a show already straining to accommodate his ambitions. (The video concept is abandoned before the tour begins.) Exhausted from recording and producing *Quadrophenia* with only Ron Nevison's assistance, incensed by Daltrey's disappointment with the album's mix and Entwistle's and Moon's displeasure at what they perceive as his dictatorial style, Townshend downs bottle upon bottle of Rémy Martin and steams ahead. The Who are famously contemptuous in the best of times; given the delivery of the album straight into the teeth of the deadline for the tour, something is bound to give. And as rehearsals grind on at Shepperton, it finally does.

Will Yaryan visits Shepperton in his capacity as MCA's new director of publicity. "I had been with Gibson-Stromberg earlier in 1973 and was envious of Stromberg's adventures on the Stones tour which he retold in the office on his trips back from the front," Yaryan says. "So when I got the job with MCA and heard about the Who tour I didn't want to miss out." He doesn't. A crew on hand to film the band rehearsing unwittingly provides what screenwriters call the inciting incident. "We'd played almost the whole of *Quadrophenia* and this film crew were all sitting on their trunks watching the show without a camera turning," recalled Daltrey. "So I just said, 'For fuck's sake, when are you lot gonna start filming? You're waiting for me to wear my voice out so you can film me when I'm flogged out.' And Pete came over to me and started poking me: 'You do as you're fucking told.' He was on his brandy and he started poking me in the chest. And the roadies, 'cause they know what I'm like—if I ever get rolling I'm a little tiger—they all jumped on me. They're holding me down."

While the roadies restrain Daltrey, Townshend hefts his Gibson Les Paul—a chunk of solid mahogany weighing fifteen pounds—and slams it into Daltrey's shoulder in retribution for, among other alleged misdemeanors, saying "that I'd taken too much control, that I'd done it all single-handedly and that I'd mixed him down in the mix and it didn't sound right and it didn't work," said Townshend. "And I was so hurt by that that I hit him." Daltrey recalled: "He starts spitting at me, calling me a little cunt. And then he says, 'Let the little cunt go, I'll fucking kill him.' So they let me go and he threw two punches." The first misses; as Townshend winds up to throw another, said Daltrey, "He was totally off balance and I hit him with an uppercut and he went six inches off the ground and passed out." Yaryan walks in just as Daltrey lands his haymaker. "All I remember of the fight was hearing [Townshend's] head hit the stage," he says. "It was loud." According to *The Kids Are Alright* documentary filmmaker Jeff Stein, Keith Moon hovers over the unconscious Townshend pleading, "Pete! Pete! If you're still alive we'll do anything you say from now on!" Townshend is revived in the hospital with memory loss. "No one was sorrier than I was," Daltrey said. "I was forced to lay one on him. But it was only one." As for the aftermath, Daltrey insisted: "It wasn't a big fight. It was like the wife hitting you with a frying pan. The next minute you're in bed fucking each other to death."

Opening night in Stoke goes about as well as can be expected given the attenuated rehearsals and lingering intramural hostilities between Townshend and Daltrey. The original plan is to present the entirety of *Quadrophenia* in repertory, all seventeen songs, bracketed by surefire hits like "Won't Get Fooled Again" and the band's longtime show opener, "I Can't Explain." Unlike the *Tommy* segment it replaces, "*Quadrophenia* didn't have songs that were immediately accessible live," says Peter Rudge. "And how do you work in those big Who standards—'Won't Get Fooled Again,' 'My Generation,' and things like that—around *Quadrophenia*, which was a much more sophisticated piece of work which had to find its own identity?"

With the album still not in stores in the U.K.—a vinyl shortage caused by the 1973 oil crisis is blamed for the delay—the Stoke audience responds politely to the opera and reserves its enthusiasm for the greatest hits, a pattern that will repeat at subsequent concerts to Townshend's growing infuriation. "The audiences were disappointed with it," says Rudge. "The Who struggled to get the reaction they'd got from *Tommy*." The first public performance of *Quadrophenia* unsurprisingly yields difficulties: Aside from Moon, who has the cues piped through headphones, it's hard for the musicians to hear the backing tapes amid the roar of their own instruments and voices. To replicate the tunings on the album, Townshend is forced to change guitars more than twenty times, slowing the already sluggish pacing. Three numbers from the *Quadrophenia* segment are immediately cut—"Is It in My Head," "I've Had Enough," and "The Dirty Jobs." The following night in Wolverhampton, Townshend tells the audience, "We played *Quadrophenia* for the first time last night and it was bloody horrible." The performance goes smoothly enough that reviewers—the press are embargoed from the Stoke premiere—give the show high marks: "a triumphantly successful evening with the fans going bananas and the band enjoying themselves just as much," according to *Disc*. At the next two performances, in Manchester, the band and audience are in high spirits—Townshend does a cartwheel introducing the *Quadrophenia* segment—as it seems the technical challenges and the band's opening-night jitters and relentless self-criticism ebb. *Quadrophenia* is finally released the day after the second triumphant Manchester concert—where Townshend in his exuberance polls the audience for requests. The band takes two days off as the album sells one million dollars' worth of copies in the U.S. its first three days in stores.

The wheels promptly come off on the first of two nights in Newcastle. The integration of the backing tapes and live playing, while improved, is as fraught as ever. Pridden, the sound engineer, comes to dread the moment when he pushes the button on the four-track, never knowing if the tapes will sync properly or simply refuse to play at all. When Townshend, singing the refrain "Why should I care?," finishes the guitar-and-vocal prologue to "5:15" fifty minutes into the show, a backing tape of Entwistle's horns and Chris Stainton's piano is supposed to fire just as Moon and Entwistle crash into the song's first verse; instead, the tape engages fifteen seconds late. When he hears the cacophony, Townshend snaps. He screams and spits at Pridden, hauls him from his post in the wings, and shoves him to the stage floor. He then pulls out fistfuls of the backing tapes before smashing his guitar into the tape deck while Entwistle, Daltrey, and Moon gape. The audience, well acquainted with Townshend's history of onstage violence, is nevertheless stunned and silent as he stalks off, followed by the rest of the band. The explosion is followed by twenty tense minutes while the audience is kept in darkness until the band returns and plays the rest of the set minus the remaining numbers from *Quadrophenia*. Simon Malia, a sixteen-year-old fan, is in the front row when Townshend erupts. "He had seemed edgy beforehand, seemingly wanting more response from the audience to the new material." Malia recalled that during "My Generation," Townshend harangues the audience for their supposed apathy—"he was swearing at us, calling us bastards. I was right down in front . . . and swearing back at him. Talk about 'The Punk [and] the Godfather.'" The show closes with Townshend destroying a second guitar and declaring he won't play live again.

The incident is covered disapprovingly in the press; particularly poignant is the letter to the Newcastle *Evening Chronicle* by four girls primly upbraiding Townshend: "His use of bad language and immature attitude was completely unnecessary and completely spoilt our enjoyment of an otherwise praiseworthy performance." Reflecting on the concert a year later, Townshend said that "I'd really decided that that was the end, that it had all become a complete waste of time. Any business where one night you can be playing before a completely ecstatic audience and the next night you're playing to an audience of complete dummies, must be a farce . . . I completely exploded . . . imagining that I would never, ever walk on the stage again. Twenty-five minutes later, there I was for the encore." So much for Townshend's foreboding, as the second night in Newcastle not only passes without incident but turns into the best performance of the tour. Seven shows in London end on a relatively high note, although a concert at the Lyceum is marred by a crush in front of the stage in which several fans pass out, prefiguring the lethal stampede in Cincinnati.

Seven days later, the Who arrive in San Francisco for the premiere of the American tour at the fourteen-thousand-seat Cow Palace. Tickets for the show—as with every city on the itinerary—sell out in hours, and anticipation for the band's first concert in America since *Who's Next* is acute. Although Bob Heil's quadrophonic sound system used on the U.K. dates isn't deployed, the band still travels with twenty tons of custom sound and lights and other staging that requires three forty-five-foot trailers and a twelve-man crew. For reasons never entirely made clear, the graphics for the tour's advertisements and backstage passes are based around the yellow-and-black civil defense fallout shelter symbol, which lends the aesthetics an ominous air, and the tour becomes known as simply Fallout Shelter by Who fanatics.

The show is essentially the same as presented in the U.K.: A flurry of oldies open and close, with "My Generation" serving as the lead-in to the eleven songs from *Quadrophenia*. Lynyrd Skynyrd, whose debut album has just been released, face fourteen thousand Who fans for their first gig in the big leagues. To calm their nerves they indulge predictably, and soon a Jack Daniel's bottle flies from their dressing room, nearly clocking Daltrey in the head. Skynyrd aren't alone in fueling up before the gig.

Before the Who take the stage, Moon shares a drink with two groupies; in the ensuing hour it will become clear he's imbibed something stronger than Mateus.

Despite the pressure of opening night and dire warnings from a doctor about Daltrey's fraying vocal cords, the concert gets off to a roaring start. Skynyrd—"shy, nervous, and overwhelmed," according to Yaryan—shake off their jitters and blaze through a swaggering set as if playing spring break in Tallahassee. The first half of the Who's set, including the eleven songs from *Quadrophenia,* goes down reasonably well until Moon starts to flag during "Drowned." He perseveres through the next three songs and nearly all of the punishing "Won't Get Fooled Again" until—during the drum-solo lead-in to the finale—he makes ready to strike a cymbal and instead falls backward off his stool, unconscious. Though Moon later claims his backstage companions had spiked his drink with PCP—the notorious animal tranquilizer at the time making its way through the rock demimonde—it's just as plausible he'd dosed himself. "Moon was with this girl who I think gave him the PCP," says Yaryan, who is backstage and watches the drama unfold in front of the cream of San Francisco's rock elite, including *Rolling Stone*'s Jann Wenner. "I doubt that he was slipped it unknowingly." Rudge agrees. "In terms of the girls giving him stuff or whether he was conscious of it, he wouldn't have blinked an eye—he would've just taken it." Rudge also notes that Moon's collapse in San Francisco wasn't an isolated incident. "Moonie was the kind of guy, bless his heart, who took speed to go to sleep and downers to wake up. So it was always there or thereabouts, the threat of him keeling over. That happened on two or three occasions—I remember Boston much more vividly than San Francisco."

However ingested, the drug flattens the normally unsinkable drummer and leaves the rest of the band fidgeting onstage. After some desultory remarks Townshend finally admits, "The horrible truth is that without him we're not a group." Backstage, Moon is drenched under a cold shower and given a shot of cortisone; twenty minutes after his collapse he appears stage right, apparently revived. By coincidence, the concert is being recorded with a two-camera black-and-white videotape system. In the murky footage that survives, as Moon tentatively steps onstage, Townshend grabs him in cartoonish fury and wrestles him to his microphone, where he berates him before the audience. Joined by Daltrey, they manhandle Moon across the stage and deposit him behind his drums as if he is a guitar Townshend is about to smash; Townshend meanwhile gives the audience a jocular thumbs-up. Even taking into consideration his understandable annoyance at Moon for torpedoing such a high-profile engagement, Townshend's rough treatment of his bandmate after what is clearly some sort of overdose looks especially gratuitous when viewed in the grainy video.

With Moon behind the drums, the band strikes up "Magic Bus," but within minutes he appears vacant-eyed, flailing at his cymbals, before passing out again, this time face-first into the tom-toms. As the band plays on, he is hoisted as if from a fishing net and carried offstage, limp and pale as a mackerel. With Moon unquestionably out of commission for the night, a frustrated Townshend marks time at the microphone. "When Keith collapsed it was such a shame," he recalled. "I had just been getting warmed up at that point . . . I didn't want to stop playing." Such is Townshend's mindset when he turns to the audience and half quips, "Does anybody play the drums?" A cheer goes up. "I mean somebody *good.*" (Presumably Bob Burns, Skynryd's pile-driving drummer, has already left the building.) In the audience near the stage is Scott Halpin, a nineteen-year-old Muscatine, Iowa, transplant who has paid for a scalped ticket and is attending with a visiting boyhood friend. When his pal hears Townshend's request, he gets the attention of the stage security and, indicating Halpin, shouts, "He can play!" Halpin in fact played in bands back in Muscatine but hasn't touched the drums in a year. Before he can protest, Bill Graham himself looms. "Can you do it?" Graham asks. The next thing Halpin knows, he's backstage downing a shot of brandy someone has handed him and being escorted to the Moonless drum set. As he settles in, Townshend reaches through the cymbals and shakes his hand. "I'm in complete shock," Halpin recalled. "Then I got really focused and Townshend said to me, 'I'm going to lead you. I'm going to cue you.'"

Given the circumstances, Halpin acquits himself reasonably well on the blues chestnuts "Smokestack Lightning" and "Spoonful," as well as the Who's "Naked Eye," before joining arms with Townshend, Daltrey, and Entwistle for the curtain call. "I really admire their stamina," he said. "I only played three numbers and I was dead." Backstage, Daltrey gives Halpin a tour jacket and pledges to pay him a thousand dollars. Whereupon Scott Halpin climbs into his VW Beetle and drives himself back into obscurity. Townshend sends him a thank-you note after the tour moves to Los Angeles, but the thousand dollars Daltrey promises never materializes. "That's a thousand dollars plus interest," he calculated twenty years later. "Let's figure it out."

On January 3, Warner Bros. Records releases Alice Cooper's "Hello Hooray," the first single from *Billion Dollar Babies,* nearly two months ahead of the album. As the single slowly climbs the charts, the band rehearses for the spring tour at the Galesi mansion. For the first time in their career, they integrate two new members into the touring band—Mick Mashbir and the keyboardist Bob Dolan—hired to facilitate the album's intricate songs but mostly to take up the slack left by the increasingly dysfunctional Glen Buxton.While visiting family in Arizona he is rushed into emergency surgery to operate on his alcohol-ravaged pancreas, raising for the first time the possibility he won't be able to participate in the crucial spring tour. He finally arrives two weeks before opening night, against doctors' recommendations, having learned none of the new songs that will dominate the show. "We busted our butts to make tapes and send them out when he was in the hospital," says Bruce. "We would call him up and Glen would say, 'Yeah, I've been working on those parts, no problem.' And when he came back we set up for the first rehearsal and he didn't know any of it." It falls to Mashbir, high school friend and now uneasy usurper, to teach them to him.

Deciding how the new musicians will be presented in the stage show is the subject of awkward negotiation with the band's ever-watchful manager. "When I first showed up for tour rehearsals, Shep asked me if I would play in a gorilla costume," says Mashbir. "I laughed and told him that he obviously didn't have a clue about playing the guitar." It is finally decided that Mashbir and Dolan will occupy a discreet corner of the huge set and wear the same white costumes, with bejeweled dollar signs sewn into the jackets, as the regular band. Other than that, they will keep a low profile. "I was not supposed to be given any extra exposure or publicity because Shep thought it was important to preserve the band's image," Mashbir says. "It was management's goal to always present the band as the fans expected it: Alice, Mike, Neal, Dennis, and Glen." Mashbir rides on the bus with the road crew from the airports to the hotels, not in the limos with the band, until late in the tour; by design, the contractually required eight Super Trouper spotlights seldom sweep Mashbir and Dolan's corner of the stage. "During songs like 'My Stars,' as I was playing lead the spotlight was on Glen," Mashbir says. "That happened many times during the show."

While the band rehearses in Connecticut, the final touches are put on the monumental Billion Dollar Babies set, constructed on a sound stage at Warner Bros. studios in Burbank, California. The set has its genesis in a conversation between Shep Gordon and Joe Gannon, who directed Neil Diamond's acclaimed Hot August Night concert series the year before, the first pop-rock show that incorporated Broadway-style moving sets and theatrical lighting and effects. "I had just gotten back from doing Neil on Broadway in 1972," Gannon says. "And Shep gives me a call and says, 'I want you to do the show called Billion Dollar Babies.' He says, 'I'll make you a producer. I'll pay you twenty-five grand to put this thing together.' So then I came back to the West Coast and thought of all of the insanity that I wanted to put in the lighting and everything else."

Built on multiple levels, the stage comprises two steel cages flanking a Busby Berkeley–inspired staircase that, per Alice's request, lights up with each step he takes. Silvered bodies hang from the superstructure, and a gilded Egyptian sarcophagus with lasers that shoot from its eyes looms behind center stage. "The drums were right in the middle of the stage," says Smith. "To my right and left were these big towers that probably went twenty feet into the air. There's four braces to the towers covered in tiny lights all the way up and down, and a huge mirror ball that hung from them. My drums were covered with half-inch mirrors, so when the Super Troupers hit them they just exploded like a billion diamonds. It was all lit up and moving, like nothing anybody had ever seen before."

Aside from Alice, the band members are not consulted on the design of the stage. "It was very cool," says Michael Bruce, "but it was like, how can they do this and not check with the band, you know? But we got over that and it was okay."

The original concept for the show was that it would premiere at the Palace Theatre on Broadway—Michael Bennett, two years before *A Chorus Line,* helped secure the theater. "The billboard was up in Times Square," says Gordon. "But they got a play they wanted and bumped us." Nothing comes of Alice at the Palace, as it is billed, other than a nice burst of pretour publicity, which may have been the point all along. But the Coopers' Ziegfeld-like stage is informed by Broadway in ways that don't become evident until it is on the road. "It was manufactured by theater people, right?" says Gannon. "And theater people are like, 'Where's it going? All right, it's going to the Winter Garden, and if it's a good run it will stay there for years.' This fucking thing was so heavy, so unroadwise. The towers were made up of two-and-a-half-inch by two-and-a-half-inch tubing that was quarter-inch steel. I mean, you could hang the Empire State Building on it if you wanted to." Crew member Ron Volz rents a theater in Port Chester, New York, for dress rehearsals while the stage is shipped from California. "It was like heavier than shit," Volz says. "It was just a monster job—these pieces of steel that made the trusses, it took eight guys to carry one piece." When the set is struck for the first time, says Gannon, "Shep and I are loading the truck in the middle of fucking winter. We're freezing our asses off, trying to break it down. We didn't have enough personnel to help us, everything is so fucking new. So he and I are loading the fucking truck. He looked at me and said, 'What the fuck did you get me into?' Needless to say, I had no fucking answer to that one."

Design flaws make themselves known. Michael Bruce repeatedly tears his costume and flesh on one of the glitter-encrusted steel towers that he must negotiate to reach center stage but is rebuffed when he complains. "I tried to tactfully see if there was some way to modify it, and it just turned into this big old rock star who is pissed off," Bruce says. "Finally I went to the guy who designed the stage and he goes, 'Oh, that? We can cut this bar here and slide the whole thing forward. No problem.' That's the downside of designing a stage where you don't try it out first." On a tour that will increasingly be fraught with unspoken tension over Alice's emerging superstardom, the stage's multilevel construction has the effect, intentional or not, of diminishing the instrumentalists. "I do believe that the size of the stage really made the band look like Alice's backing band," said Mashbir. "Everyone but Alice was set back and above the stage floor on risers. Those guys were used to front-row interaction with the fans and that can't happen when you're twenty feet from the edge of the stage, or in Neal's case twenty feet above the audience. I do think the band's performance suffered somewhat from the inability to make eye contact with each other—I never saw GB or Dennis onstage for the whole tour."

Just as they are about to launch the most important tour of their career, the band begins moving out of the Galesi mansion into places of their own. Alice is first to go, in January, to a penthouse apartment in Manhattan's East Fifties he shares with Cindy Lang. The moves are made possible by the sizable royalty checks from *School's Out* and, finally, profitable touring, as well as the inevitable pressure to invest and shelter income. "By the Billion Dollar Babies tour we were making a million dollars a month," says Smith. "Of course, we were almost spending that much, too." The departures from the mansion mark the end of five years of communal living and shared sacrifice at the moment when everything the band has strived toward is about to explode around them as Alice's individual fame looms.

Early in the band's career, Gordon took a meeting with a young publicist named Pat Kingsley—she will later become Hollywood's most powerful press agent, representing Tom Cruise. "I took all five guys to the office and about fifteen minutes into the meeting she said, 'Shep, could you have the guys step outside?'" When they were alone, Kingsley told Gordon: "I don't know how to make five guys in a group called Alice Cooper famous when there is no Alice Cooper. You give me one guy called Alice Cooper in a band, that I know how to do." In the lobby, Gordon told the band, "'She said we gotta pick one of you to be Alice Cooper.' So we picked Alice for the reason of having a person to do the press."

Having Alice become the focus of the group allowed a simplified story line to sell to the media: Alice-the-maybe-transvestite-and-chicken-blood-drinking-monster-man. Except for songwriting royalties, the band already divided their income equally, so, Gordon reasoned, any upside to pushing Alice benefited them all, at least financially. The downside to this arrangement, which would come into relief on the Billion Dollar Babies tour, was that the musicians collectively known as Alice Cooper could no longer compete with Alice Cooper the assiduously promoted star. Resentment, mostly unspoken, creeps into their relationship with Alice. "None of it was in the open," says Libert. "They talked about it behind Alice's back and Alice didn't have much to say about it, really. I'd overhear it and my comment was always, 'What's the matter with you guys? You're still making the same amount of money, what do you care?' But they did." Says Alice, "It got to the point where I was really doing all the work as far as promoting the band. I didn't care. I figured that's my job—I'm the lead singer, the lead guy. But I never, ever thought that anybody was getting nervous about me being the big star." There is among the rest of the band the growing realization that Alice can, if he chooses, walk away from the band with his stardom intact. "We weren't getting the publicity a band like the Who or Led Zeppelin was getting for all the members," says Smith. "It was always focusing on Alice, and that's fine. We knew that, we agreed to that. My only concern over all the publicity Alice was getting—even though everybody guaranteed he never would go out on his own—was that, if he wanted to step out of this, he has huge momentum from a band that all five of us created."

Mark Volman and Howard Kaylan, late of the Turtles and two years' punishing studio and roadwork with Frank Zappa, open the shows on the School's Out and Billion Dollar Babies tours as Flo and Eddie. "They had always been so close," says Volman, "and they began to see the band dissolving because Alice was now the star. There was nothing else you can say about it, the rest of them were just the backup band." Volman goes through similar psychodrama when he and Kaylan dominate the Turtles after the huge hit "Happy Together." "We were pretty much ostracized by our own group because we were becoming the power base," he says. "That's exactly what was happening with Alice. The record company was centering on him, the press was centering on him. That was not his plan—that's the way the music business works. I mean, who wants to talk to the drummer or the bass player when the guy who's being hanged onstage is very happy to talk to you?" Not to mention Alice possesses a star's magnetism and can switch on the charm, bright and warm as a Super Trouper, as effortlessly as popping a fresh Bud. "If you were a writer for the *Hoboken Times* and you encountered Alice Cooper," says Danny Markus, "Alice would make you feel like you were the first writer he had ever encountered—he had you in the palm of his hand within seconds." Alice's relations with the rest of the band are hardly helped when, once the tour is under way, Volman and Kaylan accompany him to press conferences. Not only are Bruce, Smith, Dunaway, and Buxton not invited, they are banned by managerial fiat. "Shep didn't want all the guys there," says Libert. "They just weren't good at it—it sort of diluted everything. So he told me to tell them not to come to the press conferences anymore. I was the one who had to tell everybody the bad news: 'Why, Shep?' 'That's what you get paid for, Libert. Just fucking do it.' So I did." Gordon recalls that the other band members "were always late. And they'd always say the stupidest fucking things. They used to kick and scream about doing the press conferences anyway, so it just became much easier." Says Bob Brown, "It wasn't like a Beatles situation where all of them had interesting things to say. Alice had the one-liners. Alice had the—I hate to call it corporate rap—but he had it down. He knew what had to be done."

Dress rehearsals for the Billion Dollar Babies tour move from Port Chester to shakedown performances in Canada and Rochester, New York, before the March 8 premiere at the Philadelphia Spectrum. Warner Bros. Records ponies up a $31,000 "party" budget for the tour, nearly $15,000 of which is swallowed flying forty-eight music journalists from New York to the Philadelphia premiere on *AC-1,* the band's red-white-and-blue Lockheed L-188 Electra charter with ALICE COOPER painted on its flanks and two snakes twisted into the shape of dollar signs on the tail. Champagne is poured throughout the flight, as well as at the pre- and postshow cocktail parties—the latter held on a yacht so overloaded the harbor police refuse to let it weigh anchor. The tipsy journalists are plied with endless statistics meant to invoke shock and awe and mostly succeeding: *Rolling Stone* dutifully quotes Gordon to the effect that the tour will be the largest in the history of rock, playing to eight hundred thousand and earning $4.5 million in fifty-six cities before the June 3 finale at Madison Square Garden. It says something about the state of high-flying rock circa 1973, and Alice Cooper's particular place in it, that the tour is launched with such calculated, crass overkill, and that the journalists along for the ride mostly lap it up. "With Alice," observed one junketeer, "the hype is half the art." *Newsweek* meanwhile laments that "rock music has evolved into a florid and self-conscious rococo period, which is also, sad to say, often decadent," and it singles out the "repulsive" Alice Cooper. Alice is quoted unrepentant, in what amounts to a mission statement for the *Billion Dollar Babies* album and tour: "Violence and sex sell. That's our appeal . . . We're the ultimate American band—the end product of an affluent society."

At the Spectrum an audience of nearly twenty thousand is packed to the arena's gunwales when the lights go out and the band take their places on the set. Mick Mashbir girds himself for his first gig in the big time. "The first night was a humbling experience," he would recall. "The crotch of my pants split as I climbed up to the stage. I played my first coliseum show with my balls hanging out." It's a vote of confidence in *Billion Dollar Babies* that the show is so tightly integrated with it—of the thirteen songs, eight are from the new album. "Hello Hooray," the erstwhile Judy Collins ballad now transformed into Alice's triumphant overture, opens the show as he creeps through stage fog into beams of the Super Troupers, dressed in ragged tights accessorized incongruously with a white satin cutaway. From there it's on to "Billion Dollar Babies," which Smith and Dunaway supercharge with a pummeling rhythmic punch only hinted at on the album. "Elected" segues into "Eighteen," with Alice sprawled over the lip of the stage as if too inebriated to stand, clutching a plastic cup of what looks a lot like whiskey but which he later insists is Coca-Cola. "Even though it looked like I'd been drinking onstage, I never drank when I worked," Alice says. "I drank the other twenty-two hours."

The Rolling Stones–like "Raped and Freezin'" and "No More Mr. Nice Guy," from the new album, both built around irresistible Michael Bruce guitar riffs, are combined in a medley; Bruce, Dunaway, and Buxton join Alice at center stage for a turn in the spotlights, one of the few times in the concert that all five band members interact like a traditional rock band, with Buxton and Alice sharing the mike, à la Mick and Keith, on the chorus. During an instrumental break, Alice squeezes a glob of spittle from his lips between the breasts of a headless female mannequin, then positions himself to catch it in his open mouth and spits it into the front rows. "My Stars," the band's ode to Pink Floyd's *Saucerful of Secrets,* is performed live for the first time, accessorized with lasers beaming from the mummy's eyes. "Unfinished Sweet" introduces the theatrical segment of the show, as a "dentist," played by the Amazing Randi—the professional magician behind the show's guillotine and other illusions— gleefully wields an outsize drill on Alice's mouth while the audience winces at the taped sound effects. Alice attacks a dancing tooth, played by Cindy Smith, with a giant toothbrush and tube of toothpaste.

The arena goes dark and strobe lights flash as roadies dump onto the stage female mannequin parts—heads, legs, torsos—and fight with them over Mussorgsky's *Night on Bald Mountain.* When the lights come back up, the band has changed into dark costumes; coiled around Alice as he sings "Sick Things" is a seven-foot boa constrictor. The band segues into "Dead Babies," whose opening line Alice amends to "little Betty ate a pound of Quaaludes," a bit of pander to the audience's current drug of choice. Alice prances around the stage with a mannequin's head jammed into his crotch and brings a hatchet down on the doll's neck, from which stage blood oozes. The band shifts into "I Love the Dead" as Alice yanks a black curtain back, revealing the guillotine and a hooded executioner, played by the versatile Amazing Randi, who summons Alice and locks his head in place. The preceding songs, in which Alice flaunts his perversions and sick behavior, are preamble and justification for his punishment, and vice versa. "It's a whole procession to involve the audience so they got to yell for my head," Alice said. The guillotine is designed by Randi and includes several fail-safes, but, as Smith points out, "I still own that guillotine, and I don't think I would ever put my head under that blade. It's not sharp but it's heavy as hell, and it will definitely break your neck and kill you. You have to have a lot of balls to use it, and I always gave Alice a lot of credit for doing it." Randi pulls a lever, the spot-lighted blade drops, and Alice's head disappears. In the Spectrum's audience, a young woman near the stage remarks, "I'm going to be sick." Randi dips his hands into the executioner's basket and removes them dripping with blood. He reaches back inside and pulls out by the hair Alice's bloody decapitated "head," complete with blood-smeared eye makeup, and parades around the stage with it as the band seizes Alice's headless "body" and attacks it like necrophiles. Upon glimpsing this tab-leau, the queasy young woman vomits onto the arena floor.

The opening riff to "School's Out" heralds Alice's rebirth and return to the stage in white top hat and tails. "You're all sick!" he taunts the audi-ence. "You're crazier than I am. You want me to prove that you're crazier than me?" Alice unrolls a poster of himself, shirtless, kisses his image, then tosses an armful of the posters into the front rows. The audience surges in an immediate Altamont-like frenzy; Alice leers and throws more posters until the stage front boils with writhing bodies. Alice and the band exit and return for the obligatory encore, "Under My Wheels," from the *Killer* album. For the curtain call, Bruce, Dunaway, Buxton, and Smith run in turn from the wings waving lit sparklers; Alice unfurls an American flag and waves it, Washington-crossing-the-Delaware-style, over a recording of Kate Smith singing "God Bless America," then sol-emnly salutes the colors. In some cities, a Richard Nixon look-alike wan-ders from the wings flashing the V sign and the band attacks and drags him offstage. The house lights come up. The end.

Gordon and the band's publicists make much of how "shocking" the show is, and that Parliament is considering banning the band from Brit-ain. ("Pop is one thing," thundered an MP, "anthems of necrophilia are another.") And there is little apparent redeeming aesthetic value in simu-lating rough sex with disembodied mannequin parts or decapitating baby dolls with a hatchet. But there is calculation in the show's gross-out that Alice takes all the way to the bank. "His 'offensive' performances function within certain very definite limits upon taste," observed *Creem* magazine. "Cooper's routines are designed to offend fuddy-duddies—but there are never any fuddy-duddies in the audiences. It's basically a way of preaching to the converted. No risk involved. . . . That's when it doesn't operate on the more basic level of ultraviolence as simple enter-tainment." Alice is unmoved. "We liked a little ultraviolence in the show," he said. "We didn't see anything wrong with it—thus separating us from the Buffalo Springfield." At a press conference the day after the premiere, Alice beholds the assembled junketeers and sets the party line that will hold for the three months it takes the tour to stagger back to the East Coast for the finale at Madison Square Garden. "The more people get sick out there," Alice promises, caressing a Budweiser, "the sicker the act will be."

Next stop, Roanoke.

Led Zeppelin crash into the United States in May fresh off a string of European shows with *Houses of the Holy* on its way to number one. By design, the first two dates of the tour—held in outdoor stadiums to ca-pacity crowds in Atlanta and Tampa—are meant to convey the band's new world-beating status and generate the respectful press that had gone to the Rolling Stones the previous year. Peter Grant makes as much omi-nously clear to Danny Goldberg, the band's new publicist. Goldberg seizes upon a brilliant strategy to link Zeppelin to rock's ultimate touch-stones. Tallying the capacity audience at Tampa Stadium, he notes that, at 56,800, it slightly exceeds the attendance for the Beatles' record-setting 1965 Shea Stadium show. "Of course, the contrast with Shea Stadium was a reflection of the size of the stadiums, not the relative popularity of the groups," Goldberg later acknowledged, along with the fact that rock festivals like Woodstock had drawn far larger audiences. "But I figured those crowds had been drawn by multiartist packages rather than single headliners." Goldberg types a press release in his Tampa hotel room de-claring that Zeppelin has broken the attendance record set by the Beatles for a single-artist concert and drops it off at the local UPI bureau—"where it was a slow news night." UPI dutifully moves a dispatch quoting Goldberg's statistics; the next day newspapers around the world run sto-ries with headlines blaring that Led Zeppelin is now "bigger than the Beatles."

Goldberg's coup is soon joined—at Grant's belligerent insistence—by an invented quote he attributes to the mayor of Atlanta that Zeppelin are the biggest thing to hit the city since *Gone with the Wind*. Goldberg arranges it through gritted teeth, but in the evolving rock PR ethic there is still a place for bald-faced mendacity straight out of J. J. Hunsecker's playbook. "We would make things up," admits Marsa Hightower, Goldberg's colleague at Solters who worked the Billion Dollar Babies tour and the second leg of Zeppelin's. "A lot of it was manufactured." (Such is the likely provenance of Alice Cooper's supposed Secret Service bust over the *Billion Dollar Babies* record sleeve.) Later in the Zeppelin tour, when Goldberg refuses to place a phony item that the band wants to play Shea Stadium but the Mets won't let them, his boss simply does it himself— "See?" Lee Solters chides his young apprentice when the New York *Daily News* prints the "story" unchallenged on page three. But the stupendous crowds and grosses for the Atlanta and Tampa gigs need little embellishment, and from this evolves Zeppelin's first media strategy that actually plays to their strengths. "My mantra was that whether the critics liked them or not, Led Zeppelin was the people's band, the favorite of real rock fans," Goldberg recalled. Zeppelin may not have Truman Capote, but they legitimately can claim, thanks to America's fist-pumping, lighter-waving hordes, that they are the kings of the rock and roll road in the spring and summer of '73.

The tour blasts off May 4 at Atlanta's Fulton County Stadium with 49,236 in attendance, half of them sprawled on the baseball diamond's grassy infield. The show grosses $246,000 with a six-dollar top (the same show would earn more than $1.2 million at 2012 ticket prices.) The crowd gives Zeppelin a taste of what is to come on the tour—a cream-colored, mushroom-shaped cloud of pot smoke hovers over the stadium in the still spring air. In one of the first uses of closed-circuit video in a live rock setting, close-ups of the band appear on a screen mounted next to the stage. Unlike Alice Cooper's and the Who's tour repertoires, which lean heavily on material from their new albums, Zeppelin's set usually includes only four or five songs from *Houses of the Holy*: "Over the Hills and Far Away," the dirgelike "No Quarter," "The Song Remains the Same," "The Rain Song," and, among the encores, "The Ocean." Production values don't begin to approach the spectacle of the Alice Cooper stage, but, along with swanker wardrobe (embroidered black bolero jacket for Page, a glittery open blouse for Plant) and special effects that include artificial fog and pyro that transforms Bonham's symphonic gong into a ring of fire, the band does its part to drag the rock concert once and for all out of the ad hoc Fillmore era and into the cash-and-carry seventies. In what is supposed to be a moment of transcendence, doves are released at the conclusion to "Stairway to Heaven," ostensibly to flap away over the affably stoned audience and into the Georgia night; the birds have other ideas. Atlantic Records' Jerry Greenberg is backstage when the big moment arrives. "They opened the cages and instead of the doves going out into the open they got panicky," Greenberg says, "and they all came back on Bonzo's head and were flying all around the stage. It was like, Oh, shit!"

A young musician named Joe Chambers, en route to a battle-of-the-bands contest in South Carolina, takes in the concert from the infield, where "there was not one square inch of grass to sit on. The stadium lights were on the entire concert. It almost seemed like a dream. I think my friend and I were the only two people there not completely stoned out of our minds or tripping." The band, he recalled, "sounded great," but he suspects that they may have dropped the key of "Stairway to Heaven" to help Plant manage the shrieking-Norseman cries of the finale—a harbinger for problems later in the tour and beyond. As Zeppelin leaves the stage and the crowd fires its lighters and screams for more, Chambers climbs to the top of the stadium, where he beholds "three black limos with their bright red taillights leaving the stadium lot all in a row heading toward the interstate and disappearing into the night. I remember thinking how cool it would be to have been in one of those limos . . ."

"It seems between us we've done something that's never been done before," Robert Plant deadpans from the stage the following evening. Spread before him is Tampa Stadium's record-breaking audience of 56,800. Aerial photographs of the concert defy hyperbole: The stadium—in an endorsement of the utility of festival seating—is utterly, completely, stupendously packed. (According to one fan, the actual count may be closer to sixty thousand, as he is one of an estimated crowd of four thousand who breach an eight-foot perimeter and gain access after stadium officials try to turn them away.) The concert grosses $309,000, an enormous payday for the early seventies, and every dollar, true to Goldberg's hype, is generated solely by Led Zeppelin—the band eschews an opening act for the tour and plays two and a half to three and a half hours, with no intermission. By now accustomed to performing before large audiences, they are nevertheless taken aback when they first glimpse the throng looming in the twilight. "Fucking hell, G," Plant beseeches Grant, "where did all these people come from?" Nine nights later, in New Orleans, Plant is still overwhelmed. "I think it was the biggest thrill I've had," he said. "If you do a proportionate thing, it would be like half of England's population." Noting there were no video screens, as at Atlanta, to engage the audience a half mile from the stage, Plant ventures, in his trademark post-hippie garble, that "the only thing they could pick up on was the complete vibe of what music was being done."

The audience spends the pre-performance in sunny, stoned comity, dancing to the Doobie Brothers piped over the sound system, heaving the prettiest girls into the air from blankets. Showco by then has expanded and provides the lighting for the concert as well as sound reinforcement capable of covering nearly sixty thousand in an open-air environment. For the Atlanta and Tampa gigs, the company reconfigures three of its standard traveling systems into a single titanic wall of sound. Showco's Rusty Brutsche mixes both concerts and recalls the ineffable electricity that precedes every Zeppelin show, which he does not witness again until he see Guns N' Roses perform twenty years later. "There was just something about them," he says, "there was this tension in the air before the gig. I don't know how they did it." From his mixing station deep in the audience at Tampa Stadium, Brutsche can feel the anticipation build. "It was all festival seating, kind of an unruly crowd. There was lots of drugs being used and that added to the tension."

When the band finally hits the stage to "Rock and Roll," the indispensable pile-driving opener, the reaction is standard-issue Zeppelin frenzy that, given the conditions on the field, devolves into a pileup in front of the stage. "Dare I ask that you could just cool it on these barriers here?"

Plant ventures before "No Quarter." The crowd quite predictably goes right on pushing and several topple and require rescue, prompting Plant to appeal more sternly before "Dazed and Confused": "I got to tell you this because three people have been taken to hospital, and if you keep pushing on that barrier there's gonna be stacks and stacks of people going . . . So cool it for a bit 'cause it's not very nice." Having admonished as much as is seemly for a rock star, Plant shifts back to cock-of-the-walk mode. "Now, this next song is a song that takes me back to when I was nineteen, before I got the clap or anything like that . . ."

Two nights into the tour after a month's layoff, Plant's voice occasionally frays and the band's playing varies "between brilliant and sloppy," recalled an audience member. Still, for sheer volume, both in the music played and decibels blasted, at six dollars the show is surely a bargain: fourteen songs reaching deep into all five Zeppelin albums, plus two encores including "Communication Breakdown," the Yardbirds-like double-time rave-up from the first album. Several songs are deconstructed to allow maximum improvisation: "Dazed and Confused" clocks in at a staggering twenty-five minutes and includes a six-minute Page solo played with violin bow, while his shredding étude in "Heartbreaker" quotes J. S. Bach's "Bourrée in E Minor." Bonzo somehow keeps "Moby Dick," his showcase, to a mere eleven minutes—it approaches three quarters of an hour some nights—but still manages a timpani solo and several minutes of flailing away at his Ludwig Vistalite drum kit with his bare hands.

But the band's musicianship is really beside the point. For those in the vast crowd who endure their older siblings' endless reminiscences of evanescent live rock experiences in the sixties, Zeppelin's Tampa concert offers a taste of the empowering generational solidarity a mass rock event can deliver. "I still think of it as my Woodstock," recalled Bill Studstill, who is fourteen years old in 1973 and hitchhikes the eighty-four miles from his home in Orlando. "Nothing was going to stop me from seeing this concert." And despite Zeppelin's tendency to bludgeon rather than caress, a faint aura of sixties atmospherics—mostly emanating from Plant's unashamed hippie-dippie couplets—clings to the band like incense. After the Tampa concert, one of the doves released during "Stairway to Heaven" is discovered perched on a van in the stadium parking lot. "He turned out to be completely tame," recalled the young woman who discovered it. "Not knowing what else to do with him, we brought him home with us. My friend named him Peace."

Robert Plant, en route to Tuscaloosa, would surely approve.

Chapter 8

"SHE SAID SHE LIKED THE WAY I HELD THE MICROPHONE"

A new generation of groupies waylays our heroes; calling the morning "ball scores" on the tour plane, a hat trick is not uncommon; Salt Lake City as 1973's rock and roll Gomorrah.

Although the 1973 rock and roll tour is nominally subject to the laws and customs of whatever municipality or sovereign state through which it passes, it creates its own law inside the traveling party. Behavior unacceptable to civilians is tolerated or actively encouraged within the entourage if it boosts camaraderie—a private plane is a powerful bonding device for rich young men interested in no one's agenda but their own. "Sure, it's expensive," Shep Gordon said of *AC-1,* the charter for the Billion Dollar Babies tour, "but having our own plane is good for everybody's morale. We don't have to fuck around waiting in airports, and we can do what we want once we're on the plane." Individuals from outside the entourage who gain access to the inner circle are under no illusions about the activities therein, nor what it takes to get there. The real attraction of breaching the touring party's defenses—the sullen road managers, the backstage barriers, the constant movement under chaperone—is a shot at rock star parity: If only for one night, the ordinary rules that don't apply to the band also don't apply to *you.* The dreamscape of privilege flaunted by rock stars—arriving just as a protracted recession gets under way in 1973—stokes the aspirations of tens of thousands blinking into the stage-front lights. The divide between audience and performer, reinforced by amplification so fierce and staging so immense that it subjugates even sold-out coliseums, grows to a chasm, but the wish fulfillment the platinum-plated rock world represents to the young and feckless is ever more acute. Somewhere in Danny Markus's archives is a photograph he takes from the stage of a girl hoisted into the air at a Zeppelin concert. "She pulled up her skirt to above her waist with no panties on," Markus says. "You might look at her lower extremities. But the look in her eye is what that photo was all about."

The rock and roll tours of 1973 certainly didn't create the anything-goes atmosphere surrounding musicians on the road. There is a long symbiosis of drinking, doping, and ribald carnality with traveling bands stretching back to the big-band tours of the thirties and forties and well beyond. Male-dominated closed societies historically engender off-the-menu sexual expedition—the origins of modern swinging culture are sometimes traced to wife-swapping pilots stationed at postwar American air force bases. The early rock and roll tours in the supposedly straitlaced 1950s offered feral hometown girls a chance to let their hair down— Little Richard claimed that he and Buddy Holly were in the midst of a three-way when the emcee announced Holly's name; the doomed young writer of "Not Fade Away" frantically finished his business and raced to the stage. Chuck Berry, a well-traveled connoisseur, wrote leeringly about the front-row girls with backstage designs in their "tight dresses and lipstick" in "Sweet Little Sixteen."

While Peter Noone of Herman's Hermits is said to have coined the term, Mick Jagger wrote perhaps the first rock song explicitly about groupies, "The Spider and the Fly" ("She said she liked the way I held the microphone . . ."), released as the B-side to "Satisfaction" in 1965. It is joined by a slew of others—Steppenwolf's "Hey Lawdy Mama," Lynyrd Skynyrd's "What's Your Name," the Faces' "Stay with Me," Aerosmith's "Sweet Emotion," and Grand Funk's indefensible "We're an American

Band"—as if rock bands imprisoned on perpetual tours are left with nothing to write about except their lives on the road. By the post-Beatles tours, widely available and reliable birth control and the relaxation of sexual standards have a predictable effect. Recalled a member of the Monkees' entourage during their white-hot streak of fame in 1966: "We had a regular airline charter, with a regular airline stewardess. And by the third week of the tour she was fucking in the aisle, putting on a show for everybody." Gordon claimed that the original stewardesses on *AC-1* were fired by the pilots for fraternization with the entourage. "You should have seen them—first week on the plane they double-fucked absolutely everybody on the tour." (David Libert demurs: "I think somebody might have fucked a stewardess every once in a blue moon, but with no more frequency than a regular girl.")

Thanks in part to the exertions of Led Zeppelin on their early voyages to America, where the fabled and perhaps fabulous "shark incident" is codified as urban legend, by 1973 on-the-road sexual escapades are such an integral part of tour protocol they might as well be another ledger item on the hospitality rider specifying Budweiser in cans. Bystanders brushing up the entourage are fair game, too. "We were all on a plane going to San Francisco," says Libert. "[An entourage member] was sitting next to a girl and says, 'Do you live in San Francisco?' and she says, 'No, I'm on my way to my father's funeral.' He goes, 'Oh, I'm very sorry to hear that.' A couple of beats later, he says, 'Well, what are you doing after the funeral?' He ended up with that girl, you know, later that evening."

The groupie scene, counterintuitively, is most blatant away from the coasts and big cities. Steve Borges is a San Francisco–based production manager who traveled extensively on the rock and roll road in the early seventies. "Once you got to places in middle America, like Cleveland? It was rampant," Borges says. At Swingos, Cleveland's legendary rock and roll hotel, "you'd finish the load out and [the groupies] would just be waiting. You'd take one back and have your way, open the door, she'd be on her way, and there's others cruising the hallways. A hat trick was not uncommon." Salt Lake City, of all places, turns out to have been an unheralded Gomorrah, at least when a rock and roll band hit town. Says

Borges, "They had that whole stiff, very Mormon thing. They were wild. They would line up right outside the bus for the privilege of coming in and performing oral sex or whatever." Michael Des Barres had similar experiences as a glam singer on the road in America in '73. "I found it absolutely predictable. I found the most decadent behavior was in Boise, Idaho, not in Chicago and not in New York, because they were so starved for it. The hipsters in Manhattan are too fucking stoned to get laid, to pick up a pair of handcuffs. No, that was the lifestyle of the trapped and oppressed Midwesterners." British bands in particular on their first visits to America set a formidable standard for depravity—the shark incident, in which Zeppelin's Richard Cole supposedly plumbs the vagina of a groupie with a mud shark caught from the balcony of a Seattle hotel on the band's first U.S. tour, is merely the most traveled. "A lot of things went on in the hotels with all the British bands that I can't reveal, even now, because they were so outrageous," Bill Harry, Zeppelin's first publicist, told Chris Welch thirty years after the fact.

It is little wonder that British rock musicians, raised amid the doldrums of postwar Britain, where repression was an art form, run completely amok in 1973 America. "If you are nineteen and you've gotten a blow job, perhaps, in your village behind the church, and you come to California and you meet two fourteen-year-old blond girls wearing six sequins, strategically placed, your mind is blown," says Des Barres. It is every British rock musician's dream to tour America, he says, because "they could remove themselves from judgmental England, where you're hated if you've had any degree of success." Once ashore in the States, they discover a female welcoming committee overwhelming in its abundance, beauty, and whimsy. Jimmy Page falls for Miss Pamela of the GTOs, leader of Frank Zappa's prototypical groupie clique (and Des Barres's future wife), who with Miss Christine previously performed a desperately needed style intervention for the men of Alice Cooper. The musicians, says Des Barres, "meet these acolytes, these—I was going to say virgins but that probably is not correct—and they put turquoise bracelets on their wrists and make them incredible shirts and velvet pants with stars and lightning bolts at the side and give them little antique tops with puffy sleeves. American girls were so used to quarterbacks—either sports

freaks or big, galumphing tobacco-chewing bastard children of John
Wayne—that when these skinny little Englishmen arrived, they wanted
to dress them up like dolls. So they would dress you up as a girl and fuck
you."

By the time of the '73 tour, the sex and drugs around Zeppelin have
evolved to include a full-time doctor to prescribe anything anyone in the
entourage needs to get through the night and day, plus two women in
their twenties who provide the usual comforts of broad-minded female
companionship. "They had their doctor and they had their two special
groupies," says Marsa Hightower. "And that, sort of, kept them out of
trouble." Like Carol Klenfner and other young women who work the
1973 tours, Hightower, a former Blackwell model, contends with, on the
one hand, a women's movement then in full swing and on the other a
rock culture steeped in sexism. "Jimmy [Page] and I used to have fights
in the hallways," she says. "He was very into trying to seduce women or
control them. So he didn't appreciate my lack of—my not wanting to be
controlled or to sleep with any of them, or sleep with him. And I didn't.
I never slept with a client. If you weren't a client, it was okay." Page, she
notices, is "actually really quite shy. He was very inhibited. I don't know
what he did behind hotel room doors, but he would never make the first
move on anybody. He would just wait for them to come to him." Bonham, she says, "was very stand-offish and very much more into drugs
and groupies than the other three." John Paul Jones, fiercely independent
when offstage, mostly absents himself from the entourage and its druggy,
sexual camaraderie. "He was rarely around," says Hightower. "He wasn't
always on the plane. He just sort of did his own thing, which drove Peter
crazy. And any time we were on the plane, he would always be reading a
book. I'm sure there were lots of groupies that would have liked to have
been around him. He was just by himself."

The groupies who manage to penetrate Grant and Cole's heavily de-
fended security perimeter tend toward the very young. "They *all* were,"
says Hightower. "I was always, 'Where are your parents?'" During the
tour Page commences a lengthy relationship with a fourteen-year-old
from L.A., Lori Mattix, with the consent of the girl's mother. "They were
like little kids that you wanted to slap and say, 'If you really think one of

Jimmy Page and Robert Plant dance to the first playback of "Dancing Days," from 1973's *Houses of the Holy,* during recording sessions at Stargroves, Mick Jagger's country estate outside London.

Led Zeppelin with the *Starship*, Teterboro, New Jersey, 1973. The band leases the plane—outfitted with a fake fireplace and private bedroom—for a thousand dollars a day. Bob Gruen's iconic photo comes to symbolize the glamour—and excesses—of rock stardom as defined by Zeppelin's 1973 tour. Left to right: bassist John Paul Jones, drummer John Bonham, guitarist Jimmy Page, and singer Robert Plant.

Robert Plant onstage,
Kezar Stadium,
San Francisco, 1973.

Peter Grant, Led Zeppelin's
manager, with Robert Plant at
L.A.'s Riot House, in 1973.
Grant, a former bouncer, is a
brilliant and ruthless businessman who rewrites the rules of
engagement for the rock music
industry. With Led Zeppelin's
road manager, Richard Cole,
Grant builds a fortress around
the band that few dare breach.
"The common denominator in
the operation that Peter Grant
and Richard Cole ran was fear,"
says an associate. "They were
thugs, and they ran it like thugs."

Ethan Russell

The Who rehearse *Quadrophenia* at Shepperton Studios, London, 1973. Left to right: John Entwistle, Roger Daltrey, Keith Moon, and Pete Townshend. Townshend later provokes Daltrey, who knocks out the guitarist with a single punch that sends Townshend to the hospital.

Pete Townshend and his Mercedes-Benz Pullman 600 limousine outside his house in Cleeve, where he prepares the rough tracks for *Quadrophenia* in his home studio.

Chris Morphet/Redferns/Gettyimages

Townshend onstage during the Quadrophenia tour. Diffident audience response to the opera, Townshend's most ambitious work since 1969's *Tommy,* plus malfunctioning equipment, cause Townshend to smash his guitars in frustration in several cities.

Peter Rudge, the Who's Cambridge-educated co-manager, shepherds the band through their '73 North American tour. All of his diplomacy is called upon when Pete Townshend and Keith Moon trash a Montreal hotel suite and land their entourage in jail.

Mary Beth Medley, Rudge's second in command, is among a handful of women who breach rock's boys' club in the early seventies. "It wasn't some barrier to break like belonging at Augusta," Medley says. "It was an opportunity and a love."

Alice Cooper, with photographer David Bailey, London, 1972. Alice's personal stardom becomes a source of increasing tension as the band tours nonstop in 1973. Left to right: guitarist Michael Bruce, Bailey, Alice Cooper, bassist Dennis Dunaway, lead guitarist Glen Buxton, and drummer Neal Smith.

Bob Ezrin (front center) with (left to right) Glen Buxton, Mick Mashbir, and Michael Bruce. Ezrin produces Alice Cooper's first hit, "I'm Eighteen," and is instrumental to the band's success—"our George Martin," says Alice. Mashbir is drafted for the *Billion Dollar Babies* sessions when Buxton's drug and alcohol abuse compromise his guitar playing and alienate him from the band.

Alice Cooper first enjoys the fruits of rock stardom on their European tour in 1972, touring behind the hit "School's Out." This private sex show arranged for the band in Amsterdam was typical. Starting third from the left, in rear: Cooper, Mark Volman, and Neal Smith.

The Billion Dollar Babies entourage poses in front of *AC-1*. Alice Cooper manager Shep Gordon, kneeling, in black cowboy hat, shrewdly steers the band from laughingstock to superstardom.

Cooper with Mark Volman (left) and Howard Kaylan aboard *AC-1*. As Cooper's bond with the band frays, Kaylan and Volman increasingly serve as a buffer between the singer and his bandmates. "The friendship he had with us was probably the friendship he'd had with them," says Volman.

Alice Cooper onstage at the Billion Dollar Babies tour premiere at the Philadelphia Spectrum. The band's blood-soaked stage show generates endless publicity that helps drive the album to number one in the spring of 1973.

Alice Cooper perform in Roanoke, Virginia, in the thick of the '73 tour. The $250,000 stage, designed by Broadway set designers and built on multiple levels, is unprecedented and forever raises the stakes for touring rock acts.

these guys is going to marry you and carry you off to England, you're crazy,' " Hightower says, "because that was the fantasy: 'They're going to take me away, and Robert's going to leave his wife . . . ' " Among the aspirants, there is no greater dream than to be commemorated in song—one liaison is alleged to be the source material for Plant's lyrics in "Hot Dog." But their deepest delusion and the secret justification for their supplicant's role is both eye-rollingly grandiose and pathetic in its naïveté. "We're their *muses*," more than one confessed to a tour insider, who emphatically clarified, "No, you weren't." So what, ultimately, is the appeal of a twenty-seven-year-old transient Englishman to an American high school sophomore? "What do you think?" says Hightower. "Power, money, dreams. And fantasies, of course."

Michael Bruce good-naturedly enjoys the company of many, many women on Alice Cooper's voyages, never more so than on the Billion Dollar Babies tour. "It doesn't speak for my morals, but I was a single man," he says. "I had a lot of relations but I always thought I conducted myself as a gentleman." Says David Libert, who indulges while cracking the whip on his charges, "He was always looking for women. 'Hey, Michael, did you get laid today?' He says, 'Morning no, afternoon yes, evening don't know yet.' " Among Bruce's conquests—if she can be called that—is Connie Hamzy, "sweet, sweet Connie" and groupie legend of "We're an American Band," who waylays the band at a stop on the tour. "When we pulled up to the hotel she was waiting," Bruce says. "I wanted to be first and I was." Afterward, Bruce asks her, " 'What is it with you and bands?' She goes, 'Bands are power.' So that was how she embraced power. It was very serious for her. It wasn't just fun and games." According to Bob Brown, during Alice's first solo tour two years later, "Connie hooked up with us somewhere down south and proceeded to fairly successfully have oral sex with pretty much everybody in the entourage."

The success of *School's Out* and *Billion Dollar Babies* not only fattens Alice Cooper's bank accounts, it vaults them into an entirely different stratum of backstage companionship. Says Bruce, "The smell of money was in the air. You know, we finally crossed some invisible barrier known only to women who like to be around that environment." They get their first taste on the European tour the summer before, where the entourage is treated to a private sex show at an Amsterdam club and a Warner Bros.–hosted party in Munich. "Every girl who came into the party was more beautiful than the last," Alice recalled. "I don't think anyone even got laid that night, they were all waiting for the next batch of even more beautiful girls to come in." Says Neal Smith, "You have to remember a lot of this depends on your financial worth. Yeah, there's going to be some girls around when you're still trying to break in and they like you because they are attracted to you. But when you start having gold and platinum albums, then most of the women are attracted to you just because of who you are and your success. We worked our way up on levels, even financially and sexually, I guess." During rehearsals at the mansion for the Billion Dollar Babies tour, Smith takes a call from Los Angeles in his blood-red, bemirrored bedroom. "It was this chick. I had spent time with her, we got high, talked, but it was never a romantic situation, ever. So, she called up. She goes: 'You know, I've been thinking now that you're a success, if you want to get together, I'd love to see you.' I said, 'You know what? Take this number, erase it, and never fucking call me again, you goddamned bitch.'"

Smith says the sexual tension surrounding the band has actually mellowed by the '73 tour. "Most of the guys in the band were single, but Alice had a girlfriend and was just a one-girl kind of guy. And at that time I had a fiancée and Dennis was with my sister. So it was really Mike and Glen if anybody was hanging out with the groupies. But '72 was probably the craziest year and one girl was so gorgeous—she gave me the clap in Florida and then we're recording over at Morgan Studios and she's over there and I got it again. What pissed me off the most was I couldn't drink beer for a week after that. The Billion Dollar Babies tour, we had a hell of a lot of fun, but it was nothing like what had happened in the previous years. The novelty had worn off for me and I'd been in enough free clinics and doctor's offices." Nevertheless, Smith says, "of course there was a lot of sex going on. I went into this one room, I think it was in the South somewhere, and there's a bedroom off the suite. There's a chick in there and she's fucking and sucking everybody." A member of the tour party beckons Smith to join them, but he declines. "I said, 'Think about it.' And a couple of days later he goes, 'Goddamn! I have the clap!' And I go, 'This chick is fucking like fifty guys and you wonder if she has the clap? If she didn't, she did before the night was over.'"

The titillation over sex and drugs on rock and roll tours is largely an obsession of civilians, not the musicians and their handlers. "Everything was taken in stride," says Libert. On the Billion Dollar Babies tour, he says, "everybody was doing drugs, but it wasn't as if everybody was fucked up all the time. Everybody was too busy working. After the show there was coke around, or maybe smoke a doob." Alice—who drinks like Hemingway but has no appetite for drugs, at least not yet—"didn't like any of it around him, so you couldn't smoke on the plane. So drugs was not a big thing." Says Mark Volman: "It wasn't really a tour fueled by drugs—it was an alcohol tour. We didn't smoke pot on the plane or anything like that. And because Alice was very out front with his drinking, it made it a lot easier to drink. He had no trouble making everybody feel right at home drinking."

As for groupies, "some people took it more seriously than others," Libert says. "One of the things these guys would do to entice a girl would be to say, 'Hey, we're going to such and such a town the next day, stick with me and I'll take you with me on the plane.' Well, that was a pretty good argument to get a girl. So I had to institute the following rule: If you take a girl on the plane, if there's room, she had to be eighteen and prove it. She had to prove it. Rule number one. Otherwise you get in trouble. Rule number two: If you got a girl on the plane and took her to the next town, you owed her a plane ticket back to where you got her from. Period. Couldn't just abandon a girl in another town—'Yeah, we were with Alice Cooper and we were doing drugs.' What these guys failed to remember was, you get into the next town, there's a whole slew of new girls, and like everything else it was a little bit competitive. So sometimes they get to the next town with a girl and they'd say to somebody, 'Hey, remember that girl I was with last night you thought was really cute? Well, she's available.' I had sit-downs with two or three guys at a time, sometimes, to decide what percentage of the plane ticket that person owed to get that

girl back to where they got her from. And my verdict was final, there was
no appeal, and if you didn't like it you could quit. And if you refused to
pay you got fired. And that happened once or twice. Because they said, 'I
didn't even fuck her. I'm not paying anything.' Well, you pay or you
leave." When informed that the policy sounds unusually gallant given
the blithe standards of rock star decorum, Libert clarifies, "Well, we had
to protect Alice. It could jeopardize the whole tour. It wasn't that I was so
gallant."

Led Zeppelin flies the first leg of the '73 tour in a Falcon 20, a snug
French business jet derived from the Mystère fighter. After the plane encounters severe turbulence after a gig in Oakland and terrifies the entourage, especially Bonham, already a tremulous flier, Grant leases the
just-commissioned *Starship*. A former United Airlines Boeing 720-B
owned by teen heartthrob Bobby Sherman and his manager, Ward Syl-
vester, the plane is a shortened variation of the classic 707 jetliner. Gut-
ted and retrofitted at a cost of $200,000 with tacky-chic seventies delights
including a water bed, shag carpeting, brass-trimmed bars, and a video
library stocked with everything from *Deep Throat* to *Duck Soup*, the
Starship is a hit with nouveau riche rockers who can afford it—Zeppelin
pays $30,000 to lease it during July. "There was nothing like it on the face
of the earth," says Libert. "It was sort of like Air Force One, but rock and
roll. If you could get somebody with a rock and roll mind and have them
design something as excessive and ostentatious as it could be, that would
be it." Peter Frampton, who leases the plane during his fleeting superstardom in 1976, recalled: "You drove the limos onto the runway and
went straight from the door to the plane. When you landed you didn't
get off until there were a fleet of limos waiting. And as you stepped down,
you heard the trunks popping." Not everyone is impressed. "It's so *tacky*,"
Mick Jagger gasped the first time he stepped aboard and glimpsed the
wall-to-wall Vegas. Gordon leases the plane for Alice Cooper's monthlong holiday tour at the end of 1973 but cancels midway through the
itinerary after the Pratt & Whitney engines refuse to start one time too
many. ("We're paying a lot of money for this intensive-care unit," Alice

would mutter, wrapped in a blanket as mechanics tried to light the plane's engines.)

Zeppelin take to the *Starship* instinctively—Bonzo, a hot-rod aficionado, installs himself in the cockpit and, according to Grant, actually takes the controls on occasion; Jones plays chestnuts like "I've Got a Lovely Bunch of Coconuts" on the electric organ in the midships club room. The plane's 556-mile-per-hour cruising speed allows the band to base themselves in geostrategic locations like New York and fly to gigs as distant as Pittsburgh and return the same night to their base hotel, another innovation of Grant's that will later become standard operating procedure for large-scale rock tours. The plane also figures in Zeppelin's dramatic postshow exits. As the band leaves the stage, each musician is wrapped in a prizefighter's terry robe and hustled by Richard Cole into the waiting limos and out of the arena—"the getaway," as the maneuver is known within the entourage. "We flew up to a gig in Minneapolis from Chicago," says Markus. "There was a fence and the airport was on one side and the venue was on the other. They didn't have cell phones in those days, and I remember the security guy at the hall with his two-way radio. After the getaway we drive to the tarmac, get into the airplane, take a seat—the plane is already starting to taxi—and back at the hall the security guy holds up his two-way: People are yelling, applauding. I'm being served lobster thermidor as we go down the runway and the audience in the building is still waiting for the encore."

Compared to the mighty *Starship*, the Lockheed Electra that transports Alice Cooper on the Billion Dollar Babies tour seems barely airworthy: The four-engine turboprop cruises at an anemic 373 miles per hour and can't climb above 29,000 feet, leading to forays into spectacular turbulence. Nevertheless, it is beloved by the Cooper entourage for its crash-pad aesthetics and practicality. Alice Cooper tours via traditional point-to-point routing, checking in and out of hotels daily—Oklahoma City–Tulsa–Fort Worth–Albuquerque–Tucson is typical. "Our gigs were never more than four hundred miles apart," says Libert. "That was sort of the rule of thumb. The trucks can't drive more than four hundred miles a day, really, so why did you need a plane that went five hundred fifty miles an hour? It wasn't necessary. A plane that could go three hundred miles an hour is really perfect. That's why we used the Lockheed Electra for the tour."

If the *Starship* is a rock and roll Air Force One, Cooper's *AC-1* is a flying Delta House. A reporter from *Rolling Stone* renders it thus: "The interior of the chartered, four-engine F-27 is covered with scrawled drawings, spit-stained posters and mutilated magazine pin-ups. With . . . beer cans rolling up and down the aisles and rock & roll blasting from eight JBL speakers, the 48-passenger bird is a dangerous but stone-carefree flyer." During a stopover in Colorado, Smith purchases an enormous taxidermied brown bear that won't fit in the plane's cargo hold and so is lashed to one of the seats in the cabin where it remains, partially blocking the aisle, for the rest of the tour. "We had to put little pillows on its claws so people wouldn't get hurt walking by," says Libert. The plane, Smith says, "was like a hangout. You know, like when you were a kid hanging out in the den in the basement of your house, but only now we're a little bit older and it's a plane traveling all over the United States."

The plane carries not only the Alice Cooper band and road personnel but also Flo and Eddie and their backup musicians and roadies. "The Electra had a round table in the back and that was the gambling table," says Libert. "Every square inch of the walls was covered with *Playboy* and *Penthouse* centerfolds. There was a poker game there every day." Neal Smith is the dealer. "That goes back to the early days," Smith says. "Glen, Alice, and I would play blackjack on an airplane. We'd put down the tray tables and play, even if it was for nothing."

But the poker and blackjack are actually beside the point. ("After the whole tour, and some of those stakes got pretty high, I think I made like thirty bucks," Smith concedes.) "It wasn't the game—it was the camaraderie," Mark Volman says. "It was: 'Did you see that girl last night? Did you see what was going on in the dressing room?' We were all like scouts and we'd come on the plane and relive the night before because we were all so busy that we couldn't share anything until the next day." Libert collates the morning-after gossip with a play-by-play of the previous night's indiscretions, known among the entourage as the "ball scores." Says Libert: "I had to make an announcement every morning on the plane, so I used the PA system. If somebody ended up with the prettiest girl, we would have like a 'high' for the night. I'd say, 'Let's hear it for Portland, Oregon! There were three two-ways, two four-ways, and one one-way—that was Joe Gannon there in the back.'" Alice, according to Libert, "rarely got laid on the road, he had a girlfriend. But once in a blue moon something would happen. And I remember he came up to me and said, 'Libert, I don't want to be in your goddamned ball scores—I'm serious, David, don't fucking do it. I don't want to hear my name.' All right, okay, okay. So I get on the P.A. 'Well, here's the ball scores.' I said, 'The high for the night is . . . I'm sorry, I have to be discreet. I cannot mention his name. But I'll give you a hint: He's a very big star!' No one's immune, Cooper! Don't you forget it!"

Libert comes to cherish the flights if only to relieve temporarily the crushing responsibility of keeping a thirty-member entourage on schedule and out of jail while tens of thousands of dollars in box office receipts hang in the balance daily. "The airplane was a moment of relaxation because there wasn't anything that anybody could do while you're on the plane except eat, sleep, gamble, read, hang out with your friends, listen to music, whatever," he says. "It was something everybody looked forward to because as soon as that plane landed, it all changed."

The daily flights and show-must-go-on deadline pressure inevitably result in some airborne terrors and comic relief. "There was this guy that was my projectionist, his name was Space," says Gannon. "Genius kind of guy, but he was out there, right? And the guy that was the tour accountant, we called him Elton Jew. Elton Jew would carry around paper sacks with fifty thousand dollars in cash. Everybody loved Elton. So we're coming into Minneapolis and Alice looks out the window: 'Hey, Joe, one engine is smoking and stopped.' Then the captain comes on and says, 'Well, we have a little problem but we're in the final leg of our thing so we're going to land.' We're about twenty minutes out and flying on one engine, right? So Space, in the back, jumps up. 'Oh, man. I know I'm going to die and I've got to confess. Elton, I'm sorry—I've been fucking your old lady all these years! I'm not going to lie! I've got to confess and I'm so sorry!'" The terrified passengers are instantly convulsed. "Everybody just went over the top, just over the fucking top, just laughed their asses off," Gannon says. "And we finally landed with the fire trucks and all that shit. But nobody gave a shit by then, everybody was happy."

Amid the good fellowship on the plane, the blackjack and leering decor and early-morning rounds of Budweiser, cracks in the band's relationship with Alice appear. A picture emerges of a star increasingly isolated, by circumstance of his stardom, from his collaborators and oldest friends. "He didn't have anybody in the band to hang out with anymore," Volman says. "That was just a natural extension of what was going on: Dennis was with Cindy, so Dennis never really hung out with him. And Neal would play cards with us, but Neal was in his own world. Michael never hung out with Alice—he'd check in once in a while, and I think that was probably the worst part of it. And Bob Dolan and Mick Mashbir, they're just hired guns to play on the tour. Glen and Alice were still very close. [Glen] was such a loving, innocent guy. I don't think he felt any problems with Alice being a big star. He never held any tension over Alice about something he needed out of Alice in terms of the band"— whereas the other members, especially Bruce and Smith, are acutely attuned to their status relative to Alice's.

"I always felt like we almost acted like buffers—the friendship he had with us was probably the friendship he'd had with them," Volman says. "We kind of become a part of this family he didn't have anymore. The guys had always been like family to each other, and all of a sudden the band is starting to dissolve around him—there's this animosity starting to grow because he was being singled out—and so he was able to just hang with the two of us; we didn't need anything from him and we didn't care he was the big star." Says Mashbir, "Alice always retreated to a 'neutral corner' when he could. Mark and Howard were great company and could easily distract Alice from the growing tensions within the band." Libert notices the fissures but adds a caveat. "All of that is true except that it didn't create a lot of tension on the plane, because that wasn't anything that was ever talked about."

For the young men and handful of women in the early 1970s who run them, rock and roll tours offer an irresistible parallel reality: the opportunity to live like a rock star even as they help define the genre in a thousand rented limos, Holiday Inns, and concrete-block "dressing rooms" at athletic arenas across North America. Danny Markus describes a split screen, one depicting life on tour, the other civilian life. "Rolling up through the gate and out to the tarmac, you get out of the car and walk up the stairs to the plane and somebody hands you a drink. The other screen is you wait in line, you get your boarding pass, you go through security, you show your boarding pass, 'Oh, you're not in the right row.' That whole thing. I'd be out on the road with Led Zeppelin for a month and end up at the airport. I'd jumped off the tour and I'm looking at this boarding pass thinking, 'What the fuck is this? What did I do wrong?' It was like I was being penalized." In the midst of the Billion Dollar Babies tour, Gannon wakes up in a panic because he can't remember where he is or why. "I have no idea. I wasn't drunk. I wasn't stoned. I wasn't anything." Gannon finally ascertains his location from a hotel matchbook at his bedside. "So that's the insanity of the tour when that's how you realize where you were: 'Shit, you're in Chicago, man. Get your shit together.'" When Yaryan, then a newspaper reporter in Pasadena with a wife and two small children, gets the call to work for Atlantic Records as a publicist, "it was as if I had been jerked out of the doldrums and sent to deepest Africa on a genuine adventure. The participants I knew in the music scene were either interested in the money that could be made, the power they could exert, or they loved the music and wanted to get as close to it as they could without actually being a musician. I was among the latter." Says Chip Rachlin: "What was important was the access, the fun—the circus comes to town! That's what appealed to me. You know, to be part of the circus and not the guy shoveling elephant shit."

Invested as it is in an aggressively unprogressive male-dominated culture, the high-grossing rock and roll road of the early 1970s nevertheless makes room for women in its ranks more interested in the business than with scoring a night with Robert Plant. More accurately, the women simply make room for themselves. As a group they are smart, resourceful, and possess personalities that brook no disrespect but don't threaten the fragile egos of the boys on the plane. Several of the decade's most effective and influential publicists come from their ranks—among them

Marsa Hightower, Carol Klenfner, Jane Ayer, Bobbi Cowan (said to be the model for the Bobbi Flekman character played by Fran Drescher in *This Is Spinal Tap*), and Susan Blond, who like Cowan and Ayer forms her own successful PR company. Many punch their tickets at the Warner-Atlantic-Elektra labels, possessed of some of the rock business's greatest artists and most distinguished executives, among them Ahmet Ertegun, Mo Ostin, and Jerry Wexler. Lynn Volkman, one of the first woman tour managers in rock, shepherds everyone from the Rolling Stones and the Who to James Taylor and Cat Stevens. Volkman conceives the idea for the wireless microphone, developed by her boyfriend, Kenny Schaffer, one of Alice Cooper's earliest publicists and an electronics whiz; the Schaffer-Vega wireless microphone and guitar attachment revolutionize live rock performance when they go into wide use in the late seventies.

Mary Beth Medley started booking rock acts in 1969 while an undergrad at the State University of New York at Stony Brook. Four years later she becomes Peter Rudge's right-hand woman at Rudge's Sir Productions. She meets Rudge through the New York booking agent Frank Barsalona, who, outside of Bill Graham, is the most influential figure in creating the modern rock concert experience. "Frank was like my mentor," Medley says. While a junior agent at the old-school GAC agency, Barsalona booked the Beatles' first U.S. concerts and in 1964 founded Premier Talent, the first agency to focus exclusively on rock acts. Barsalona worked closely with managers to build an audience for bands who were gaining exposure on the new FM radio format but lacked top-forty singles, starting at smaller venues like Tea Party in Boston—an early coup for Led Zeppelin—and onward until his acts were headlining Madison Square Garden. "We had to create this whole underground—as if it were the Internet of its time," says Rudge. "It was people like Frank Barsalona, Don Law in Boston, Tom Donahue in San Francisco. It was built from the roots up as an alternate thing, and it became big business." By the end of the sixties, Barsalona represented the cream of post-Beatles rock artists and wielded tremendous influence. "Frank pretty much dictated who would be successful and who wouldn't," says Rachlin. "Woodstock couldn't have happened without Frank." Barsalona delivered several careers through his ability to supply bands with incessant, high-profile roadwork that fueled their record sales, among them Humble Pie and, later, the band's lead guitarist, Peter Frampton. (Humble Pie later bought Barsalona a Rolls-Royce in gratitude.)

After graduation, Barsalona encouraged Medley to become an agent; instead she went to work for Bud Prager and Gary Kurfurst, managers of Mountain—the band that embarrassed Showco's first sound system— and booked their tours in the U.S. and Britain. By the time Rudge hired her, Medley had spent three years touring the United States with whatever bands passed through the Prager-Kurfurst management company. "When I went to work with him I knew the halls, I knew the promoters," Medley says. Planning a national tour in an age before cell phones, email, and even the widespread use of credit cards to guarantee reservations requires dedication. "When we were planning tours I would use a Rand McNally standard mileage calculator, a map of the United States, and index cards," Medley says. "Heather Daltrey"—Roger's wife—"said to me a few years ago, 'How did we do it in those days? It was just the roadies, the sound guys, and you with your clipboard, and we still managed to do the gigs.' It was just so much simpler."

Rudge, Medley says, "didn't really care whether you were a man or a woman as long as you did the job. And he validated me in many ways when I was doing the deals for the Stones and the Who. There were certain promoters that would say, 'I don't like this deal—I want to speak to Peter.' And Peter would pick up the phone—he called me Mother—and he'd say, 'What's the deal Mother gave you?'" Rudge would listen, unimpressed, and inform them, "Well, that's it. I can't do any better." Medley credits this support less to the egalitarianism of men like Barsalona and Rudge and more to a pragmatism exercised at a moment in which the values of the sixties and those that will define the seventies briefly commingle before diverging for good. "I never thought, 'Oh, you're a woman, you can't do that,'" Medley says. "I never felt like I was given any special treatment because I was a woman—or that it was extraordinary at the time. Ina Meibach, the Who's lawyer for years and years, and Barbara Skydel, who was a top agent then, neither of them went into the music business because it was a frontier for women. It wasn't some barrier to break like belonging at Augusta; it was an opportunity and a love. We were all very equal then, or at least thought we were." Says Klenfner: "It was a given going in if you were young and pretty you were perceived as a groupie and available. Being at Gibson-Stromberg and being made head of the New York office, professionally I didn't feel a lot of discrimination. But there were times when, because of the whole groupie thing, they just didn't want you around unless you were a groupie. They were getting down to a different kind of business that I have nothing to do with."

The fact is, in the early seventies so much of the script for rock culture—and the culture at large—is still very much a work in progress. "It was an amazing time," Medley says. "The whole business—radio stations, record shops, clothing stores—all just bloomed. There weren't really parameters. You created what you could create. There was nobody saying, 'You can't do that.' The music business at that time was so small. In the early seventies you knew every promoter in the United States. You knew every record company promotion man because there wasn't one in every city. You knew the heads of the labels, you knew the agents. There were maybe four agents at Premier, maybe four agents at William Morris, there weren't hundreds. And they stayed the same year after year." That nearly all of them are generational peers with shared values rooted in the music they create together encourages an empowering optimism that it will always be thus. As it happens, 1973 is both the peak for the sensibility and its twilight, though that won't be evident to those living the moment for several more years. It finally strikes Medley mid-decade when she realizes "the hippie era died, so the feeling that came along with that—that late-sixties freedom—was gone." And with that, the music business, once an emporium for a generation's dreams, became just another business. "You could sell shoes," Medley says, "or you could sell a rock and roll band."

Chapter 9

"I'M JUST TRYING TO GET THROUGH THIS TOUR ALIVE"

Pete Townshend and Keith Moon run amok in Montreal; Led Zeppelin storm the provinces in the Starship; Alice Cooper's boa constrictor nearly suffocates him as the band dodges M-80s, bottles, and darts.

On Thursday, November 22—Thanksgiving Day—the Who stagger into Los Angeles after their disastrous premiere in San Francisco for a two-night stand at the Forum, where Alice Cooper and Led Zeppelin played some of the best shows of their careers just months earlier. The opening night audience numbers 19,500. *Quadrophenia* is now a month into its release; the following week it will reach number two, its peak, denied number one by Elton John's unstoppable *Goodbye Yellow Brick Road*. Meanwhile, the album's first U.S. single, "Love, Reign O'er Me," never makes it past number seventy-six on the charts but receives heavy airplay on FM stations, which is far more important to the album's long-term prospects. It is pouring rain in Los Angeles the day of the show— a good omen, per Townshend's experience cutting "Drowned" at Ramport when Chris Stainton's piano booth filled with rainwater. "Ever since that night we've got this thing that if it rains, it's gonna be a good night," Townshend says the afternoon of the show. Will Yaryan, newly installed as director of publicity at MCA Records, orchestrates a frantic press junket at the Century Plaza hotel. In a nod to the protocol now demanded by even the Who, the most press-friendly band in rock, at least one prospective interviewer claims he is led blindfolded from the green room to Townshend's suite. (Yaryan doesn't recall anybody being blindfolded but acknowledges that "I was indulging myself at the time" and can't rule it out.) Townshend is, as ever, polite and cordial, "not tense, not sarcastic," one of his interviewers that afternoon notes. "He answers all questions thoughtfully, deeply." Nevertheless, Townshend admits, "I'm really drained from *Quadrophenia*."

That night the Who, in a return to form after the Cow Palace debacle, tear though a five-song opening volley of muscular hits, starting as always with their first, "I Can't Explain." After a warmly received "My Generation," Townshend cautiously addresses the audience regarding an "album we spent the last fifty million years of our lives composing, recording, working on, predicting, *surviving*." It's a story set in London, he continues, "about the time we started our career. It's not so much a looking back as it is a summing up of what's happened to us, and what's happened to our audience and all that sort of shit." The crowd at the Forum, between the rebel yells that plague every band touring the U.S. in the early seventies, laughs appreciatively; hearing their acknowledgment, Townshend seems to relax. "I think I need a bit of *atmosphere*," he italicizes, "a kind of a *quadrophonic* atmosphere." From Bob Heil's massive bass drivers and radial horns flanking the stage comes the sound of crashing waves from "I Am the Sea"—the infamous backing tapes, tonight, at least, arriving on cue—as Townshend announces, "Here, playing for the first time, *Quadrophenia*, for you." When the audience cheers for a full fifteen minutes after the house lights are turned on, the band performs Marvin Gaye's "Baby Don't You Do It," a chestnut from their Maximum R&B days. Townshend closes the show in classic fashion, sacrificing one of his Les Paul Deluxe guitars—each emblazoned with a number to delineate its tuning for *Quadrophenia*'s endless key changes— "bringing it down on the stage with a resounding crash time and time again until it cracked around the 12th fret," *Melody Maker* noted with admirable precision.

Friday's concert at the Forum is by most accounts even better played.

It also begins the controversial practice by both Townshend and Daltrey of annotating the *Quadrophenia* material with lengthy expositions of each song's place in the opera's story. Townshend's introduction to "I'm One" begins, "I don't know if you ever get the feeling that maybe there's somebody else that's a little bit better looking than you, a little bit better dressed than you, a little bit smarter . . ." and digresses into the etymology of the pronoun *one* as used by royalty before he mercifully stops talking and starts playing. Daltrey footnotes "Helpless Dancer" with "That song was basically about the frustrations that happen when you get mixed up with dirty things like politics . . . anyway, from there the kid is very disillusioned and like a lot of kids today, and when we were Mods—which we never really were—he runs away from home and he runs down to the seaside." Finished? Not quite. "He goes to Victoria Station—there was only trains in them days . . ." And so on.

Daltrey defends the commentary. "It was my idea. It helps people follow the new material. In a couple of months when everybody knows the album, we wouldn't have to explain." Townshend, as always and almost reflexively when it comes to Daltrey, demurs. "I think the story line isn't so complicated it bears much explaining: a kid sits on a rock and remembers the things that have happened in the last few days. I think if you explain the story line too much it demeans all the other things in the music, makes it too *Tanglewood Tales*. When Roger gets too literal about the story, I have to cut in and make it lighter." Townshend later admitted, "I found it so embarrassing to have to explain the album in between numbers. It's a bloody admission of growing old, to stand up and talk about 'When I was nineteen . . .'" Yet he and Daltrey persist with the introductions throughout the tour, which seem to baffle the audiences as much as enlighten them.

Reviewing the Forum concerts, the *Los Angeles Times*'s pop music critic Robert Hilburn praises the Who's "precision, power and desire that made it one of rock's most rewarding and influential bands"; however, he can't reconcile "the troubling impression that the group's momentum—and therefore importance—is waning." Hilburn confirms Townshend's obsession, hand-wringingly expressed in a hundred interviews prior to the tour, that the Who seem trapped by their past. But far from acknowledging that *Quadrophenia* can be the band's passport to a future unencumbered by their sixties legacy, Hilburn instead seizes on the concert's *Quadrophenia* material as evidence of the band's stasis and even retrogression. "I kept feeling I was being asked to relive a 1960s experience . . . At a time when rock is in serious need of new direction, the Who seems part of rock's past." Townshend and the Who, Hilburn concludes, "have contributed too much to fully write them off at this point, but these concerts were not encouraging."

As the tour moves to Dallas—the weakest performance of the itinerary, according to Daltrey—thence Atlanta, St. Louis, and Chicago, the reaction to the twelve-song *Quadrophenia* segment, comprising three quarters of the concerts, rarely moves beyond polite tolerance as audiences cheer most avidly for the *Who's Next* and *Tommy* selections that open and close. *Rolling Stone* notes the Dallas concert's generational dissonance: "ten thousand college and high-school-age Texans" watch "four men in their late 20s . . . perform powerful crashing music about events in 1965." But even in deepest Dallas, the Who's sterling rock-elder-statesmen credentials keep the heckling down to a lone bellowed "rock and roll!" while Townshend shambles through yet another mise-en-scène from *Quadrophenia*. The goodwill the Who enjoy among their new-found younger audiences is in fact tinged with their nostalgia for a past never lived; the band, along with the Rolling Stones, is among the last links to the legendary sixties fandango that they missed by dint of birth order but are determined to sample on the hoof while they still can. The irony is that the part of the concert they like the least—*Quadrophenia*—is about nothing but the origins of that scene.

Townshend comes to believe that younger audiences will not accept the Who's near-mythical sixties legacy as a reason to buy concert tickets, and that the band must evolve to suit shifting tastes or wither. This he has exactly right and exactly wrong—the Who-besotted sixteen-year-old of 1973 waits in line overnight in San Francisco and L.A. and Dallas specifically to experience that myth and the songs associated with it, none of which appear on *Quadrophenia*. These punks may not like what Townshend has toiled for the last year to deliver, but they are not about to disrespect their Godfather—so long as he and his band also play "See

Me, Feel Me" and "Won't Get Fooled Again." At the same time they have—and will continue to have—only passing interest in new material from the band. *Quadrophenia,* for all its flaws, proves to be the last Who album that strives for contemporary relevance and achieves any measure of it.

What Townshend can't see in 1973—any more than can Mick Jagger or Jimmy Page, whose bands' creative critical mass soon dissipates in exactly the same fashion—is that the Who's future earning power and long-term plausibility are about to be uncoupled from the popularity of their current output. The cultural equity of the Who is tied to a run of perhaps five albums recorded over as many years, and these will return to the band dividends that will allow them to perform profitably for the next four decades and repurpose the material in repertory—as in the Broadway production of *The Who's Tommy: The Musical* and the 1996 Hyde Park performance of *Quadrophenia*—in ways that aren't imaginable or palatable by the lights of 1973. ("Won't Get Fooled Again" as the theme music for *CSI,* to cite but one particularly lamentable example.) Thirty-nine years after *Quadrophenia* and Townshend's crisis of confidence in the band's future, the remnants of the Who will perform the opera on a well-received tour of Europe and North America.

Townshend later cites the concerts in Chicago and Montreal as the high points of the Quadrophenia tour. There is something about Chicago's International Amphitheatre—a ramshackle barn dating to 1934 on the city's South Side conceived as a showcase for livestock from the adjacent stockyards—that encourages audacious rock and roll performance; the Rolling Stones turned in a pair of barn burners at the hall the previous year. The sheer volume and power of the Who's playing, and the blithe tolerance among Chicago audiences for idiosyncratic material and performers, so long as they rock—David Bowie is as big here in the seventies as he is in New York—bode well for the Who and the *Quadrophenia* songs. "The din from the stage was incredible, the din from the audience matching that and then some," reported the *Chicago Tribune.* The crowd shrugs off Daltrey and Townshend's song introductions—"Fuck it," an exasperated Entwistle cuts off Daltrey during one—which are rendered superfluous by the Amphitheatre's punishing acoustics as well as the absurdity of trying to explicate the libretto of an opera in a venue smelling of cow shit and pot smoke. The audience instead concentrates on absorbing the gale-force impact of the band's playing, which when in top form compares to nothing in rock. "I say to this day, there was nothing like the original four members of the Who on stage," says Rudge. "I mean, none of them played particularly well, but it didn't matter. That raw energy and emotion that came off that stage was something that I have never seen with any band." The Who, concluded the *Tribune*, "are in the final analysis pure, raw energy."

The Who flies commercial during the tour, which means the band interacts with civilian travelers at airports and in the air. The bubble theory of advancing a rock entourage—hotel to limo to private plane to hall to hotel to limo to plane—is harder to pull off at, say, O'Hare International Airport, where the Who, shepherded by the resourceful Peter Rudge, arrive the day after their Chicago gig to catch a flight to Detroit. "Rudge was a lovely guy and it was always a pleasure dealing with him rather than [Zeppelin's] Cole or Grant," says Yaryan, who runs press interference throughout the tour.

For the flight to Detroit, Keith Moon emerges from his limousine at O'Hare bearing a life-size inflatable sex doll, which he takes on the plane. Like Zeppelin's John Bonham and the many rock drummers for whom aggression is an asset to their craft, Moon is a heavy drinker and doper and given to unpredictable behavior, though his outbursts are in general less sullen and more theatrical than Bonzo's, and more inclined to entertain than abuse. "He was the court jester," says Rudge. "It was a game with Moonie. We all wondered how far he'd go. He was the soul of the Who in that sense. If you're on the road and bored and it's eleven o'clock at night, what better thing than to go down to the bar and have a drink with Moonie because always something would happen."

Moon's chief distraction is flushing M-80s and later dynamite down hotel toilets, which, in conjunction with his driving a Lincoln—by some accounts a Cadillac—into the swimming pool of a Holiday Inn in Flint, Michigan, gets the band banned from the chain for life. "A cop would be hired to guard him and he'd say, 'Let me buy your hat,' and he'd buy that and whatever else and run around the hotel in a policeman's uniform," says Danny Markus, whom Rudge would hire to work the band's 1975 North American tour. "He'd go to somebody's room on the tour and bang on the door, and they'd open up and see a policeman and scare the shit out of everybody."

When the band's relationship with Rudge begins to fray, Markus finds himself alone with them in a private hotel dining room. "I was [Rudge's] guy. Moonie stands up and says, 'Everybody that would like Daniel Markus to leave stand up.' And everybody stood up. So I realized I shouldn't be in this room." As Markus makes his exit, "Moon takes out a dagger from behind his neck and throws it at my chair—not at me, but I felt the breeze as it went by and it stuck in the chair." Later that night Markus is awakened by a knock on his door. "It was Pete. He said, 'Danny, we're really sorry.' Each of them came up individually and apologized." Yaryan has a similar experience while waiting for the band's flight to Detroit "when Moon began to attack me. I don't recall his words but I got up and started to walk away. He came after me, shouting. And then, surprisingly, he cooled down and effusively apologized. I tried to stay out of his way from then on." Says Rudge: "It was fun that sometimes turned into a serious problem, and it eventually killed him."

While in Detroit, Yaryan is visited by a friend from California. "He managed an unsuccessful group but was known for his coke. I called him Mr. Bolivia and took him with us to Montreal, where he shared my suite at the hotel. I'm sure he wasn't the only drug dealer in the traveling party, but his services were appreciated." Mr. Bolivia, his product, Moon, Townshend, and the frustrations of a tour that is so far at best a qualified success coincide the next night in a penthouse suite at Montreal's Hotel Bonaventure, where another chapter in the Who's and rock and roll's litany of outrages is delivered to history.

The show in Montreal is just as raucous as Chicago and the audience even more emphatic. "They were crazier than you in Chicago," Townshend taunts as they hoot and holler over his introduction to "I'm One." "After the [Chicago] show somebody said to me, 'That was like the French Revolution.' And the promoter said, 'Wait till you get to Montreal!'" Jim Chisolm, who attends the show, would recall: "The audience was very chatty and noisy and Pete took offense to this." Townshend, he said, took off his guitar and, brandishing it like a hockey stick, asked "'if we thought this was a fuckin' 'ockey game.' Well, in another building that might have meant nothing but in the Montreal Forum it was like picking a fight. So he motors around the stage stick-handling an imaginary puck as if he's Guy Lafleur and the crowd goes nuts." Recalled Donald Adler: "My greatest memory of the show was all the tension that had built up just before the Who came on. When they came onstage, Pete came running out and slid on his knees across what seemed like the entire stage. At that moment two or three fistfights broke out around me. Then the music began." Even with the tour's inevitable technical snafus—tonight Daltrey's hand microphone cuts out just as he delivers the climactic scream at the end of "Won't Get Fooled Again"—"the entire set was a powerful performance," recalled Adler.

At the Hotel Bonaventure, Yaryan makes ready for a reception in the penthouse suite he has reserved for the occasion. "Usually I would have a reception after shows and mostly writers, DJs, and company men came; the band was not much interested in schmoozing or doing interviews." Tonight is no exception. "I had the usual party with celebrities from the Quebec rock scene, but nobody from the Who." After most of the guests have left, Townshend and Moon wander in looking for food and drink. By this time only Rudge, Yaryan, Mr. Bolivia, and "two Canadian girls who had attached themselves to us" remain. "Pete and Keith were recounting old stories of hotels in other cities—like the trashing of the Holiday Inn that got them banned," Yaryan says. "I must say I egged them on, wanting to hear the worst of it. I think in the back of my drink-and-drug-addled mind I wanted to be part of a Who adventure."

Yaryan is about to get his wish. "I remember somebody, I can't remember who, challenging Moonie to repaint the room in ketchup," says Rudge, and "the room starting to take on a red glow at some point." Says Yaryan: "It began with Keith taking down an innocuous print from the wall, tearing out the contents and rehanging the frame. Then he picked up a ketchup bottle and slung some into the center of the frame and proclaimed it beautiful art." The next thing Yaryan knows, "Pete and Keith—

the rest of us just watched and probably applauded—picked up the marble-topped coffee table and attempted to throw it through the window. But it was winter and the window was double-glazed so the table just stuck between the panes." Moon and Townshend eventually dispatch the table, though Yaryan admits, "my memory starts to fog over here—maybe it was the TV. I think the table made it outside but not the TV." Fortunately, the table lands not twelve stories below on the Rue de la Gauchetière but on the rooftop directly outside the suite. "And then there were complaints from other guests, obviously," says Rudge.

"By then the party was over," says Yaryan. "Mr. Bolivia and I went into the bedroom and got into bed with our groupies. I recall being concerned and ready to accept my fate, certain that eventually something bad would happen. I heard people walking on the roof, their feet crunching on broken glass, and commenting on the damage. We told the girls to leave before they got in trouble." Not long after, there is a furious banging on the door. "It was the police," Yaryan says. "They had surrounded the entire hotel and rounded up everyone in the Who party, about two dozen people. Daltrey, who generally kept himself aloof, was very pissed off, since he had gone to bed early."

The entourage is taken to the police station, booked, and placed in custody. Because the devastated suite is registered in Yaryan's name, he is the assumed ringleader and put in a cell by himself. Moon and Townshend occupy the cell next to his and spend the rest of their incarceration laughing and singing soccer songs and metaphorically rich selections like "Don't Fence Me In." Yaryan says, "I was too wasted to worry and assumed money would change hands. It did, finally, after a couple of hours." The show's promoter is roused from bed at four A.M., orders a fleet of limos to the station, and arrives with six thousand dollars cash. Rudge, who is jailed along with the rest of the entourage, is made to understand that the band, still larking and singing, would be well advised to shut up and exit Canada immediately. "We were taken to several limos in the basement which drove out through the crowds of fans who'd heard about the Who's arrest," says Yaryan. "First we were taken to the hotel to collect our things. Luckily my bedroom had a separate entrance. When I passed the living room the door was open and the wrecked room was full of TV crews and reporters. The limos drove us straight to the airport and the flight to Boston. It was not their best show."

Following their record-breaking Atlanta and Tampa concerts, Led Zeppelin steam slowly west through the month of May: Tuscaloosa, St. Louis, Mobile, New Orleans, Houston, Dallas, Fort Worth, San Antonio, Albuquerque, Denver, Salt Lake City, and San Diego, until they reach their traditional strongholds on the West Coast, Los Angeles and San Francisco. In New Orleans, the keyed-up crowd reacts with such unrestrained vigor to the opening fanfare of "Rock and Roll" that management at the Municipal Auditorium freaks out and turns on the house lights, to which Robert Plant rejoins: "It's pretty pointless, us bringing our own lights . . . Mr. Cole, can you take your dress off and get these lights turned down, please?" A drug casualty in the audience tumbles from the balcony into the mezzanine, but the band keeps playing.

As the tour wears on, Bonham's drum showcase, "Moby Dick," metastasizes to lengths that will try the patience of the hardest-partying headbanger; tonight it clocks in at a staggering nineteen minutes and seventeen seconds, second only to "Dazed and Confused" at nearly half an hour. (The idled members of the band soon discover an altogether pleasant diversion to pass the downtime; as Bonham flails away, young women from the audience bestowed with backstage passes prior to the show join them for a moment of appreciation, an innovation handed down through the decades to Def Leppard, Mötley Crüe, and other bands created in Zeppelin's image.) The encore is "Communication Breakdown," stalwart from the first album leavened tonight with a detour into the Isley Brothers' "It's Your Thing" before Plant renders the heartfelt benediction, "Good night, New Orleans. The best city in the States."

Atlantic chairman Ahmet Ertegun, who signs and nurtures many of the city's R&B legends, pulls out the stops for his label's highest-earning act with a party at Cosimo Matassa's Jazz City recording studio; entertainment is provided by an array of New Orleans R&B greats including Ernie K-Doe, Snooks Eaglin, and Art Neville. Jerry Greenberg, a professional drummer before joining Atlantic, sits in with Atlantic exec Phil Carson on bass and John Paul Jones on organ. Ertegun, says Greenberg, "loved the band. He loved going to the shows and always felt it was important to show the band that the label cared." It helps that Ertegun himself commands respect from even the flinty Zeppelin principals "as the guy that produced Ray Charles, wrote the songs—I mean, he was one of them."

Zeppelin is scheduled to play two shows in Los Angeles, but the first is canceled at the last minute when it is reported that Page has sprained the ring finger on his left hand on a fence at the San Diego airport. Or perhaps not. The band as always check in to the Riot House on the Sunset Strip, whose rock and roll bona fides and reputation for anarchy the band more or less invent. There ensues a party on the hotel's rooftop pool with Plant, Page, Dewey Martin of Buffalo Springfield, and members of the Zeppelin road crew during which Martin is tossed into the pool by Richard Cole along with Page, who thereby injures his priceless playing hand—a chain of events that if nothing else better conforms to the Zeppelin story line of anarchy in the U.S. than a blunder into an airport fence. Meanwhile the second show proceeds, made possible by Page submerging his injured hand in ice water in the hours before the concert. Despite Page's fragile condition, the show goes down respectably, though some in the audience who are veterans of earlier Zeppelin shows note that the top end of Plant's voice is not what it was on previous tours. It also happens to be Bonham's twenty-fifth birthday, as Plant informs the audience before "Moby Dick": "Considering it's the gentleman's birthday, I think it's only fair that we should let him bang his balls out, right?" Which he does for a few seconds shy of twenty minutes, including a three-minute interlude playing without sticks and a timpani solo. After the concert Atlantic throws a party for the band in Laurel Canyon, former home to Plant and Page's heroine, Joni Mitchell, and L.A.'s original folk rockers. George Harrison—in drunken expat mode—pushes birthday cake into Bonham's face, which leads to the beefy drummer tossing everyone except Grant into the pool. "Lowell George hid in the closet so he wouldn't suffer the same fate," says Yaryan. "I think the house we rented was destroyed."

After a two-day break, Zeppelin arrives in San Francisco to play Kezar Stadium, an anachronism tucked into a corner of Golden Gate Park, until recently the home of the 49ers football franchise. Promoting as always is Bill Graham, whose disdain for Zeppelin, aside from his showman's weakness for the cash they generate, only deepens when he is told the band is en route from L.A. via private aircraft but that Page at the last minute has insisted on flying commercial "because he had gotten bored with flying on the private plane," Graham recalled. "He wanted to be with just regular people. So he was coming separately on United Airlines." Grant finally arrives with the band two hours late while Page circles San Francisco Airport. "The fans were chanting, 'We want Led Zeppelin!'" Graham recalled. "I realized I had to say *something*." Biting back his contempt, he tells the audience that Page is having trouble with his signature double-necked guitar—without which he cannot perform "Stairway to Heaven"—and that "he really wants to get it just right for you." The audience applauds fervently. "They loved that. If Jimmy wanted them to hang for him, they were happy to go on hanging. Eventually he got there and went onstage. I was livid all day long."

The show grosses $320,000 from a fifty-thousand-strong gate—six thousand short of capacity, the only show on the tour that does not sell out—but it tops the $309,000 gross from Tampa and thus becomes the then-highest-grossing single performance by the band, albeit with several warm-up acts. The *San Francisco Chronicle* notes that perhaps half the audience is drawn from outside the Bay Area proper, who "were here to have a high time with the Zeppelin, not necessarily to generate the communal-like atmosphere that distinguished performances by locally based groups." A hard-core druggie vibe infests the decaying stadium; during Zeppelin's performance a girl, drowning in psychedelics, strips naked and has sex with a bystander, then wanders off, leaving her clothes behind.

Graham is so dispirited by the concert and the thuggish Zeppelin entourage—"Peter Grant sitting backstage with his twelve bodyguards, Jimmy Page flying *United* so he could be with the *regular* people"—and how bands like Zeppelin increasingly set the tenor of an industry Graham's taste once dominated, that he admits, "I didn't want to be a part of this anymore." As Zeppelin slog away, Graham harbors a fantasy in which a helicopter evacuates him from Kezar—with the day's receipts, of course—while he gives the loutish performers and party-hardened audience the finger and the entire stadium is consumed by flames; instead, the concert ends, as at Atlanta, with the release of white doves. In another iconic Zeppelin photo that emerges from the '73 tour, Neal Preston captures Plant smiling beatifically at the dove that has just landed in his right hand onstage, with the endless audience as backdrop.

The following day the entourage flies south—amid the terrible turbulence that prompts the leasing of the *Starship*—to play a makeup date for the canceled Forum concert. *Rolling Stone* has just published the "Limp Blimp" review of *Houses of the Holy*, prompting Plant, while introducing "The Song Remains the Same," to snipe: "I think we better dedicate this to the toilet paper that people buy in this part of the world called the *Rolling Stone*." Despite Page's still-recovering finger, the show—the last before they return to Britain for a one-month break—is one of the finest of the tour and their careers. "I have seen everybody from Prince to the Clash to the Rolling Stones," says Michael Des Barres. "And I will tell you straight off, Led Zeppelin was absolutely transcendent when they played. Jimmy and Robert were Hedy Lamarr and Marilyn Monroe and it was the most glorious thing I have ever witnessed." Says Greenberg, "Listen, I signed Gary Moore. I signed [Free's] Paul Kossoff. I know guitar players. And the slam-dunk top guitar solo of all time, to me, is Zeppelin and 'Stairway to Heaven.'" Showco's Rusty Brutsche, mixing sound for this and all subsequent Zeppelin tours, is impressed that no matter what mayhem Bonham has gotten up to the night before, "he always came in every day and tuned his drums. He was extremely particular about the way they sounded," especially his Gretsch snare drum, "which must have been ten inches deep." At the start of the tour, Mick Hinton, Bonzo's drum tech, orders a gross of Ludwig's heaviest hickory drumsticks; some nights, Bonham hits so hard his bass pedal goes straight through the drumhead. "He was loud," Brutsche says, "but his technique was good. He was a precise musician, a solid and very intricate drummer." With John Paul Jones, he comprises "an unbelievably great rhythm section. The way the two of them played together, that to me was the core of the band. And when you layered Jimmy and Robert on top of that you had a really magical sound."

Given their collective talents, the critical vitriol directed at the band seems at best misplaced, at worst a conspiracy of bias. The beating Led Zeppelin take in '73 while at the height of their popularity, Des Barres says, is cover for critics burnishing their credentials—"in order for you to maintain your hip status you must hate it"—although he concedes that "Robert's lyrics, shall we say, are not that challenging. But that's not the fucking point. The point is that he was gorgeous. He had great thighs and Jimmy had the best wrists and fuck off anybody who criticizes them to make their bones." The nineteen thousand at the Forum for the makeup gig surely agree. For the encore, "The Ocean," the microphone is passed to Bonham, whom the crowd join in bellowing his now famous count-off, "We got four already . . ." Instead of ending the show as usual after "Communication Breakdown," John Paul Jones plays an organ solo that segues into the rarely performed "Thank You," a wistful ballad from the second album that accompanies untold makeout sessions. Tonight it becomes an emotional farewell and encomium to Zeppelin's hardest-core fans.

When the tour resumes with a pair of shows in July at Chicago Stadium, the first night is marred by near-continuous fistfights throughout the eighteen-thousand-strong capacity audience. Plant's voice, even after a month's rest, is again fraying and he clearly wearies of having to use it to mediate the brawls between the audience and security. Near the end of the show, after several appeals for peace, he snaps, "Right, now listen. I've never seen so much heaviness and violence, so cool it, for goodness' sake. Can you dig that?" Evidently not. "Zeppelin takes no glee in ringside chaos," the *Chicago Sun-Times* writes in a glowing review. "Crowd antics to them are like asking George Shearing to play 'Melancholy Baby.'" The *Chicago Tribune* is less effusive and notes that "Plant seemed tired—a man doing what is, after all, a job."

With the *Starship* at their disposal, Zeppelin hunker down in their suites at Chicago's Ambassador East and fly to and from gigs in St. Paul, Milwaukee, and Detroit. The plane's comforts and convenience are a revelation after the terrors of the Falcon 20 charter; the *Starship* also serves as a diorama for the band's high-flying hubris and protectionism against critics, journalists, and even their own support staff. The first time Danny Markus steps aboard the *Starship*, "Bonzo walks up to me and—he used to do this to everybody—he would grab a hold of your nipple and squeeze it as hard as he could. I mean, this still hurts now, okay? Or he would hit you in the solar plexus, just out of the clear blue." As for the motivation, Markus has no doubt. "He was testing you. He wanted to see how your reaction was. And the next time he did it, I'd flinch. He got a kick out of that."

When Markus boards the *Starship*, he is wearing a pair of distinctive custom-made eyeglasses. Bonham, he says, approaches him without pre-amble, plucks the glasses from his face, and "puts them on the floor and stomps on them." Danny Goldberg, the tour publicist, is mortified and offers to buy a new pair on the spot; Markus, in the formative stages of his never-let-them-see-you-sweat Zeppelin stratagem, shrugs off the in-cident. The next night, he wears a fresh pair of the same glasses on the flight to Detroit. When Bonham approaches him menacingly, Markus launches a preemptive strike: "I took them off and *I* stomped on them." The gesture, pathetic in its appeasement of a bully's prerogative, never-theless levels the dynamic between star and supplicant. "And that was it, he never forgot that, and I was in for the rest of his life," Markus says. "He thought that was the funniest thing he'd ever seen and put his arm around me, and he never hurt me again."

Atlantic's Greenberg is rarely on the *Starship* but witnesses an attack backstage by Bonham against one of his staff. "The guy made a very sim-ple remark, okay? One simple remark. He said, 'When am I getting the next single from you guys?'" Wrong question. "First of all, they ain't a singles band. It just struck Bonzo the wrong way." To which the drum-mer responds by lifting the man by his throat preparatory to clocking him. "He was gonna hit him, and I had to break it up," Greenberg says. The incident's overriding presumptuousness—Bonham clearly fears no consequences for assaulting the man—gnaws at Greenberg. The next day he calls Grant and demands that Bonham apologize. "I remember Ahmet said, 'You're gonna call up Peter Grant and tell him *what*?' I don't know how many people would go to the biggest act in the world and tell the drummer he's gotta apologize. I said, 'Fuck him. I was there. I ain't letting him get away with that. He is out of fucking line and nobody can do that to one of my employees. I'll never show up backstage again.' "

Greenberg gets his apology, but it is a rare instance of anyone outside Zeppelin's inner circle holding someone in the organization, let alone one of the four principals, accountable for his behavior. Carol Klenfner flies on the *Starship* as the plus-one of her husband, Michael, an executive at Atlantic. "Michael dragged me along—I'd just had a miscarriage the week before—to fly the Led Zeppelin jet to Pittsburgh or something," she says. "People were doing a lot of drugs." As she surveys the entourage, she spies Peter Grant holding court. "He took a handgun out and flashed it around while we were in the air. It was pretty crazy." Meanwhile, it develops that Plant needs a hairbrush before the gig and borrows Klenfner's. "So that was a thrill," she says.

When Zeppelin pack up from the Ambassador East prior to moving their base camp to New York and a run of shows leading to the three-night finale at Madison Square Garden, Bonham has a parting gift for the hotel staff. "What happens is that when they check out of the hotel, security goes to all the rooms to make sure before they leave that there isn't any damage," says Markus. "Bonzo wanted a pool table so they had put a full slate pool table in his suite. When they opened the double doors to the suite—well, what he had done was he'd torn the sheets and emptied the room carefully. He didn't do any damage to anything. He lowered everything that was in the room down to the garden in the atrium behind the suite. I'm talking about the couch, all the pictures, all the furniture. And when they opened the doors to the room, the only thing that was visible was a cue ball on a carpet. There was no furniture, no bed, no coffee tables, everything had been carefully lowered down to the atrium." Markus allows that the story might be apocryphal; on the other hand, this is a band that, when staying at the Riot House, "would rent an entire floor," says Yaryan. "They liked Dom Pérignon and Atlantic bought them a few cases at fifty dollars and up a bottle; empty bottles were thrown out the window in a sometimes successful attempt to hit the billboard across the street. Then they suggested transportation from one end of the hallway to the other—usually Plant had the suite at one end and Page the other. We got them a wheelchair, a bicycle, and a motorcycle. They were happy campers after that."

There is no monthlong break for Alice Cooper during the spring and summer of '73. The Billion Dollar Babies tour charges out of Philadelphia into a brutal string of one-nighters that keep the band in constant motion throughout March, April, May, and the beginning of June, setting box office records in Baltimore, Indianapolis, and Roanoke along the way. When the tour hits Atlanta, Alice is approached by members of a local glam band who present him with a pair of thigh-high leopardskin boots with six-inch soles and heels. Alice is delighted: "Aren't these *horrible*?" The next night he adds them to his standard stage costume: filthy ripped tights and top smudged with stage blood, a psychosexual offender on the lam. Deploying the precarious boots on the multilevel Cooper set is practically an act of valor, given that the show requires Alice to race up and down stairs blinded by Super Troupers wielding an ax and sword while butchering a baby doll, sexually molesting mannequin parts, and fending off an attack by Michael Bruce during "Sick Things." "Everybody says, What's the most dangerous thing you've done in your life—probably the guillotine, the snake, the hanging," says Alice. "No, it was a half a bottle of VO and those boots. Because I could have fallen off those boots and it was a long fall down." (The boots now repose in the Rock and Roll Hall of Fame Museum.)

Other southern cities—where the pall from the burning of Beatles records after John Lennon's 1966 "more popular than Jesus" quip still hangs in the air—are openly hostile to longhairs, let alone transient and apparently transvestite specimens whose advance publicity is 100 percent negative. As Alice alights from the tour plane in Shreveport, he is confronted by a caricature of a southern sheriff who advises, "Ah heerd aboutchoo killin' them chickens, an' ah heerd aboutchoo slippin' them posters 'tween you legs lahk they was your you-know-what. Yew do anything that ah even *theenk* is lewd, and ahm gonna slap yew in jail so fast yer ears are gonna fall off." That night, Alice performs what amounts to a staged reading of the usual show. "I couldn't even touch a mannequin," he complained, "or he would have slapped me behind bars." At other cities in the South, the band are warned not to indulge in some of the show's standard outrages, even mild contrivances like Alice's soliciting insults and then handing the microphone to audience members. ("You haven't got a dick!" is a girl's typical rejoinder in Atlanta.)

Like Led Zeppelin and the Who, Alice Cooper soon apprehend that the audiences that pack the arenas in '73 are restless, demonstrative, drug-flecked, and violent. The difference between even the previous year's School's Out tour is marked enough for Neal Smith to speculate after the tour ends, "I don't know if it was because the kids were more violent or because we were playing to larger audiences, so the odds of violence breaking out were higher. But by the middle of the tour we were thinking about wearing football helmets." Shep Gordon's gruesome image-building and Alice's taunting stagecraft guarantee that the band already attracts more than its share of bent arrows—Alice famously took a pineapple upside-down cake to the face while performing at the Midsummer Rock Festival in Cincinnati in 1970, and Glen Buxton forever carries a floating bone fragment in his knee after being struck by a hammer hurled onto the stage in Ohio. Too, the band have a history of heaving props into the audience, from the feather pillows they stole from motels and ripped open to lend low-tech drama to their early finales to the posters and giant balloons filled with talcum powder and dollar bills tossed to the crowd at the climax of the Billion Dollar Babies shows.

Still, the volume and ferocity of the ordnance launched at the band during the '73 tour is striking: Alice takes a bottle to the head in Seattle; an M-80 in Toronto detonating between Dennis Dunaway and Smith "nearly blew us off the stage," Smith recalled; two shows later, Alice dodges another bottle that shatters against Smith's bass drum; a firecracker lands in Michael Bruce's shoulder-length hair but doesn't explode. In Chicago, at the notorious Amphitheatre, Smith feels a sharp sting in his back during "Hello Hooray." Moments later his roadie beholds blood seeping through Smith's satin stage jacket, a dart lying on the ground and another harpooned in Mashbir's guitar amp. ("I had no idea who had done it, but I turned around and threw about twelve drumsticks behind me," says Smith.) "Neal was kind of upset about it," says Bruce, who secures one of the darts after the show. "The next morning when Neal came out of his room there was a dart stuck in the door with a note saying—you know how they cut out letters from the newspaper?—DON'T EVEN KID YOURSELF, IT'S ONLY STARTED. Neal's playing it cool like he doesn't care, but I know he was looking around when he checked in to his room because I would be right next to him—he'd check under the bed and behind the curtain before he'd get comfortable. After a week or two I ran out of ideas and I told him I was the one that did it and he goes, 'Oh, I knew it was you all the time.'"

The worst incident occurs during the Coopers' Holiday Tour in December. In Toledo the audience rises up and pelts the band with raw eggs (one hits Alice squarely in the chest), rocks, cigarette lighters, and another ubiquitous M-80, which sends one of the crew crumpling to the stage. After only two songs, Alice adamantly refuses to continue the show. "Alice said, 'Fuck this' and walked off and wouldn't go back on," says David Libert. The audience is kept in darkness while the band returns to the hotel and Libert pries the night's receipts from the promoter. "I had Shep on the phone and he's trying to talk Alice into coming back on stage," Libert says, "and Alice says, 'I'm not going on.'" Gordon seethes, "Goddammit, Libert! Get him on that stage!" to which Libert replies, "Shep, I got the money." "What?" "I got the money already." Gordon reverses course faster than Alice pops the top on a fresh Bud. "Well, fuck these people. Alice shouldn't go onstage. He could get killed out there."

The macabre nature of the stage show lends itself to perils offstage as well. Before the gig in Indianapolis, Alice is warming up Eva Marie Snake, his latest boa constrictor. Suddenly Eva wraps herself around Alice's torso and, in an alarming return to instinct, starts squeezing. In seconds Alice can no longer speak and is barely able to breathe. In desperation he staggers into the living room of the suite, where his bodyguard initially fails to grasp the gravity of the situation; by then the snake is resolutely coiled around Alice's midsection. After attempts to unwind the snake fail, the bodyguard deploys a pocketknife and, gruesomely, cuts the snake from Alice's wheezing body. Just another afternoon on the road.

The difficulties with Glen Buxton do not resolve once the tour starts. Weakened from surgery, forbidden to drink even a beer, the guitarist, when not on the plane or at the arenas, withdraws to his room, where he whiles away his band's triumphant tour apparently getting high. Buxton's dysfunction is a daily nightmare for Libert, who must run the tour with Rommel-like precision. There is so little slack in the itinerary—in May alone the band plays six back-to-back one-nighters covering 2,400 miles, followed by ten more consecutive shows—that a single glaringly late curtain can mean thousands of dollars in union overtime and danger-ously delay the load-out of the elaborate stage and its erection in the next city. In a worst-case scenario, the delays cascade into the cancellation of a show and the forfeiture of tens of thousands of dollars in box office receipts. So Libert keeps the entourage on a tight leash.

"I had a good grip on those guys because I didn't take any shit from them," he says. "That was the problem with the road manager before-hand. They would test him. They'd push him around all the time. And I realized from day one that I could never, ever let them do that or they would never listen to me, and if I couldn't be in control, I couldn't have the job. It was real black-and-white to me. So we had rules in the morn-ing. I do wake-up calls to the band, someone else called the rest of the crew. What happened was after you got your phone call, you have to stick your bag outside the door in the next half hour. Somebody would pick it up, put it on the truck. There was a system to make it easy for everybody." Says Michael Bruce, "I sound like Howard Hughes, but I would only use the top drawer and wouldn't put stuff all over the room so I'd have to search for it, so I could pack it pretty quickly."

The band, aware that the show can't go on without them, mostly re-spect Libert's early-morning musters. "Alice, always on time, never a problem," Libert says. "Neal Smith, he was okay. Dennis Dunaway was absolutely perfect. Michael Bruce, depending on what he did the night before, 'Come on, Michael. We're going.' 'Okay. I'll be right down.'" Then Libert gets to Buxton's name on the manifest. "Glen Buxton wouldn't even answer his phone. So the routine was, I'd knock on his door, there's no answer. This is after I called him and he didn't answer. So I would ei-ther get a passkey from the desk or just kick his door in. And if I had to kick his door in, he had to pay for the door. And the reason he wouldn't answer the phone or the door was he was up all night doing drugs or whatever and his shit would be all over the room, unpacked. So if he was sleeping, I simply turn the mattress over so he would fall out on the floor. I would bring in two roadies who would have some kind of burlap bags and just fill these bags with everything that was all over the room and physically throw him on the limo that took us to the airport. This was my daily routine with Glen Buxton."

Buxton never completely masters the new material from *Billion Dollar Babies* before the tour begins, diminishing his already precarious performances. It is a testament to the professionalism of the other band members that the concerts are, in general, taut and well played. The years and years of unsparing roadwork and invaluable tutelage by Bob Ezrin turn the band, once written off as a novelty act by their mentor, into a model of rock and roll efficacy and drive. Tapes recorded off the sound boards in random cities from the tour evidence the band playing with remarkable consistency, night after night, whereas their contemporaries on the road in '73, including the mighty Led Zeppelin and the Who, are given to wide fluctuations in quality. "The show really came together every night," says Mark Volman. "I mean, it was played well, every night they were great."

Buxton still has his moments—he plays a lengthy solo in "I'm Eighteen" and is featured in "School's Out," along with his signature opening riff, and on the encore "Under My Wheels." But Mick Mashbir and Bruce cover most of the guitar solos, even as Buxton basks in a spotlight. When Buxton was more functional, says Bruce, the band could accommodate his desultory work ethic. "Glen was like, 'I'll be right back,' and two days later we're like, 'We wrote a couple of songs, drop by when you get the chance.' It wasn't a big deal, nobody was mad. We were totally prepared, forged ahead and then he would catch up. When his health caught up with him, those days were kind of like over for Glen. They should have been, anyway." Now, as Buxton falls further and further behind, it becomes increasingly difficult to hide his incompetence from the audience. "We tried to keep him out of the limelight," says Joe Gannon. "He was there on the stage, but nobody paid any attention to him. I mean, nobody would know the difference if he was on." Buxton's performances some nights are so erratic that drastic measures are taken. "He just was not capable of playing after a while," says Libert. "He didn't have a clue. So they turned him off." Says Smith, "A lot of times when Glen didn't know the song that well, he would be up there and look like he's playing but his microphone was actually turned off in the mix. So you would be hearing Mick playing the guitar part that he should have been playing. That, unfortunately, was the reality we had."

Billion Dollar Babies hits number one on the Billboard album chart just as the band swings into Florida for three dates followed by a rare two days off. "The night that we found out that it went up to number one, we were down at Fort Lauderdale," says Smith. "It was Spring Break. I re-member Alice and I were in a limo together and we said, 'Let's go get a drink.' There's kids all over the place, and we just stop at a bar and the limo parked out front. I went to the bartender and said, 'What's your big-gest glass you have in here, like a beer glass?' And he has like a thirty-two-ounce glass. I said, 'Fill it with vodka.' And he goes, 'It's like a dollar a shot, you want this?' I go, 'I don't give a fuck what it is, fill it up with vodka.' And all I know is by the time I was about halfway through that glass, Alice and I were dancing on the dance floor and throwing chairs at people, just trashing the place. I had to be carried out." One monumental hangover later, Smith is unrepentant. "After all the bullshit we'd fucking gone through, now there was nobody in the world that had a bigger album than we did. So from that standpoint, personally, I can't talk about the rest of the guys, but personally it was like everything I'd ever hoped for." Alice marks the occasion and two-day vacation from the tour with a forty-eight-hour poker game in his hotel room. "When it was over there were broken chairs, beer bottles, and torn sheets all over the floor," Alice would say proudly when the tour pauses in Tulsa. "You would have needed a steam shovel just to clean the room."

In Detroit, the band sells out two shows at the cavernous Cobo Arena, a homecoming near the farmhouse outside Pontiac where Bruce wrote the band's first hits. "Detroit was where we broke and we always knew Detroit was going to be the best hard-rock city," says Alice. Backstage is Alice's beehive-hairdoed mother. "Alice has always been unusual," she shrugged when asked about her son's career path. "Alice has always done exactly what he's wanted to do." Indicative of the magnitude of the band's success, Warner Bros. chairman Mo Ostin presents the band with gold albums for *Killer* and *School's Out* at an after party at the Roostertail nightclub. Detroit is the eighteenth city of the tour, to which Alice, the former long-distance runner, commented, "We're only one-third finished and I'm already forty-seven years old." Eternally glib when required by the job—and it is beginning to seem like one more and more as the tour and his publicity duties accumulate—Alice begins to show the strains of being Alice. At the Howard Johnson's Motor Lodge, he makes what he calls "my last statement on autographs" by exposing himself to two teenage girls who ambush him on his way to his room. In another instance of his chasing the personal stardom that is wearing him out while cleaving him from the rest of the band, he arrives in Detroit from a side trip to New York and the unveiling of a hologram of his skull by Salvador Dalí.

Alice Cooper work their way west throughout May—Oklahoma City, Albuquerque, Tucson, sometimes followed by Led Zeppelin playing a hall they'd sold out only days earlier. Concerts in Houston and Fort Worth are filmed for what will become the only redeeming parts of *Good to See You Again, Alice Cooper,* a movie released straight to drive-ins the next year that presents them in fighting trim in the thick of the tour. In Los Angeles, where the band began and very nearly ended its career five years before, two sold-out shows at the Forum await. The sense of vindication in conquering the city that rejected them so utterly that they were forced to leave is palpable. "When we got to the Forum, I remember the limos pulled down this long ramp into the coliseum," says Bruce. "We were still driving in, but we could hear the people. They were stomping, the whole building was vibrating. It was incredible. Because this was L.A., and everybody was usually real reserved and stuck-up, I couldn't believe it. It was two days of crazy."

As the tour reverses course for the string of dates leading to the New York finale, the strain on Alice becomes obvious. The endless beers during the day, interrupted only by the ninety minutes onstage, would seem untenable but are probably therapeutic. "The key to Alice's drinking," says Volman, "was that he'd hold on to the Budweisers until they got warm and then he'd just set them down and get a fresh one, and then he'd sip on that. By nighttime he'd have a pretty good buzz on. He functioned very well with his alcohol. He was in a comfortable haze. He'd drink Budweiser from the minute he woke up until around six o'clock, and then he'd start in on the whiskey, and he would drink that until he passed out at night. And he was still always able to put on a great show." Considering that before Shep Gordon's earlier intervention, Alice was downing two fifths of VO a day, this is progress.

Alice blames his truly heavy drinking, which finally lands him in rehab, on not compartmentalizing the doll-chopping Alice from his own mostly amiable offstage personality. "He was the easiest guy to get along with," says Libert. "He never gave anybody a hard time—he just didn't have it in him. I remember in Vegas he was waiting for his food in the suite and I said, 'You're Alice Cooper, give them shit! Get pissed, Alice!' And he called up said, 'Hello, this is *Alice Cooper* . . . ' and then he said, 'I can't do this.' He wanted everybody to like him." Alice admitted, "I tried being Alice for a while. Offstage. I started believing I had to be Alice all the time . . . till I realized, 'What am I doing this for? Bela Lugosi doesn't go biting people in the neck offstage.'" The Alice character may be killing himself with booze, "but why do I have to go, too? Why am *I* involved? I don't even know him that well." When Gordon informs him that his drinking is destroying his personality, he has the epiphany that Alice the rock star caricature is suffocating Alice the wisecracking punk from Arizona. "That was the last thing I wanted to do," he said. "Because I really like me. The whole Alice trip is like *The Three Faces of Eve*." By the Billion Dollar Babies tour, Alice mostly knows who he is and isn't and plans accordingly. Bob Brown, the tour publicist, is careful not to schedule interviews with him directly prior to or following the shows. "He was fine until about thirty minutes before the show and about thirty minutes after. At that point he morphed into Alice and I wouldn't get anywhere near him. He would lash out if you disturbed him. So I learned early on, that period of time, to leave him to himself because he needs to make the transition. Which is understandable when you understand that Alice is a character."

Even factoring in Alice's wit, self-awareness, and nominally curtailed booze intake, the travel, press conferences, and near-nightly shows where he is—by his own choice and temperament—the star place him under pressures not shared by the other members of the band. "I was the one focal point," says Alice. "By the time the rest of the guys got up, I had already done eight or nine interviews. It got to the point where I was really doing all the work as far as promoting the band." On previous tours, Bruce, Dunaway, Buxton, and Smith had been far more integrated into the show's narrative—Alice and Smith re-create the knife fight out of *West Side Story* on the School's Out tour—easing the load. Now that the choreography and stage emphasize Alice alone, who is constantly trailed by eight Super Troupers, the concerts are one-man shows save for Libert's use of the plural pronoun when introducing the band. Unsurprisingly, the Bud that Alice sips constantly during the day is supplemented with plenty of Canadian whiskey after he retires to his suite. "I was drinking heavily every night," Alice admitted. "That was my release."

While Alice takes pride in not drinking onstage, neither is he altogether sober when he hits the boards in his six-inch leopard-skin platforms, with predictable consequences. "In the fight scene onstage I've broken my elbow, two knuckles, and a rib," he said in Detroit. "The other day in Texas I counted thirty-one bruises on my body. I'm usually so drunk I don't feel like I'm getting hurt." A year after the tour, he elaborated, "I was bandaged all over my upper body. It was one of those things where you hit something, like the mike stand"—as he does violently when transitioning from "Hello Hooray" to "Billion Dollar Babies"—"and you don't feel it. Or you fall down those stairs, all the way down the stairs, and you don't feel it. And you get off the stage afterwards and they say, 'What a great show' and all of a sudden I look at my arm and my arm is broken, I touch it and I can feel the bone."

For Alice—natural celebrity, class clown, and shameless show-off who lives for the empowerment of an adoring audience—the price the Billion

Dollar Babies tour extracts in order to satisfy those compulsions ought to be, despite his nightly oblivion, sobering. For now, there is another wake-up call, another press conference, another show. As Alice remarked wearily before shoving off from Detroit for Pittsburgh, "I'm just trying to get through this tour alive."

Chapter 10

THREE FOR THE ROAD

Alice Cooper ponders the meaning of Madison Square Garden (or is it Oklahoma City?), Led Zeppelin count their money and come up $180,000 short, and the Who go out with a bang and a whimper.

As the bands near the rendezvous with their closing nights—Led Zeppelin and Alice Cooper at Madison Square Garden, the Who at the Capital Centre in Largo, Maryland—there is the matter of whether they've achieved what they'd set out to accomplish. All three tours have unquestionably been moneymakers—though given the overheads, especially on the Cooper tour with its $250,000 stage, profits are not quite what the impressionable fans might imagine as they watch the limos trail into the night. Add the trashed hotel rooms, the thousand-dollar-a-day lease on the *Starship,* and petty cash outlays for incidentals like buying off furious innkeepers, and the expenses for all three tours chip away at the bottom line like so many razors on a rock of cocaine. Just before the end of the Billion Dollar Babies tour, Gordon estimates a gross of $4.5 million from total paid attendance of 820,000. Expenses, including production costs, travel, and salaries excluding the band members and managerial partners, are approximately $3.5 million. Based on this accounting, the five members of Alice Cooper split a payday of approximately $1 million before Gordon's 20 percent commission, or around $150,000 each, not including their cut of concessions, a profit center in its infancy in 1973. This is not bad money for what amounts to three months' work, but it is far from the riches most assume bands in the Zeppelin-Cooper-Who weight class earn for their exertions.

As for advancing the cause of each band's image and career, the results are mixed. *Quadrophenia* does not turn into the cultural juggernaut or capstone of the Who's sixties legacy that Townshend has fought so hard to summon. His uncharacteristic anger at audiences on the tour that don't take his new opera emphatically enough to heart is for him unprecedented, and the mindless party-on ethic that supplants previous Who fans' enthusiastic high spirits for the band, the music, and each other seems to mystify him. In Philadelphia, the day before the tour's finale, he observes that "*Quadrophenia* has been getting blamed for our troubles this tour, but I don't believe that anymore. I think the audience has changed. We've been so self-involved the last two years we've missed—I think for the first time—the changed experience of the audience. It wasn't till we got here to the U.S. that we found out that such acts as Alice Cooper have not only come but gone." The ever younger audiences, he discovers, "seem more demanding, more skeptical . . . We won't necessarily be going home unhappy, though there have been emotional outbursts among us that reflect a sense of dissatisfaction."

Led Zeppelin starts the '73 tour incensed that their massive popularity does not translate into critical acceptance or mainstream fame. *Houses of the Holy* does little to reverse the former, but the tour's record-breaking attendance—shrewdly framed by Danny Goldberg's publicity as a referendum on the band's appeal to a new generation by invoking the Beatles, sacred cow of the old—goes a long way toward satisfying Grant's agenda and Robert Plant's hunger for unambiguous stardom. To that end, with only three dates remaining, the band and Grant commission the director Joe Massot to film the Madison Square Garden concerts for a feature film. *The Song Remains the Same*, as the movie will eventually be titled, will sit on the shelf for the next three years once the band gets a look at their fatigued performances at the tour's end and the mortifying "fantasy" footage of each member shot later. But for the moment, lean and sassy on the *Starship,* with the end of the tour on the horizon, Led Zeppelin's trajectory must seem to them unlimited.

Coming on the heels of the fiasco in Montreal, where the band spent the night in prison and missed their original flight, the Who's Boston concert is rife with references to their incarceration. Townshend questions whether the Royal Canadian Mounted Police who arrested him could stand onstage after seven hours in a cell the night before—"fuck their fucking arseholes." Daltrey, who slumbers in his suite when the hotel is vandalized but is arrested anyway, says: "About ten hours ago this gig was absolutely fucking impossible. So this one is for ... the police in Montreal. We're here and it's good to be here and this is for them: 'Won't Get Fooled Again'!" The Boston audience has little patience for *Quadrophenia* and belligerently yells requests during the quieter passages, which provokes another of Townshend's lectures. According to Rob Boffin, who was in the audience, "the Who left the stage pissed off and did not perform an encore." The next night in Philadelphia, recorded for broadcast on the *King Biscuit Flower Hour* syndicated radio program, the aimless introductions sandbag the *Quadrophenia* segment while backing tapes trip up Townshend before "I Am the Sea," though this time it is he who comes in early rather than the tape commencing too late. During Moon's vocal turn in "Bell Boy," he ad-libs, "Remember the place in Canada that we smashed?" As usual, the crowd responds to the classic Who material as if prodded by a hot poker—their eight-minute ovation after "See Me, Feel Me" is finally rewarded with the encore "Naked Eye." As the song crashes to a close, Moon upends his drums for the last time on a tour that seems to frustrate audience and performer in equal measures.

The Who check in to the star-crossed Watergate hotel the day before their farewell performance in suburban Largo, where a skeptical *Washington Post* interviews Daltrey—the only one of the band Will Yaryan can muster—at midnight. The conversation, refereed with increasing exasperation, offers a glimpse of the ennui that ensues when a rock star with less finesse than Townshend fences with an unsympathetic reporter from outside the music press. The topic of the Montreal hotel trashing is broached, to Daltrey's dismay. From the *Post:*

> "I 'ope you are not going to talk about that," says Daltrey dolefully. In a doleful mood Daltrey looks like the archangel Michael with a stomachache. "Those newspaper stories about the 'oo are greatly exaggerated. They said, for instance, we caused ten thousand dollars worth of damage. Untrue." How much? "Six thousand," said Daltrey.

Yaryan, in damage control, interjects that wrecking a hotel room really doesn't hurt anybody. "Daltrey snorted, 'Course it does. Course it 'urts someone.'" At one particularly deep lull, "Daltrey reached over for a grinning toy monkey," the *Post* observed. "He pushed a button and the monkey began to cackle and crash a pair of cymbals together. This went on for about two minutes while Daltrey gazed benignly at the creature."

The final concert of the Quadrophenia tour before 17,500 "largely suburban" fans sporting "a plethora of platform shoes," according to the *Post*'s review, "was not up to the group's proven standard of excellence." While allowing for closing-night fatigue, "the band sounded tired and sloppy—almost like a second-rate rock outfit trying to imitate the Who—an echo of an old tidal wave." This is precisely the opposite of what Townshend intends for *Quadrophenia;* instead of transcendence, the critics see only nostalgia in the opera's Mod setting, where actual Who songs from the era like "I Can't Explain" and the even more temporal "My Generation" are given a pass. It must gall Townshend to have the opera itself so completely and regularly misconstrued. And so at the end of the Largo concert Moon ritualistically wrecks another drum kit and the Who return to Britain, the only band on either side of the Atlantic in 1973 capable of going out with both a bang and a whimper.

On the eve of Zeppelin's Madison Square Garden concerts, Peter Grant is in fine form backstage at the Baltimore Civic Center, upbraiding the building manager after he discovers that unauthorized photographs of the band are being sold in the arena. *"How much of a kickback are you getting?"* Grant demands, massive as always, the turquoise outcroppings on his rings menacing. Robert Plant's wails are heard faintly through the concrete-block walls in the dismal "dressing room," the chafing dishes arrayed amid sinks and urinals, as Grant relentlessly hectors the man. The scene is captured by Massot in one of the more compelling moments in *The Song Remains the Same*. (Some patient soul later calculates that Grant says *fuck* and *cunt* a combined eighteen times during the exchange.) Even allowing for the opportunity to preen, Grant's tirade over what is probably at most a five-hundred-dollar loss to Zeppelin's income stream seems completely in character—one can only imagine how he would have handled the matter were Massot's camera not turning. Grant's nose for cash fails him only once during the tour, and spectacularly so: Three nights later, before Zeppelin plays their final show, $180,000 is stolen from a safe at the band's hotel. Richard Cole, who discovers the theft, is initially suspected but cleared. The crime is never solved.

The last gigs at Madison Square Garden are competent, but the strain of performing a three-hour nightly concert with no opening act is evident. "It's really been an incredible tour but we're all terribly worn out," said Page. "I went past the point of no return physically quite a while back but now I've gone past the mental point." As Plant tells the audience closing night, "You could call this gig a fitness test just to see that we can really still do it." What is remarkable, viewing footage of the concerts today, is just how rudimentary the staging and primitive the stagecraft are for this, 1973's top concert draw. Aside from mirrors arrayed haphazardly behind them, the band plays on a bare stage littered with amplifiers and cables, the roadies and hangers-on in plain view in the wings, while the musicians cluster around Bonham's drums and each other as if for warmth. Anyone in the audience who toils in a garage band (with no doubt several Zeppelin covers in their repertoire) recognizes the tableau instantly—it's what they look like when *they* play, huddled close, watching each other for cues and changes, admiring friends gathered around them like a comforting blanket. Despite the *Starship* and limos and thuggish entourage, Zeppelin's unwitting ability to allow its primary audience to read the band as both larger and smaller than life, in a venue as immense as Madison Square Garden, accounts for much of their bond with their fans. The Houses of the Holy tour will be the last Zeppelin performs with such intimacy—future tours will emulate the example set by the Billion Dollar Babies stage and incorporate lasers and a giant electric LED ZEPPELIN that blinds the audience after the encores.

But tonight, for the last time, Zeppelin present themselves pretty much as they do in 1969 at the Whisky or Kinetic Playground or Cheetah or Tea Party—one singer, two guitarists, and an artillery battery for a drummer attacking their repertoire as if it owes them money. The seventeen-song set includes a thirty-one-minute "Dazed and Confused" and a twenty-minute "Whole Lotta Love," plus three encores. As in Los Angeles at the end of the first leg of the tour, the evening's final encore is the elegiac "Thank You," followed by Plant's endearingly mispronounced benediction: *"As-salamu Alaykum"*—may peace be upon you.

When the lights go down at the Garden for Alice Cooper's final shows, Mick Mashbir, Stratocaster slung over his shoulder, climbs the stairs to the stage in darkness. As the crowd seethes and the lighters flicker, Mashbir leans over to Michael Bruce, who stands nearby in the darkness, "to say congratulations and that we had made it to the end unharmed." Just as David Libert announces "America's Billion Dollar Babies, Alice Cooper!" and Neal Smith counts off "Hello Hooray," Mashbir slips in a puddle of oil leaking from the fog machine and performs a dead fall, knocking himself unconscious. "I split my ear open and was lying there on my side as the lights came up," he says. Mashbir awakens to a roadie hauling him to his feet and starts playing before Alice snarls the third line of the first verse. Then Mashbir notices spots of blood on his white satin jacket. "I bled on myself through the whole show and I now have a rock and roll warrior scar that I wear proudly today." Considering Mashbir split his pants climbing to the stage opening night in Philadelphia thousands of miles ago, there is poetic symmetry to the mishap.

The Billion Dollar Babies tour is conceived as a blitzkrieg across the country, playing as many cities as possible to make it seem as if the band is everywhere. Even to the very end, Gordon keeps adding dates—the Garden concert is followed by add-ons at the Nassau Coliseum before the tour finally wraps at the Providence Civic Center June 7. But in 1973, the Garden is the most prestigious rock venue in the world, and ending one's tour with a sellout there is the de facto gold standard, unquestionably announcing that you and your band have arrived. Not that it matters to the exhausted musicians. "If you would have said, 'You're in Oklahoma City tonight,' and we were at Madison Square Garden, we would have gone, 'Okay,'" says Alice. "Honestly, it just didn't matter to us—we were going to do the same show that night." Says Michael Bruce, "It kind of seemed like it was never going to end. We just thought we were going to be on the road forever."

The Billion Dollar Babies tour permanently ups the ante for presenting live rock at the arena level. The costumes, the multilevel stage, the props and theatrical lighting are expensive upgrades to the rock experience that Alice Cooper absorbs while charging its audience the same $6.50 top commanded by outfits like Grand Funk, who perform with only their amplifiers and dubious charisma as the draw. "Nobody had ever used truss lighting before," says Alice. "Nobody had ever used Vari-Lites. We made that stage look like a Broadway show." Says Gordon, "We took it way past what even we thought was possible. It really set the model for everything we see today. Everybody's doing production shows, and that didn't exist before. Until Alice, nobody in the contemporary music world was thinking about stuff like that."

As *Billboard* reports, in the aftermath of Alice Cooper's 1973 tour, "Increasingly, rock stars feel they have to put on a show of some sort." The story cites a 1973 performance by Elton John at the Hollywood Bowl, introduced by Linda Lovelace of *Deep Throat* fame, in which the lids of four grand pianos are opened to disgorge flocks of homing pigeons as John walks onstage wearing giant spectacles that spell out his name in lights—all pages from the Alice Cooper playbook.

For all that the Billion Dollar Babies show is complicit in elevating Alice as the star, it is also the expression of the entire band's vision, born when they would throw feathers (and the odd unfortunate chicken) into the audience—anything to get a reaction, anything to show that they were not just another shambling rock band but stars in need of only a little burnishing, which they shamelessly supplied themselves until the rest of the world did it for them. "I loved that show," says Neal Smith of the Billion Dollar Babies tour. "I loved everything about it. Our challenge was to be creative and different but still make it a commercial success, and we did that." Observed the *New Musical Express* at the tour's end, "the whole Alice Cooper thing is the biggest practical joke in the history of rock and roll . . . Alice Cooper told everybody right up front what he was going to do, and [everybody] still fell for it. It really leaves one dumbfounded with admiration."

Alice Cooper's first—and, it will turn out, last—show at Madison Square Garden goes off in a barrage of fireworks and a stage front crowded with faces painted in emulation of Alice's ghoulish makeup. Backstage, Alice informs a bystander matter-of-factly that "I haven't thrown up today." It is unclear whether this is good news or bad. Onstage Alice takes command with his usual provocation. "This my hometown, New York. And yet I haven't been insulted yet." The jeers go off like the flashbulbs filling the arena: *Fuck you, Alice! Up your ass, Alice!* Alice smiles, satisfied. "*That's* what I like." The rest of the show clicks off the outrages like clockwork: the snake, the doll, the body parts, the beheading, ending as usual with Alice saluting the colors while Kate Smith warbles over the PA and, tonight, the Richard Nixon impersonator is pummeled and dragged offstage. When the houselights come up, one of the bepainted Alice acolytes hands a Cooper roadie a garter snake and begs him to give it to Alice as a gift. It turns out to be dead.

Much later that night, wearing a T-shirt emblazoned I'M ALICE—BLOW ME, Alice makes a hero's return to Max's Kansas City, where Bob Ezrin three years ago shook off his provincialism and had the epiphany that the misfits writhing onstage before him could become stars. And tonight, Michael Bruce, Dennis Dunaway, Glen Buxton, Neal Smith, and Alice Cooper are unquestionably who they set out to become when they clawed their way out of Topanga Canyon as the most hated band in L.A. Yet there are omens, which they glimpse grinding to and from Charlotte and Shreveport and Oklahoma City and Amarillo and San Bernardino, that the calculus will change for everyone in the band except its singer and true star, leaving the others with bruised feelings and lifestyle consequences never entirely resolved. But tonight the five men of Alice Cooper are the toast of New York's rock demimonde—even if Alice complains at Max's that he can't get drunk after having been carried out to his limo the night before. As Neal Smith reflects forty years later: "The music was great, the show was great, the plane was great. I had the biggest set of drums and we were all on top of the world."

EPILOGUE

The '73 tours have consequences, immediate and long term, that change the lives and careers of the Who, Alice Cooper, and Led Zeppelin in ways mundane and profound. Having spent six months of every year since 1969 on the road, Led Zeppelin commences an unprecedented eighteen-month hiatus from live performance. John Paul Jones—who always holds himself at a remove from band camaraderie—seriously considers quitting the group during the sabbatical. He drolly tells Grant on the eve of recording Zeppelin's next album, *Physical Graffiti,* that he is considering applying for the job of choirmaster at Winchester Cathedral. The fact that Jones invokes a job so comically opposite his rock star existence is telling. The sessions are postponed before Jones reconsiders and joins the group at Headley Grange, where Ron Nevison cuts eight tracks for the album. The delay caused by Jones's cri de coeur forces Nevison to depart the sessions due to a prior commitment to record the soundtrack for the Who's *Tommy* movie. "They weren't happy about that," says Nevison. "No one had ever quit Led Zeppelin before."

As Robert Plant's hit-or-miss vocals throughout the '73 tour make plain, singing full throttle night after night for the past four years has ravaged his voice. During the tour Plant finesses the punishing falsetto portions of "Stairway to Heaven" by dropping an octave, and several songs are reconfigured in lower keys so that he can manage them live.

Much later Plant reveals he underwent throat surgery during the band's hiatus; Zeppelin scholars detect a noticeable attenuation in his voice upon the release of 1975's *Physical Graffiti* and subsequent albums and tours. The band's first double album is a mixed bag of new material and leftovers from the Stargroves sessions for *Houses of the Holy* and introduces the last great Zeppelin anthem, "Kashmir," a swaying Middle Eastern epic anchored by one of Bonham's greatest drum figures. A winter and spring tour of North America, the band's first since '73, is hampered when Page injures his hand in a train door just before the premiere and Plant battles the flu during the early dates. But overall the tour and album—which soars straight to number one and sells eight million copies in the United States—are well received, and Zeppelin finally attain the unqualified renown and critical acceptance that had eluded them since 1969.

The rest of the seventies are an unfolding nightmare for Led Zeppelin. Plant and his family are severely injured in a car accident in Greece, forcing the cancellation of an American tour and delaying their seventh album, *Presence*. Released in March 1976, the album's jarring, flinty, ultra-hard-rock repertoire receives a cool reception from critics and fans. *Presence* has the misfortune of being released into the thick of Britain's punk movement, which casts Zeppelin as its chief object of ridicule and explicitly rejects the ponderous rock star excesses the band personifies. In lieu of touring, the band releases *The Song Remains the Same*, shot mostly at the 1973 Madison Square Garden concerts and shelved after the rushes are viewed as unsalvageable; it is savaged by critics but does respectable box office. Most ominous, in the U.S. Zeppelin's now college-age core audience has shifted its enthusiasms and money to the softer melodic rock practiced by the likes of Fleetwood Mac, reconstituted with a sleek L.A. sound. Peter Frampton replaces Page as the cohort's guitar hero as Frampton's freakishly successful 1976 live album blasts from dorm rooms across the land while *Presence* languishes in cutout bins. For the first time, Led Zeppelin is no longer hip with its chief constituency.

Zeppelin nevertheless remains a potent concert attraction; with no new album to promote and only their legacy as a draw, the band sells out a lucrative spring and summer U.S. tour in 1977, playing before a record-setting audience of 76,229 at the Pontiac Silverdome. While the tour comprises some of their best performances, it is plagued by unruly fans, injuries, and arrests. The mood within the entourage is increasingly dire and paranoid; the motorcade to and from the arenas now numbers six limos, one for each band member and Grant plus one for groupies. (According to Markus, for the Madison Square Garden shows the band deploys a staggering thirty-two limousines—"I think the first one arrived at Madison Square Garden just as the last one was leaving the Plaza.") On the third show of a four-night stand in Chicago, Page takes the stage obviously indisposed. "He looked weird and the vibe was weird—something was wrong," says Neal Preston. "All of a sudden [Grant] comes out from the wings waving his hands, like, 'Stop, stop.' I run backstage just as Richard is dragging what looked to me to be almost a lifeless Jimmy Page right in front of me. He shot me a look like 'Don't even think of photographing this.'" The official explanation for Page's collapse is food poisoning. The following evening Page performs dressed as a Nazi storm trooper, with leather boots and an SS officer's cap cocked jauntily atop his curls. By now so spectrally thin that he appears malnourished, Page cuts the repellent figure of a decadent wastrel. He is photographed on *Caesar's Chariot,* successor to the *Starship* in Zeppelin's private air force, wearing the SS cap while a Texas groupie favored by Robert Plant nuzzles his scrawny neck.

The Waterloo for the tour and the band comes at two Bill Graham–promoted Day on the Green concerts at Oakland-Alameda County Coliseum. Tensions run high throughout the first show as Zeppelin's crew randomly assault Graham's personnel, knocking out a stagehand. When a misunderstanding arises over the removal of a dressing room sign involving a Graham employee and Grant's young son, Bonham kicks the man in the crotch; he is later lured to a trailer, where—as Richard Cole menaces Graham's security with an aluminum pole—Grant and John Bindon, a notorious Zeppelin security thug, beat the man so severely he believes he will be killed. Following the concert, Zeppelin's attorney implies the band will not perform the next day's sold-out show unless a document is signed absolving Grant, Bonham, Cole, and the rest for the incident. Graham finally signs, fearful of a riot if the concert is canceled, and meanwhile quietly arranges for the perpetrators to be arrested after the show. Graham's own security spoil for a fight. "Bill," one of them informs him, "we're tellin' you up front. Before the show tomorrow. After the show tomorrow. We're gonna do somethin' about it. We're gonna *do* these guys." They agree to hold off when Graham tells them about the impending bust.

When Zeppelin takes the stage the next day an hour and twenty minutes late, "they were totally behind enemy lines," Graham recalled. "No one spoke. No one smiled. The only thing moving were people's eyes." The next morning Grant, Cole, Bonham, and Bindon are arrested at the San Francisco Hilton and transported to Oakland, where they are handcuffed, booked, and briefly jailed before posting bond. They later plead nolo contendere and receive modest fines and suspended sentences; a $2 million civil lawsuit is settled out of court. As Graham's stage manager later recalled, "When we started looking into it, there were incidents like that across the country on that tour. Trashed hotel rooms. Trashed restaurants. Literally like twenty thousand dollars' worth of damages at some restaurant in Pennsylvania. Really outrageous stuff. Like where they physically abused waiters and people in the restaurant and then just bought them off. The accountant would open up the valise as the guys were zooming off in their limousines and say, 'Okay. How much?'"

After Oakland, Zeppelin is scheduled to appear before eighty thousand at the New Orleans Superdome. The show never goes on. After checking in to the band's hotel, Plant receives the news that his son, Karac, has died suddenly of a viral infection. The rest of the tour is canceled and Plant, accompanied by Bonham and Cole, flies home to England. In San Francisco, Bill Graham receives a phone call from Peter Grant. "I hope you're happy," Grant tells him, perfectly serious. "Thanks to you, Robert Plant's kid died today." After eleven tours and 337 shows, the Oakland fiasco becomes the band's legacy in the country that delivered them to superstardom. Led Zeppelin never again plays America.

Two years pass before Zeppelin performs again. During the hiatus Plant mourns his son and in 1979 a new album is released, *In Through the Out Door,* a partial return to form after *Presence.* The band plays two shows before a combined 350,000 Britain's Knebworth Festival, reassuring them that their audience is still there. *In Through the Out Door* debuts at number one in the U.S. and revives the fortunes of a record industry in a prolonged slump following the collapse of disco. In the summer of 1980 Zeppelin embarks on a no-frills tour of Europe and lays plans for a monthlong return to America in October. Rusty Brutsche, as ever, mixes sound. "They had been through the wringer and did Europe with a lot of trepidation," he says. "They actually sounded good and kind of came back together again." Following a rehearsal for the American tour at which Bonham is almost too drunk to play, the band stays at Page's house in Windsor for the night. The next morning, Brutsche waits at a London soundstage for the band to arrive for rehearsals; instead, there is a phone call from Benji Lefevre, Plant's vocal tech. "He said, 'The rehearsal's not gonna happen today,' and I could just tell from the way he said it that it was something really, really bad." Showco's Dallas office calls with the news that John Bonham is dead. The drummer has been discovered in bed at Page's home by Lefevre, having choked to death on his vomit after consuming, it is later determined, more than a liter of vodka. He was thirty-two years old. After rumors circulate that the band will carry on with a replacement drummer, Zeppelin issues a statement on December 8, 1980: "We wish it to be known that the loss of our dear friend [has] led us to decide we could not continue as we were."

In the ensuing years Page and Plant perform together and separately, most visibly on MTV's *Unledded* in 1994, playing acoustic versions of the Zeppelin canon without inviting or even informing John Paul Jones. With Bonham's son Jason on drums, Plant, Page, and Jones play the Atlantic Records Fortieth Anniversary concert and at Zeppelin's induction into the Rock and Roll Hall of Fame in 1995. The four reunite under the Led Zeppelin name in 2007 for a concert honoring Ahmet Ertegun at London's O2 Arena that draws more than twenty million requests for tickets. The show is so well played there is speculation a reconstituted Zeppelin will tour, but Plant refuses. In 2012, the surviving members receive the Kennedy Center Honor; thirty-nine years after the band started agitating for mainstream credibility and respect in the summer of '73, Page, Jones, and Plant, in black tie and wearing medals presented earlier at the White House, are seated not far from Barack and Michelle Obama.

Peter Grant, meanwhile, retreats to his moated Sussex estate, where he mourns the loss of Bonham and succumbs to his cocaine addiction while battling diabetes. Already divorced from his wife, he now loses touch with the surviving members of Led Zeppelin. Plant makes it known he will seek new management when he launches his solo career. In the late eighties, Markus invites Grant to tea at the Mayfair Hotel in London and is shocked by his decline. "He looked awful. He looked like an old man. He was living alone, his clothes were soiled, and he just didn't smell good." Grant eventually cleans up, loses weight, and reenters society. Taking stock of his legacy, he is moved to tears when Bill Graham's damning account of the Oakland beatings is published and confides to an associate, "I don't want to be thought of as a bad person." Though no longer managing them, he reconnects with Page and Plant informally. He is scarcely recognizable to those who know him from his buccaneering Zeppelin days.

Tony Mandich, head of artist relations for Atlantic Records, spots Grant backstage at a concert in L.A. and invites him to dinner after the show. "My God, he'd probably lost a hundred and fifty pounds," Mandich says. Before dinner, Mandich orders a glass of champagne. "I said, 'Peter, have a drink.'" Grant orders a fifth of Stolichnaya. "I was shocked because in the car he was complaining that his doctor told him he was going to die if he didn't stop drinking." Mandich orders a bottle of champagne for himself and he and Grant spend hours reminiscing. Grant thanks Mandich for looking after Zeppelin over the years—including niceties like making sure the band's preferred booths at the Rainbow were always available when they were in town—and tells him that this will be his last visit to America. As they leave three hours after the restaurant closes, there is perhaps a finger of vodka left in the bottle Grant ordered. He gathers around his shrunken frame the scarves and enormous woolen trench coat that for years had been his manager's mufti. Mandich never sees him again. Peter Grant dies of a heart attack on November 21, 1995, while driving home with his son Warren. He was sixty years old.

•   •   •

Alice Cooper has scarcely unpacked from the Billion Dollar Babies tour before they are back at work recording *Muscle of Love*, the follow-up to *Billion Dollar Babies*. After the tour wraps, Alice would recall, "I couldn't get out of bed for a week, even to go to the bathroom, 'cause I was shaking. It was like when you turn your car off and it keeps going. That's exactly what happened. I was at home, in my apartment, and I was calling room service. And Cindy, my girlfriend, would say, 'What're you doing?' I had to catch myself. It started getting serious. You can't keep on that level, going that fast all the time."

Nevertheless, by October, Alice is in daily attendance at New York's Record Plant, laying down lead vocals for *Muscle of Love*. Producing the album is Jack Richardson, subbing for his former assistant Bob Ezrin, who declined the project after deeming the songs insufficient. Exhausted from the tour, the band presents the new material to the producers at Richardson's Nimbus Nine studio in Toronto. "Bob, at the time, was going through a divorce," says Michael Bruce. "He comes in while we are doing 'Big Apple Dreaming'"—a song later to appear on *Muscle of Love*—"and the first thing out of his mouth is not, 'Hi, how are you guys?' It's like, 'No, no, no, that's not what it is. Stop. Stop. Stop. That's not how you play that.' And we all turned and looked at one another and we're like, 'Oh, God, it's happening again.'" Dennis Dunaway recalled, "We started playing it and we didn't even get past the intro and Bob stopped us and wanted to change it. We were laughing but Michael Bruce took offense and said, 'We don't want to change it.'" It escalated rather quickly and Bob said, 'Well I guess you guys don't need me, then.' Michael replied, 'I guess we don't.' We were standing there looking like, 'Wait, we do need Bob.'" Says Alice, "It was getting to the point where Mike wouldn't listen to Bob. Neal didn't want to really listen to Bob. Whereas before, whatever Bob said was gospel. All of a sudden, everybody got a little bit arrogant: 'Well, we're the big rock stars and we know what we are doing.' And we didn't."

With the droll and easygoing Richardson at the helm, the *Muscle of*

Love sessions proceed apace. Meant to be a return to the band's garage rock roots after the gothic complexity of Ezrin's productions, the album nevertheless ends up bejeweled with stunt guest stars—Liza Minnelli and the Pointer Sisters sing backup—and ultimately suffers from a lack of the thematic continuity that propels *School's Out* and *Billion Dollar Babies*. "The songs were all good individually, but they sounded like they all belonged to other albums," says Alice. Even the album's packaging—a cardboard box printed with a faux grease stain—seems to not know what it wants to be. Despite his differences with Ezrin, Bruce comes to understand that "as diverse as *Muscle of Love* was, and Jack Richardson did a really good job, Bob wasn't there and we were all missing him. I would have taken the stress to have him there because I could know that it would be done right. I knew he wouldn't let anything out that wasn't just extraordinary." *Muscle of Love* ships one million copies when it is released in November and generates a modest hit single, "Teenage Lament '74," but books two hundred thousand returns, some of them from retailers believing the stain on the cover is real and that the album is damaged goods. Compared to *Billion Dollar Babies,* perhaps it is.

Alice Cooper embarks on a monthlong U.S. tour in support of *Muscle of Love* in December. Aside from changing the band's costumes to sailor suits—to coincide with the album's inner sleeve depicting the band on a rampaging shore leave—the tour is essentially the Billion Dollar Babies show, right down to the snake and guillotine. Glen Buxton, who does not play at all on *Muscle of Love,* is in no better condition than on the last tour, and Mick Mashbir once again is tapped to cover his parts. The concerts sell out despite the gas shortage gripping the U.S., and the band plays solidly at every date. "We were really up to speed and playing much better than we had on the Billion Dollar Babies tour," says Mashbir. But the overall mood is dour. Bob Greene notices that Alice pulls back from the most vicious elements of the show, no longer taunting the audience and only going through the motions of chopping the doll and serenading the snake. "I feel as if I've done this before," Alice observes on opening night in Nashville. "Do we really have to go out there tonight?" Just before stepping onstage, he turns to Greene, yawns, and says, "As you can see, I'm a bundle of nerves."

Alice's isolation from the band, apparent on the Billion Dollar Babies tour, is now exacerbated by an aggressive bodyguard who shadows him everywhere, even when he practice-putts in the safety of his locked suite. Alice is, incongruously, now an avid golfer and arranges side trips from the tour to play without the others. Bruce finally asks Alice "why he was drinking all this beer, playing golf, doing this whole Dean Martin trip. And he said he's been doing what we're doing for the past nine years, and he's sick of it. He said he's ready to do something else." Says Alice, "I was slowly drifting away from the band." After the tour Alice said, "Up to *Billion Dollar Babies* it was fun but then it got grueling and everyone lost their sense of humor."

Shep Gordon is already working behind the scenes to broaden Alice's celebrity beyond the confines of a five-man rock band and, ultimately, to remove him from it. Bob Brown finds that dealing with the band makes him uncomfortable "because I knew what was happening. I knew that this"—the Muscle of Love tour—"was kinda gonna be it." Alice is photographed mingling with mainstream celebrities, which during the buildup of his vicious image would never have been allowed but is now orchestrated just as minutely. "Playing golf with Johnny Mathis was not done by accident," says Brown. "Hooking up with Groucho Marx was not done by accident. *Hollywood Squares*"—Alice appears on the game show with tired, toupeed "stars" like Paul Lynde—"was not done by accident. It was all part of the transition of Alice the band to Alice the individual, the solo artist."

The Muscle of Love tour wraps New Year's Eve, 1973, in Buffalo, followed in March and April by a five-date cash-grab tour of Brazil—an uproarious gig in São Paulo is attended by 150,000. After the tour, the tensions that had been steadily building throughout the past year surface. "The guys called a band meeting and said they wanted to do solo projects," says Gordon. "They weren't happy with the way things were going. They felt that people weren't appreciating them for their musicality and they didn't want to do the theatrics anymore. Alice was the only one who really was willing to play the character; they were almost embarrassed by it. It created tension every single night because they didn't want to go on in the costumes or do the guillotine. And I can understand their point of view. They were musicians and wanted to be appreciated and loved for their music. But our guitar solos didn't get a lot of standing ovations, and the hanging did every night." Neal Smith counters that "the band didn't break up because we didn't like the theatrics or we didn't like the clothes. There's nobody more theatrical than me. I'm as much as Alice if not more. I would have the most outrageous drum set in the world, and an even bigger one on the next tour."

At the meeting, Gordon says, he reminds the band that "we all made a commitment that [Alice] was going to take on the burden of doing all the press and he gets the exact same amount you guys do. But if you break this bond, I want you to understand that he's got the name Alice Cooper, so he is Alice Cooper. That's the way we created it, and that's why we made our deal that nobody would break from the other guy because we were giving him a very big advantage. So if you call this off, you have to understand what you're letting loose. And I want you to know that as far as I'm concerned, I'm gonna be going with him because I'm not interested in the musicality. I'm interested in the theatrics." Alice says that "the thing that really drove the stake through the heart of it was when Billion Dollar Babies was done and everybody was fairly exhausted, I was already thinking, 'I've got an idea for a show that's gonna be bigger and take two years of solid touring. The moment we stop, Bowie or somebody else is going to step up and take over. We cannot stop right now.'"

In the end, the band takes a year off, during which Michael Bruce can record a solo album. "We were just going to take it easy and then a year later, we were going to get back together and record the next album," says Smith. They never do. In 1974 Alice records Welcome to My Nightmare, produced by Ezrin, that is also the soundtrack to a TV special, Alice Cooper: The Nightmare. "The minute I heard about Alice doing a solo album, I said, 'Well, that's it,' " says Smith. "If he has any kind of success, he has all the momentum of the name behind him."

Released in 1975, Welcome to My Nightmare is a sizable hit and spawns a top-ten single, "Only Women Bleed." After that, there is no more talk of the original band regrouping. Bruce says calls to Gordon go unreturned. "Then the phone rings and it's Shep," says Bruce. "And Shep says,

'Alice says you will no longer be working together.'" David Libert cites Bob Greene's unsparing insider account of the Muscle of Love tour, published in 1974, as the decisive factor in the breakup. "The book came out and that changed everything. Alice read the book and said, 'I don't want to work with these guys anymore.'" Alice legally changes his name from Vincent Furnier to Alice Cooper. "Now what do you got?" says Brown. "You got a person named Alice Cooper and a band named Alice Cooper. And you can't copyright a personal name that's been changed."

Outmaneuvered at every turn, the remaining band members consider their options. "We [jointly] owned the name," says Smith, "and we had to work something out legally because of that." Says Bruce: "We would have to sue and none of us wanted to do that. I mean, we got close. I wasn't going for it. Glen had nothing to lose. Dennis didn't want to and Neal was on the fence because it would change the relationship forever. And it will be long-drawn-out and the lawyers are going to make the money. So we figured, let's just go on with our lives and just let them run with it." Says Smith, "There was never going to be a lawsuit because a lawsuit would never really fix anything. It just makes everybody hate each other more."

The remaining members of Alice Cooper change their name to Billion Dollar Babies and, with Mick Mashbir, record the album *Battle Axe,* a commercial flop, before disbanding in 1975. Alice tours successfully behind *Welcome to My Nightmare* with a band that includes Dick Wagner and Steve Hunter, who played on *Billion Dollar Babies* in lieu of Buxton; the tour's support personnel—Joe Gannon, Libert, Brown, and the rest—are essentially unchanged. (Bruce is bitterly amused when he hears that the new band are disgruntled because they aren't in the spotlight enough.) Alice's drinking meanwhile progresses to full-blown alcoholism—footage from the Nightmare tour depicts him barely able to stand, and he badly injures himself after a fall headfirst off the stage in Vancouver. After the tour, Brown is dispatched to L.A. to live with Alice at his new home on Lookout Mountain in Laurel Canyon—the neighbors include Harry Nilsson and Micky Dolenz of the Monkees, who along with Keith Moon and Ringo Starr comprise a drinking club, the Hollywood Vampires, who congregate at the Rainbow nightly. "Bob had to babysit him," says Linda Bischoff, hired as Brown's aide-de-camp. "You couldn't leave the guy alone." Says Brown, "He needed someone to drive him more than anything because at that point he had never driven. That was my job when we weren't on tour—that and take him to the Rainbow."

Alice struggles with alcohol throughout the seventies and early eighties. "I was costume mistress on the tours," says Bischoff. "He would come offstage and I would have to take his two-piece leotard off and put on another. And I couldn't have done it if it wasn't for [two Cooper roadies] holding him up. I don't think he really wanted to do it anymore, and that was the way he coped." Alice goes through rehab twice before finally cleaning up for good in the mid-eighties. (He later becomes a devout Christian.) For the next thirty years he releases a string of solo albums and tours regularly but never entirely eclipses his work with the original Alice Cooper band, which features prominently in his shows. When the Rock and Roll Hall of Fame finally inducts Alice Cooper in 2011, it is the original five-member band that is honored. At the ceremony, Alice, Michael Bruce, Dennis Dunaway, and Neal Smith—with Steve Hunter substituting for Glen Buxton, who had died of pneumonia in 1997—perform "I'm Eighteen," "Under My Wheels," and "School's Out." It is the first time all the surviving members have played together since the breakup in 1974. "One thing I do know," Neal Smith says a year after the induction, "is that sooner or later, except maybe for the Rolling Stones, every band breaks up. And breaking up at the top of your career is not the worst thing in the world. I'd rather do that than be dragging a guillotine into a bar somewhere in Indiana and getting five hundred bucks a night doing a whole Alice Cooper set, you know?"

Chiseled into a black granite gravestone in Clarion, Iowa's Evergreen Cemetery are two bars in the key of E minor:

In a fitting memorial to Glen Buxton, his epitaph in the obscure Midwestern town where he spent the last years of his life commemorates the eternal contribution he makes to Alice Cooper and to rock and roll: the bouncing, belligerent opening riff to "School's Out."

The Who play out the seventies after *Quadrophenia* amid personal upheaval and public and private tragedy. Townshend wrestles with drink and drugs while trying to answer once and for all whether it is possible for the band to remain relevant. *The Who by Numbers,* the band's first new material since *Quadrophenia,* is released in 1975 to indifferent reviews and sales. The album is dominated by Townshend's soul-searching over his addictions ("However Much I Booze") and fields a minor hit in "Squeeze Box," a near novelty record with naughty punning lyrics and a banjo solo from Townshend.

After a three-year hiatus during which the band members work on solo projects, the Who regroup and record *Who Are You.* Released in 1978 with the English music scene dominated by punk, the album features stronger material and yields the band's last major hit in the title track, the opening verse of which recounts Townshend's being rousted by a policeman after passing out drunk in a Soho doorway. Within a month of the album's release, Keith Moon dies suddenly after ingesting an overdose of the drug meant to wean him from alcohol. Moon had been in decline throughout the decade as he ramped up his booze and drug intake to lethal levels; unlike Townshend, the definition of a functioning alcoholic, Moon's playing deteriorated to the point that his drum part had to be wiped from one of *Who Are You*'s tracks. His stomach is so distended from brandy that he sits for the album's cover photo in a chair labeled, in brutal coincidence, NOT TO BE TAKEN AWAY. Kenney Jones, the affable former drummer of the Faces, replaces Moon in the band. "Keith was a very positive musician, a very positive performer, but a very negative animal," Townshend said a year after Moon's death. "He needed you for his act, on and off stage. Kenney fits in very well as a person with the other guys in the band." Nevertheless, part of the Who dies along with Moon and is never recaptured.

Tragedy continues to stalk the band when, at a sold-out concert in Cincinnati in December 1979, eleven audience members die of asphyxiation before the concert in a crush outside the arena doors. A contributing factor is festival seating, the profit-maximizing strategy launched when rock concerts were upscaled from ballrooms to arenas in the early seventies. With the entire main floor of the arena given over to standing room, a sizable crowd had gathered outside Riverfront Coliseum prior to the concert in order to secure good spots. When the band performs a sound check, some in the crowd mistakenly assume the concert has started and surge toward the entrances; however, the doors are still closed. Before they finally open, eleven fans are dead and several dozen more injured in the melee to reach the stage front.

When the concert starts, few in the eighteen-thousand-strong audience—along with the Who—realize the incident has occurred. Cy Langston is backstage when word finally reaches the entourage about the deaths. "The count was getting higher and higher. We had to make a decision. Well, what do we do? We can't pull the band offstage, because it could cause a riot. So in the end Bill Curbishley, the tour manager, and myself decided we can't tell [the band] until after they've done the show. It wasn't until they came off the encore that we sat them down to tell them." The band are stunned but elect to continue the tour. As Townshend recalled, "I watched Roger Daltrey cry his eyes out after that show. I didn't but he did . . . It was, fuck it! We're not gonna let a little thing like this stop us. That was the way we had to think. We had to reduce it. We had to reduce it, because if we'd actually admitted to ourselves the true significance of the event, the true tragedy of the event—not just in terms of 'rock,' but the fact that it happened at one of our concerts—the tragedy to us, in particular, if we'd admitted to that, we could not have gone on and worked."

By the early eighties, Townshend seems destined to follow Moon as his depravity reaches heroic levels even as he releases a well-received solo album, *Empty Glass*, with its top-ten single "Let My Love Open the Door," and the Who issue *Face Dances*, the first album recorded with Jones. Townshend's inebriation finally bleeds into his performances—he famously nods off at an Amnesty International benefit; infuriates Daltrey, Entwistle, and Jones by launching desultory improvisations during a London concert; and nearly expires after collapsing at a club after an injection of heroin. Townshend later credits his dissipation in part to his "inability to deal with the [Who]. I felt that the band wasn't facing up to reality. I should have said to the band, 'I'm leaving. I've had enough of rock and roll. Good-bye.' But I didn't. I couldn't deal with that emotionally at the time." Although *Face Dances* yields the hit "You Better You Bet," Townshend decrees the album subpar. The follow-up, 1982's *It's Hard,* is hailed by *Rolling Stone* as the band's "most vital and coherent album since *Who's Next.*" But between Townshend's addictions and contracting sales—the albums sells a fraction of *Who Are You*—the Who, confirming Townshend's obsession since *Quadrophenia,* no longer seems of its time.

Townshend finally cleans up and the Who embark on a successful "farewell tour" in 1982 that later becomes farce as the band, without Jones and including a host of sidemen including Townshend's brother on guitar, tours in 1989, 1996, 1997, 1999, 2000, 2002, 2004, 2006, 2007, 2008, and 2009, in addition to numerous one-off shows, including the Concert for New York City, a benefit for first responders to the 9/11 attacks that the Who dominate with a powerful performance. Eight months later, on the eve of a U.S. tour, John Entwistle dies of a cocaine-induced heart attack while in the company of a middle-aged groupie at the Hard Rock Hotel in Las Vegas. He is fifty-seven. As with the tragedy in Cincinnati, the band elects to continue the tour, and Entwistle is replaced with the session bassist Pino Palladino. Townshend later reveals he only agreed to the tour to help Entwistle—deeply in debt—and afterward plans to no longer perform as a member of the band. Entwistle's death instead breathes life into Townshend's fraught relationship with Daltrey and encourages him to carry on with what is left of the Who. "I felt it was like a gracious gift from John . . . though his passing was really tragic. Roger and I were thrown together. We had been respectful and friendly to each other, but we had never been great friends. We had never managed to find a way to live with how different we are, and how differently we think and work. With John gone we were on our own, no distractions, no excuses."

And so Townshend, who ties himself in knots over the Who's place in the rock and roll continuum, finally is content to let the band's legacy define his own. In 2010 the Who play a rapturously received performance of *Quadrophenia* in its entirety at the Royal Albert Hall that serves both to gentrify the opera for new generations—Pearl Jam's Eddie Vedder makes a cameo as the Godfather—and to give it, finally, the proper staging that eluded the band so tragicomically during the '73 tour. Reviewing the concert, the *Guardian* observed, "They really don't make albums like this anymore, and while there's undoubtedly a reason for that, you can't help being glad someone once did." In 2011 Townshend presents the lovingly curated "director's cut" boxed set of *Quadrophenia* that leaves no doubt of his devotion to the opera that no one seemed to love except him when it escaped at the tail end of 1973, itself a year of cultural schizophrenia that teetered between the sixties and seventies, steeped in both and resolving neither.

It doesn't take long for the last of the sixties atmospherics to evaporate from the music industry once 1973 is past. Cocaine ceases being a fey and fashionable pick-me-up and devolves into a full-scale scourge, destroying bands and corrupting relationships professional and personal at every level of the music business. "The excesses of that time were directly tied to senior management's ability to identify with the artist," says Chip Rachlin. Which means what, exactly? "Who did drugs with whom." After the *Quadrophenia* tour, Will Yaryan, having adopted the vices of his rock star charges, endures one more year of soulless toil on behalf of music that increasingly reflects the cynical turn of the industry—albums and drugs are now interchangeably referred to as "product"—before he can take no more. "My marriage didn't survive the nights at the Troubadour, Roxy, and Whisky, and by the end of 1974 I quit by locking myself in my office and listening to music until the gold-chain-wearing head of the office fired me. It took me a year to get the speed and coke out of my system." Yaryan moves to Santa Cruz and later to Thailand and rarely looks back.

Marsa Hightower logs untold hours in the *Starship* and in backstages in every major metropolitan market on the map throughout the seventies. "One could encapsulate the entire era into a single motif—the circus," she says. "The ladies flying through the air enticing all around, the tightrope walkers trying to maintain balance, the daredevil trapeze artists. Then, of course, there was the aroma of elephant dung in the background, lending a certain decadence to the experience. And the audience, enraptured, wanting to be part of the circus but also waiting for the spectacular falls and missteps." The industry's total capitulation to the drug culture in the mid-seventies, coinciding with spectacularly successful albums like *Frampton Comes Alive!* and Fleetwood Mac's *Rumours,* begets a fall-of-Rome decadence that disquiets Hightower even as she maneuvers through the business in L.A.

"There was a dealer named Howard, who first was the coke guy. Then he was the freebase guy. Then he was the heroin guy," she says. "You'd go to parties and you always knew when the drug dealer came in because everybody would be following him or her." As the decade grinds on, the nights when Hightower hosts dinner parties at her house on Shoreham Road above the Sunset Strip—when her friend Keith Moon is still capable of being charming and the drugs are mostly kept at bay—become a memory as the scene turns irreducibly hostile. "The thrill was gone, as were many friends and acquaintances. There are a lot of them I can't believe lived through it, Jimmy [Page] being one of them. Don't get me wrong. I enjoyed it. But I knew there was a possibility that if I stayed in it much longer, it was going to happen to me, too. And it was like, I'm getting out of here. I'm done."

On a street lined with sycamores in Los Angeles's Mid-Wilshire district is a whimsical mock Tudor cottage of the sort that Charlie Chaplin stashed his mistresses in during the twenties. Inside, the shelves are crowded with miniature Spanish galleons, the walls hung with coats of arms and neatly framed gold albums. In the backyard above a koi pond covered with plywood to foil a persistent peregrine falcon, a pirate's skull and crossbones flutters atop a flagpole in the afternoon breeze.

Ron Volz, Alice Cooper's first full-time roadie, opens the front door and leads the way to a table in the dining room piled high with hundreds of hotel keys that Volz pocketed as keepsakes on his voyages around the world with Cooper in the seventies. The battered leather briefcase he carried on tour is open nearby, overflowing with backstage passes, long-lost itineraries, and his original laminated crew pass from the Billion Dollar Babies tour, with its purple image of Alice in his stage makeup. Volz stirs the keys and selects one embossed CONTINENTAL HYATT HOUSE—Led Zeppelin's fabled Riot House, the mother of rock and roll hotels. He stirs some more. Here are keys from the Intercontinental Hotel in Berlin, from Rotterdam, Amsterdam, Hamburg, Copenhagen, Lund, Essen, Frankfurt, Vienna, Munich, Paris, Antwerp, London, Liverpool, Perth, Melbourne, Brisbane, and Auckland. Running through the pile are dozens of the peculiar oblong fobs once the trademark of Holiday Inn, "The Nation's Innkeeper" and Keith Moon's, too, until he drove a Lincoln (or maybe it was a Cadillac) into one of their swimming pools.

Volz became a roadie after he hitchhiked from Cincinnati to the Woodstock Festival at nineteen and somehow insinuated himself backstage. Alice Cooper hired him when they passed through Cincinnati during one of their first, primitive tours. Filling in for an absent Dennis Dunaway, he played bass the night Michael Bruce fashioned the first crude version of "I'm Eighteen" in an empty club in Ohio. Two years, four gold albums, and eight tours later, Volz was on hand as Alice Cooper gathered their Rolls-Royces and Jaguars and moved out of the Galesi mansion into mansions of their own. Not long after, the mansion burned to the ground. Volz, by then living in an apartment above the garage, watched as firefighters futilely tried to save the house that launched Alice Cooper on their final adventure.

Forty years later, Volz stirs the keys in front of him as if they are embers from a life that warm him still. After his days with Cooper, he became a successful art director for music videos with stars as big as the band that first opened the door to a world he could scarcely imagine when he was growing up in Ohio. But he never forgets his first brush with the rock and roll American dream, when the music stepped out of its hand-sewn sixties hippie vestments and into limos and arenas and *Starship*s, during the twelve barnstorming months in 1973 when he, too, was a Billion Dollar Baby.

"Wherever they were, wherever things were going on," Volz says, "I was there."

ACKNOWLEDGMENTS

Special thanks to Julie Grau, Ryan Doherty, Laura Van der Veer, Janet Wygal, Christopher Zucker, Will Georgantas, and all at Spiegel & Grau. Thanks also to Hilary de Vries, Colman Andrews, Merle Ginsberg, Jane Ayer, Will Yaryan, Cary Baker, Owen Phillips, Barbara Graustark, Stuart Ross, and Hilary Elkins. I am grateful to my literary agent, Daniel Greenberg, for his tenacity and unrelenting good humor during the conception and writing of this book.

NOTES

Introduction

xiv **"Everybody was like the 1927 Yankees"** Andy Greene, "John Fogerty: My Anger Towards My Creedence Bandmates Has Faded," *Rolling Stone,* Oct. 25, 2011.

xiv **"a fucking flying gin palace"** Steven Davis, *Hammer of the Gods* (New York: William Morrow, 1985).

xv **"We were playing sets"** William S. Burroughs, "Rock Magic: Jimmy Page, Led Zeppelin, and a Search for the Elusive Stairway to Heaven," *Crawdaddy!,* June 1975.

xv **"I remember that tour"** Cameron Crowe, liner notes, *The Song Remains the Same* soundtrack, 2007.

xv **"the best music I've ever written"** James Jackson, "Pete Townshend on *Quadrophenia,* Touring with the Who and the Mod Revival," *The Times* (U.K.), April 20, 2009.

xvi **"every teenager wanted more stereos"** Alice Cooper and Steve Gaines, *Me, Alice* (New York: Putnam, 1976).

xvi **"overindulgence and affluence"** ibid.

xvi **"We wanted to blitz the public"** ibid.

xvii **"In the end"** ibid.

xvii **"I'm just trying to get through this tour"** Bloom, Howard, "Alice Quits the Stage," *Circus,* July 1973.

xvii **"the exact same fights"** ibid.

xvii **"I fought my way through that tour"** ibid.

xviii **"Billion Dollar Babies took the life out of the band"** ibid.

Chapter 1: Gentlemen, Start Your Egos

4 **"My producers and I often joked"** James Schamus, *The Ice Storm: The Shooting Script* (New York: Newmarket, 1997).

5 **"In 1973, in the collective mind"** Danny Goldberg, *Bumping into Geniuses: My Life Inside the Rock and Roll Business* (New York: Gotham, 2008).

6 **"Zeppelin forced a revival"** Susan Fast, *In the Houses of the Holy: Led Zeppelin and the Power of Rock Music* (New York: Oxford University Press, 2001).

6 **"Led Zeppelin was the first big group"** Goldberg, *Bumping into Geniuses.*

7 **"That would have been Zeppelin"** Jeff Beck, http://www.youtube.com/watch?v=t6UykU1TG2c.

7 **"There was this slightly out of control egomaniac"** Chris Welch, *Peter Grant: The Man Who Led Zeppelin* (London: Omnibus, 2002).

8 **"When rock radio came along"** Goldberg, *Bumping into Geniuses.*

9 **"We had appalling press"** Mat Snow, "Apocalypse Then," *Q* magazine, Dec. 1990.

9 **"It felt like a vacuum"** George Case, *Led Zeppelin FAQ* (Milwaukee: Backbeat, 2011).

11 **"After all this crap"** Dave Schulps, "Interview with Jimmy Page," *Trouser Press,* Oct. 1977.

11 **"Look at all the press the Stones got"** Goldberg, *Bumping into Geniuses.*

12 **"other than my closest friends"** ibid.

13 **"We affect the little teenage boys"** Stephanie Gross, "Where Are the Chickens?" *Rolling Stone,* Oct. 15, 1977.

13 **"Even hippies hated us"** Alice Cooper and Steve Gaines, *Me, Alice* (New York: Putnam, 1976).

14 **"We did it before Bowie"** East Valley, Arizona *Tribune.*

14 **"It shocked me"** Ian Fortnam, *Classic Rock,* June 2004.

14 **"people would expect a blond folk singer"** Ken Kelley, "*Penthouse* Interview: Alice Cooper," *Penthouse,* Sept. 1974.

15 **"one of the finest"** *Rolling Stone,* Jan. 6, 1972.

15 **"Alice and I were long-distance runners"** Fortnam, ibid.

15 **"by this point we had really started"** ibid.

16 **"The Billion Dollar Babies concept"** ibid.

16 **"As soon as the announcer says, Alice Cooper!"** ibid.

17 **"was reflecting the decadence"** ibid.

17 **"It was the best thing for their careers"** Bob Greene, *Billion Dollar Baby* (New York: Atheneum, 1974).

18 **"I was keyed up"** Cameron Crowe, "Pete Townshend: The *Penthouse* Interview," *Penthouse,* Dec. 1974.

19 **"It was almost like there was too much good press"** *New Musical Express,* May 11, 1974.

19 **"We wanted to play"** Crowe, "Pete Townshend: The *Penthouse* Interview."

20 **"It was such a big jump,"** Michael Walker, "The Resurrection of *Tommy,*" *Los Angeles Times,* July 5, 1992.

20 **"There were a lot of brilliant young players around"** Steve Rosen, "Townshend Talking," *Sound International,* April 1980.

21 **"I had no other recourse"** ibid.

21 **"pilled-up Mods"** Michael Walker, "See Me Feel Me Touch Me Stage Me," *Boston Globe,* May 16, 1993.

21 **"When 'I Can See for Miles'"** Roy Carr, "The Punk as Godfather," *New Musical Express,* May 31, 1975.

22 **"What I feel is very important about *Tommy*"** ibid.

22 **"*Lifehouse* was an incredibly ambitious project"** Crowe, "Pete Townshend: The *Penthouse* Interiew."

23 **"I've always felt that *Quadrophenia*"** Press conference for *Quadrophenia: The Director's Cut,* Nov. 9, 2011.

Chapter 2: Hope I Get Old Before I Die

24 **"We'd had such a fabulous couple of years"** ITV, "London Tonight," 2011.

25 **"I'm constantly thinking about age"** Crowe, "Pete Townshend: The *Penthouse* Interview."

25 "There's people that grew up with the Who" ibid.

25 "In Los Angeles, that third wave stretched" ibid.

25 "the Who's first ordinary album" Richard Barnes, *The Who: Maximum R&B* (Richmond, UK: Eel Pie, 1982).

25 "we'd lost one bollock" ibid.

25 "artists churned out new records" *Quadrophenia: The Director's Cut*, Geffen.

25 "I began to depend on having brainstorms" ibid.

26 "the Who would from then on always need" ibid.

26 "provide us with a show" *Quadrophenia: The Director's Cut* video interview, part 2.

26 "a project that would clearly demonstrate" ibid.

27 "it sounded like a shadow" Chris Welch, "Talking 'Bout My Generation," *Melody Maker,* Oct. 27, 1973.

27 "I read it and I thought bloody hell" *Quadrophenia: The Director's Cut* video interview, part 2.

27 "The feeling came flooding back" ibid.

28 "young Mod, hopeless" ibid.

28 "My first audience in the Mod days" ibid.

28 "Rock and pop fans don't want" ibid.

28 "deliberately unstructured and accessible narrative" ibid.

29 "I mean, if someone like Bowie" Charles Shaar Murray, "Four-Way Pete," *New Musical Express,* Oct. 27, 1973.

29 "When it came to *Quadrophenia*" ITV, "London Tonight."

29 "Keith Moon was buying a Rolls-Royce every week" ITV, ibid.

29 "Keith Moon showed up with a different girl every day" *Quadrophenia: The Director's Cut* video interview, part 2.

30 "I'm thinking of calling" Charles Perry and Andrew Bailey, "The Who's Spooky Tour: Awe and Hassles," *Rolling Stone,* Jan. 3, 1974.

30 "Schizophrenic? I'm bleeding" *Quadrophenia* album jacket.

30 "There was a bit of confusion" *Quadrophenia; The Director's Cut,* part 2.

30 "What the story is about" ibid.

31 "Even if one can get away with it" Crowe, "Pete Townshend: The *Penthouse* Interview."

31 "What I think will hurt me" ibid.

31 "In '73, what we had was Electric Light Orchestra" ITV, "London Tonight."

32 "I kind of knew punk was coming" ibid.

32 "I wanted to get the band back" ibid.

32 "at the same time, I knew" ibid.

32 "In the U.S., you know" Perry and Bailey, "The Who's Spooky Tour."

32 "I've often said I was moved" ibid.

33 By the time he fetches up on the *Quadrophenia* sessions Some details and background on the recording of *Quadrophenia* are taken from Richie Unterberger, *Won't Get Fooled Again: The Who from* Lifehouse *to* Quadrophenia (London: Jawbone Press, 2011).

33 Wishing to capture an authentic cello sound ibid.

34 "I had my own studio" Ken Sharp, "Look Who's Talking: A Conversation with Roger Daltrey," *Goldmine,* July 8, 1994.

34 "I was extremely fond of Kit" *Quadrophenia: The Director's Cut* video interview, 2011.

35 "All the time we were recording" Pete Townshend, recording notes, *Quadrophenia,* 1973.

35 "Just as we were about to start it off" Bruce Pollock "On the Case: The What, When, Where and Why of Pete Townshend of the Who," *Rock* magazine, Jan. 14, 1974.

36 "They were really starting to boogie" ibid.

37 (**"Record companies like to put out albums at Christmas"**) ITV, "London Tonight."

38 **"It's incredibly weak"** Sharp, "Look Who's Talking."

38 **"We ran out of models"** Perry and Bailey, "The Who's Spooky Tour."

38 **"Roger thought of the idea"** Unterberger, *Won't Get Fooled Again.*

39 **"Obviously I was delighted"** ibid.

40 **"just how fucking efficient it was"** *Quadrophenia: The Director's Cut* video interview, part 2.

Chapter 3: Live from the Cooper Mansion

42 **"Every wall was painted"** Geoff Emerick and Howard Massey, *Here, There and Everywhere: My Life Recording the Music of the Beatles* (New York: Gotham, 2006).

43 **"I thought we might capture something really unique"** Jaan Uhelszki, "Babies on Fire," *Guitar World,* 2008.

43 **"We were under pressure"** ibid.

43 **"We didn't know if Alice Cooper was a guy"** *New Musical Express,* Aug. 18, 1973.

44 **"Here's this guy Alice Cooper"** ibid.

44 **"I leapt into it without any knowledge"** Larry Leblanc, Celebrity Access Mediawire, http://www.celebrityaccess.com/news/profile.html?id=534.

44 **"I knew it would be a hit"** *New Musical Express,* Aug. 18, 1973.

45 **"We were getting voted"** Alice Cooper and Steve Gaines, *Me, Alice* (New York: Putnam, 1976).

47 **"Offstage I'm like Ozzie Nelson"** Harry Swift, "Inside Alice," *Rolling Stone,* May 10, 1973.

49 **"Michael's songwriting"** Uhelszki, "Babies on Fire."

50 **"Things would come up that were difficult to play"** ibid.

50 **"Glen was my best friend"** ibid.

51 **"I made people feel uncomfortable"** Cooper and Gaines, *Me, Alice.*

52 **"He pulled the melody out of songs"** ibid.

52 **"the discipline of recording, rehearsing material"** Leblanc, Celebrity Access Mediawire.

53 **"Basically I was the arbiter"** Serene Dominic, "Once More, Mr. Nice Guy," *Phoenix New Times,* April 19, 2001.

53 **"I was always the crusader for the avant-garde"** Ian Fortnam, *Classic Rock,* June 2004.

54 **"a crippled guy from Canada"** Dominic, "Once More, Mr. Nice Guy."

55 **"one of the most poetic songs I ever wrote"** *Good to See You Again, Alice Cooper,* DVD commentary (Eagle Vision, 2005).

55 **"when it got to that tail end"** Uhelszki, "Babies on Fire."

57 **"When we heard the album back"** ibid.

Chapter 4: Dancing Days

58 **"The drummers would then play like crazy"** Brad Tolinksi, *Light and Shade: Conversations with Jimmy Page* (New York: Crown, 2012).

59 **"Look at the Beatles"** ibid.

59 **"a marriage of blues, hard rock"** ibid.

59 **"I wanted artistic control"** ibid.

60 **"Finally I had to scream"** ibid.

60 **"because I didn't want"** ibid.

60 **"When it came time for the lead guitar parts"** eddiekramerblogs.tumblr.com.

61 **"just flying around on a small console"** Dave Lewis, *The Complete Guide to the Music of Led Zeppelin* (London: Omnibus, 1994).

61 **"I told him exactly what I wanted to achieve"** Tolinski, *Light and Shade.*

61 **"We could relax and take our time"** ibid.

61 **"We tried 'Levee' in an ordinary studio"** ibid.

61 **"The key to Zeppelin's longevity"** Cameron Crowe, "The Durable Led Zeppelin," *Rolling Stone,* March 15, 1975.

62 **"Bonzo started the groove on 'The Crunge'"** Tolinksi, *Light and Shade.*

64 **"You can really hear the fun we were having"** ibid.

64 **"We had no set ideas"** Richie Yorke, *Led Zeppelin: From Early Days to Page and Plant* (London: Virgin, 1999).

65 **"The lads were really happy there"** eddiekramerarchives.com.

65 **"to try to get a completely neutral acoustic environment"** ibid.

65 **"wearing a V-necked cardigan"** ibid.

65 **"The recording setup for Bonham was simple"** ibid.

66 **"One of the marvelous things about John Bonham"** National Public Radio, "Guitar Legend Jimmy Page," June 2, 2008.

66 **"carrying this picture"** Tolinski, *Light and Shade.*

Chapter 5: "We Know How to Make the Money"

70 **"looked to his dad for business advice"** Debbie Geller, *The Brian Epstein Story* (New York: Faber and Faber, 2000).

71 **"nail [Stigwood] to his chair"** Johmmy Rogan, *Starmakers and Svengalis: The History of British Pop Management* (London: Transatlantic, 1988).

71 Details of Peter Grant's early life and his transition to managing Led Zeppelin are taken from Chris Welch, *Peter Grant: The Man Who Led Zeppelin* (London: Omnibus, 2002).

71 **"suicide might be better"** Rogan, *Starmakers and Svengalis.*

74 **"Peter Grant cared solely about his artists"** Danny Goldberg, *Bumping into Geniuses: My Life Inside the Rock and Roll Business* (New York: Gotham, 2008).

76 **"Peter's intentions were to be protective"** Pat O'Day, *It Was All Just Rock 'n' Roll* (Seattle: RnR, 2002).

77 **"What I didn't like about Led Zeppelin"** Bill Graham and Robert Greenfield, *My Life Inside Rock and Out* (Cambridge, MA: Da Capo, 1992).

77 **"I do remember when we first arrived"** ibid.

77 **"egos and territories"** ibid.

79 **"We were stumped"** Alice Cooper and Steve Gaines, *Me, Alice* (New York: Putnam, 1976).

80 **"When the audience screamed 'Get off!'"** ibid.

80 **"clapping like a seal"** ibid.

80 **"I had never seen such a strong negative reaction"** Bob Greene, *Billion Dollar Baby* (New York: Atheneum, 1974).

80 **"All right, I'm a Jew"** Cooper and Gaines, *Me, Alice.*

83 **"The next day, the word spread"** ibid.

85 **"It's not a bad idea"** ibid.

85 **"Shep Gordon was very shrewd"** Gary James, classicbands.com.

88 **"a pill-popping publicist"** johnpidgeon.com.

89 **"Kit was the ultimate Barnum and Bailey con man"** *Amazing Journey: The Story of the Who* (Universal Studios, 2007).

89 **"My problems with the Who"** Richieunterberger.com

89 **"Very early on Kit and I realized"** ibid.

90 **"I would say to Kit, I really want to write a fucking opera"** ibid.

91 **"He left me holding the baby"** Mark Wilkerson, *Amazing Journey: The Life of Pete Townshend* (Raleigh, N.C.: Lulu.com, 2007).

93 **"We used to find bands on the road"** Ken Sharp, "Look Who's Talking: A Conversation with Roger Daltrey," *Goldmine*, July 8, 1994.

93 **"Here was this band"** Al Kooper, *Backstage Passes and Backstabbing Bastards: Memoirs of a Rock 'n Roll Survivor* (Milwaukee: Backbeat, 2008, rev. ed; first published 1977).

Chapter 6: On the Road for Forty Days

96 **"For years only Elvis could sell out"** Pat O'Day, *It Was All Just Rock 'n' Roll* (Seattle: RnR, 2002).

96 **"It would be nearly a decade"** ibid.

98 **"What happened was I started renting Hammond organs"** Bob Heil, www .musiciansfriend.com, July 27, 2010.

99 **"Hey, man, I heard you have"** Dan Daley, "The Night That Modern Live Sound Was Born," *Performing Musician*, Dec. 2008.

100 **"There were about a dozen flagpoles out there"** Tom Ross, www.artistshousemusic .org/videos/tom+ross.

100 **"Friday night in Texas"** ibid.

101 **"most artists were paid on the flat"** ibid.

101 **"If they said the rent was twenty percent"** ibid.

101 **"a lot of the costs that promoters would charge us"** ibid.

105 **"The record companies believed"** Bobbi Cowan, www.bobbicowan.com/b2.html.

105 **"Guests were greeted at the door"** Alice Cooper and Steve Gaines, *Me, Alice* (New York: Putnam, 1976).

107 **"I would have liked to have seen Teddy Kennedy"** Robert Greenfield, *STP: A Journey Through America with the Rolling Stones* (Cambridge, MA: Da Capo Press, 2002) (first published 1973).

110 **"We still want as much, maybe even more"** Charles Perry and Andrew Bailey, "The Who's Spooky Tour: Awe and Hassles," *Rolling Stone*, Jan. 3, 1974.

110 **"I like getting drunk with the guys"** Crowe, "Pete Townshend: The *Penthouse* Interview."

113 **"I didn't laugh—I wept"** The Edge, *It Might Get Loud*, Sony Picture Classics, 2009.

113 **"Fifteen-minute guitar solos"** ibid.

Chapter 7: Let the Show Begin

115 **"The Who had always prided themselves"** John Swenson, "The Who Puts the Bomp," *Crawdaddy*, Dec. 7, 1971.

116 **"Once you were playing with a tape"** Ken Sharp, "Look Who's Talking: A Conversation with Roger Daltrey," *Goldmine*, July 8, 1994.

117 **"We'd played almost the whole of *Quadrophenia*"** ibid.

117 **"that I'd taken too much control"** *Q*, Sept. 1994.

117 **"He starts spitting at me"** Sharp, "Look Who's Talking."

117 **"Pete! Pete!"** Wilkerson, *Amazing Journey*.

117 **"No one was sorrier"** Sharp, "Look Who's Talking."

117 **"I was forced to lay"** Wilkerson, *Amazing Journey*.

118 **"It wasn't a big fight"** Sharp, "Look Who's Talking."

118 **Opening night in Stoke** Details and audience reactions to the U.K. Quadrophenia performances are taken in part from the Concert Files, quadrophenia.net.

118 **"We played *Quadrophenia*"** quadrophenia.net.

119 **"He had seemed edgy beforehand"** Simon Malia, the Concert File notes, quadro phenia.net.

120 **"I'd really decided that that was the end"** Crowe, "Pete Townshend: The *Penthouse* Interview," *Penthouse*, Dec. 1974.

121 **"The horrible truth is"** wolfgangsvault.com.

122 **"When Keith collapsed it was such a shame"** Charles Perry and Andrew Bailey, "The Who's Spooky Tour: Awe and Hassles, *Rolling Stone*, Jan. 3, 1974.

122 **"He can play!"** Sam Whiting, "Who's Drummer," San Francisco *Examiner*, Oct. 17, 1996.

126 **"I do believe that the size of the stage"** Jaan Uhelszki, "Babies on Fire," *Guitar World*, 2008.

129 **"With Alice," observed one junketeer** "Check Your Guillotine, Sir?" *Rolling Stone*, Dec. 1973.

132 **"We liked a little ultraviolence in the show"** *Good to See You Again, Alice Cooper*, DVD commentary (Eagle Vision, 2005).

132 **"Of course, the contrast with Shea Stadium"** Goldberg, *Bumping into Geniuses*.

133 **"My mantra was"** ibid.

134 **"there was not one square inch of grass"** Joe Chambers, ledzeppelin.com, concert timeline.

135 **"Fucking hell, G"** Mick Wall, *When Giants Walked the Earth: A Biography of Led Zeppelin* (New York: St. Martin's Press, 2008).

135 **"I think it was the biggest thrill I've had"** Mary Campbell, "Led Zeppelin on $3 Million Tour," Associated Press, 1973.

135 **"Dare I ask that you could just cool it"** Paul Iorio, ledzeppelin.com, concert timeline.

136 **"I still think of it as my Woodstock"** Bill Studstill, ledzeppelin.com, concert timeline.

137 **"He turned out to be completely tame"** ibid.

Chapter 8: "She Said She Liked the Way I Held the Microphone"

138 **"Sure, it's expensive"** Harry Swift, "Inside Alice," *Rolling Stone*, May 10, 1973.

140 **"We had a regular airline charter"** Bob Greene, *Billion Dollar Baby* (New York: Atheneum, 1974).

140 **"You should have seen them"** Swift, "Inside Alice."

141 **"A lot of things went on in the hotels"** Welch, *Peter Grant*.

144 **"Every girl who came into the party"** Greene, *Billion Dollar Baby*.

146 **"You drove the limos onto the runway"** Steve Kurutz, "Flying High," *New York Times*, Sept. 21, 2003.

146 **("We're paying a lot of money")** Greene, *Billion Dollar Baby*.

Chapter 9: "I'm Just Trying to Get Through This Tour Alive"

155 **"Ever since that night"** Bruce Pollock, "On the Case: The What, When, Where and Why of Pete Townshend of the Who," *Rock Magazine*, Jan. 14, 1974.

156 **"not tense," "He answers all," "I'm really drained"** ibid.

157 **"I don't know," "That song was basically," "He goes to Victoria"** quadrophenia.net.

157 **"It was my idea"** Charles Perry and Andrew Bailey, "The Who's Spooky Tour: Awe and Hassles," *Rolling Stone*, Jan. 3, 1974.

157 **"I think the story line isn't so complicated"** ibid.

157 **"I found it so embarrassing"** Crowe, "Pete Townshend: The *Penthouse* Interview."

161–62 Pete Townshend comments from quadrophenia.net.

162 **"The audience was very chatty"** Jim Chisolm, "The Who Concert Guide," thewholive.net.

162 **"My greatest memory of the show"** Donald Adler, www.thewholive.net/concert/index.php?id=178&GroupID=1.

164 **"It's pretty pointless"** Led Zeppelin Concert Files, Dave Lewis, Simon Pallett, Omnibus Press, London.

166 **"because he had gotten bored with flying on the private plane"** Bill Graham and Robert Greenfield, *My Life Inside Rock and Out* (Cambridge, MA: Da Capo, 1992).

166 **"The fans were chanting"** ibid.

166 **"Peter Grant sitting backstage"** ibid.

167 **"I think we better"** ledzeppelin-reference.com.

168 **"Right, now listen"** Led Zeppelin Concert Files.

171 **"Aren't these horrible"** Lisa Robinson, *Rock Scene,* 1973.

171 **"Ah heerd aboutchoo killin' them chickens"** Howard Bloom, "Alice Quits the Stage," *Circus,* July 1973.

171 **"I couldn't even touch a mannequin"** ibid.

172 **"I don't know if it was because"** Barbara Graustark, "Neal Smith Tells Terrifying Tales About the Band," *Circus,* Oct. 1973.

172 **"nearly blew us off"** ibid.

176 **"When it was over there were broken chairs"** Bloom, "Alice Quits the Stage."

177 **"Alice has always been unusual"** Harry Swift, "Inside Alice," *Rolling Stone,* May 10, 1973.

177 **"We're only one-third finished"** Loraine Alterman, "Killer Comes Home!" *Melody Maker,* April 17, 1973.

177 **"my last statement"** Bloom, "Alice Quits the Stage."

178 **"I tried being Alice for a while"** Ken Kelley, "*Penthouse* Interview: Alice Cooper," *Penthouse,* Sept. 1974.

178 **"That was the last thing"** ibid.

179 **"I was drinking heavily every night"** ibid.

179 **"In the fight scene"** Bloom, "Alice Quits the Stage."

179 **"I was bandaged all over my upper body"** Kelley, "*Penthouse* Interview: Alice Cooper."

180 **"I'm just trying to get through this tour alive"** Bloom, "Alice Quits the Stage."

Chapter 10: Three for the Road

182 **"*Quadrophenia* has been getting blamed"** Charles Perry and Andrew Bailey, "The Who's Spooky Tour: Awe and Hassles," *Rolling Stone,* Jan. 3, 1974.

183 Townshend, Daltrey, and Moon stage patter: quadrophenia.net.

185 **"How much of a kickback"** *The Song Remains the Same* (concert film)

185 Page and Plant stage patter: ledzeppelin-reference.com.

186 **When the lights go down at the Garden** Details of the Billion Dollar Babies tour finances and Alice's arrival at Max's Kansas City following the Madison Square Garden concert are taken from "Tolling the Take," *Rolling Stone,* July 5, 1973.

188 Alice Cooper backstage and onstage patter: *Sounds,* June 16, 1973.

Epilogue

194 **"Bill," one of them informs him, "we're tellin' you up front"** Bill Graham and Robert Greenfield, *My Life Inside Rock and Out* (Cambridge, MA: Da Capo, 1992).

194 **"they were totally behind enemy lines"** ibid.

194 **"When we started looking into it"** ibid.

194 **"I hope you're happy"** ibid.

196 **"I don't want to be thought of as a bad person"** Welch, *Peter Grant.*

197 **"I couldn't get out of bed for a week"** Kelley, "*Penthouse* Interview: Alice Cooper."

197 **"We started playing it and we didn't even get past the intro"** Jeb Wright, "The Quiet

Observer: An Interview with Rock n' Roll Hall of Famer Dennis Dunaway," classicrock revisited.com.

198 **"I feel as if I've done"** Greene, *Billion Dollar Baby.*

199 **"why he was drinking all this beer"** ibid.

203 **"Keith was a very positive musician"** *Amazing Journey: The Story of the Who* (Universal Studios, 2007).

204 **"I watched Roger Daltrey cry his eyes out"** Greil Marcus, interview with Pete Townshend, *Rolling Stone,* June 26, 1980.

205 **"inability to deal with the [Who]"** Crowe, "Pete Townshend: The *Penthouse* Interview."

205 **"I felt it was like a gracious gift from John"** Kathy McCabe, "The Who's Pete Townshend Talks Over Life, Love and New Tour," *Sydney Daily Telegraph,* March 27, 2009.

BIBLIOGRAPHY

Barnes, Richard. *The Who: Maximum R&B*. Richmond, U.K.: Eel Pie, 1982.

Case, George. *Led Zeppelin FAQ: All That's Left to Know About the Greatest Hard Rock Band of All Time*. Milwaukee: Backbeat, 2011.

Clapton, Eric. *Clapton: The Autobiography*. New York: Broadway, 2007.

Cooper, Alice, and Steven Gaines. *Me, Alice*. New York: Putnam, 1976.

Cooper, Alice, with Keith and Kent Zimmerman. *Alice Cooper, Golf Monster*. New York: Crown, 2007.

Davis, Stephen. *Hammer of the Gods: The Led Zeppelin Saga*. New York: William Morrow, 1985.

Des Barres, Pamela. *I'm with the Band: Confessions of a Groupie*. New York: William Morrow, 1987.

Doggett, Peter. *You Never Give Me Your Money: The Beatles After the Breakup*. New York: HarperStudio, 2008.

Emerick, Geoff, and Howard Massey. *Here, There and Everywhere: My Life Recording the Music of the Beatles*. New York: Gotham, 2006.

Fast, Susan. *In the Houses of the Holy: Led Zeppelin and the Power of Rock Music*. New York: Oxford University Press, 2001.

Goldberg, Danny. *Bumping into Geniuses: My Life Inside the Rock and Roll Business*. New York: Gotham, 2008.

Goodman, Fred. *The Mansion on the Hill: Dylan, Young, Geffen, Springsteen, and the Head-On Collision of Rock and Commerce*. New York: Random House, 1997.

Graham, Bill, and Robert Greenfield. *Bill Graham Presents: My Life Inside Rock and Out*. Cambridge, MA: Da Capo, 1992. First published 1990.

Greene, Bob. *American Beat*. New York: Atheneum, 1983.

———. *Billion Dollar Baby*. New York: Atheneum, 1974.

Greenfield, Robert. *S.T.P.: A Journey Through America with the Rolling Stones*. Cambridge, MA: Da Capo, 2002. First published 1973.

Harris, Mark. *Pictures at a Revolution: Five Movies and the Birth of the New Hollywood*. New York, Penguin, 2008.

Kent, Nick. *Apathy for the Devil: A 70s Memoir*. Cambridge, MA: Da Capo, 2010.

Kooper, Al. *Backstage Passes and Backstabbing Bastards: Memoirs of a Rock 'n Roll Survivor.* Milwaukee: Backbeat, 2008. Revised edition. First published 1977.

Lewis, Dave. *Led Zeppelin: The Complete Guide to Their Music.* London: Omnibus, 2010.

———, and Simon Pallett. *Led Zeppelin: The Concert File.* London: Omnibus, 2005.

Norman, Philip. *Shout! The Beatles in Their Generation.* London: Corgi, 1981.

O'Day, Pat. *It Was All Just Rock 'n' Roll: A Journey to the Center of the Radio and Concert Universe.* Seattle: RnR, 2002.

Richards, Keith, and James Fox. *Life.* New York: Little, Brown, 2010.

Rogan, Johnny. *Starmakers and Svengalis: The History of British Pop Management.* London: Transatlantic, 1988.

Schulman, Bruce J. *The Seventies: The Great Shift in American Culture, Society, and Politics.* New York: Free Press, 2001.

Townshend, Pete. *Who I Am.* New York: HarperCollins, 2012.

———. "Two Stormy Summers." In *Quadrophenia: Directors Cut.* Universal Studios, 2011.

Unterberger, Richie. *Won't Get Fooled Again: The Who from* Lifehouse *to* Quadrophenia. London: Jawbone Press, 2011.

Walker, Michael. *Laurel Canyon: The Inside Story of Rock and Roll's Legendary Neighborhood.* Faber and Faber, 2006.

Wall, Mick. *When Giants Walked the Earth: A Biography of Led Zeppelin.* New York: St. Martin's, 2009.

Weintraub, Jerry, with Rich Cohen. *When I Stop Talking, You'll Know I'm Dead: Useful Stories from a Persuasive Man.* New York: Twelve, 2010.

Welch, Chris. *Peter Grant: The Man Who Led Zeppelin.* London: Omnibus, 2002.

The following websites provided invaluable research resources:
alicecooper.com
alicecooperechive.com
artistshousemusic.org
ledzeppelin.com
led-zeppelin.org
ledzeppelin-reference.com
quadrophenia.net
sickthingsuk.co.uk
thewho.com
thewho.net
wolfgangsvault.com

INDEX

ABOUT THE AUTHOR

MICHAEL WALKER is the author of the national bestseller *Laurel Canyon: The Inside Story of Rock-and-Roll's Legendary Neighborhood* and *What You Want Is in the Limo*. His writing has appeared in *The New York Times,* the *Los Angeles Times, The Washington Post,* and *Rolling Stone,* among other publications. He lives in Los Angeles.